ADAPTATIONS

A vast majority of Academy Award-winning Best Pictures, television movies of the week, and mini-series are adaptations, watched by millions of people globally. *Great Adaptations: Screenwriting and Global Storytelling* examines the technical methods of adapting novels, short stories, plays, life stories, magazine articles, blogs, comic books, graphic novels and videogames from one medium to another, focusing on the screenplay. Written in a clear and succinct style, perfect for intermediate and advanced screenwriting students, *Great Adaptations* explores topics essential to fully appreciating the creative, historical, and sociological aspects of the adaptation process. It also provides up-to-date, practical advice on the legalities of acquiring rights and optioning and selling adaptations, and is inclusive of a diverse variety of perspectives that will inspire and challenge students and practitioners alike.

Alexis Krasilovsky is Professor of Screenwriting and Media Theory and Criticism at California State University, Northridge, teaching courses in Screenplay Adaptation and Film as Literature. Krasilovsky is a member of the Writers Guild of America, West, and is writer/director of the award-winning global documentaries *Women Behind the Camera* (2007) and *Let Them Eat Cake* (2014). She is also author of *Women Behind the Camera: Conversations with Camerawomen* (1997), and co-author of *Shooting Women: Behind the Camera, Around the World* (2015). Krasilovsky's narrative film, *Blood* (1976), was reviewed in the *Los Angeles Times* as "in its stream-of-consciousness way, more powerful than Martin Scorsese's *Taxi Driver*." Visit Alexis Krasilovsky's website at www.alexiskrasilovsky.com

GREAT ADAPTATIONS

Screenwriting and Global Storytelling

Alexis Krasilovsky

NEW YORK AND LONDON

First published 2018
by Routledge
711 Third Avenue, New York, NY 10017

and by Routledge
2 Park Square, Milton Park, Abingdon, Oxon, OX14 4RN

Routledge is an imprint of the Taylor & Francis Group, an informa business

Library of Congress Cataloging-in-Publication Data
A catalog record for this book has been requested

ISBN: 978-1-138-94917-1 (hbk)
ISBN: 978-1-138-94918-8 (pbk)
ISBN: 978-1-315-66926-7 (ebk)

Typeset in Sabon
by HWA Text and Data Management, London

Contents

Foreword
On Adaptation

The Columbia University professor Sidney Morgenbesser used to compare the three leading schools of philosophy to the three leading schools of umpiring the game of baseball. Picture a man in black standing behind the home plate. Here are the ways he decides what is a strike, and what isn't:

- One: I call them as I see them.
- Two: I call them as they are.
- Three: They are because I call them.

In some ways, the work of a screenwriter adapting a book is not at all unlike the work of Morgenbesser's umpire:

- One: I call them as I see them. Meaning: I look for the truth of the book, its essence rare – and I work to preserve that truth even as I sell everything else down the river. I here think of that pre-eminent adapter of literary novels, Ruth Prawer Jhabvala (*Howard's End*, *The Remains of the Day*, *The Golden Bowl*) who would read the book, then put it utterly aside, and refrain from opening it during the entire process of writing and rewriting the screenplay.
- Two: I call them as they are. Meaning: I just take the book and make it a movie, simple. Perhaps the greatest exponent of this approach was John Huston, who adapted Hammett's *Maltese Falcon* in the most literal sense. As Huston described it, and I quote "You simply take apart two copies of the book, paste the pages, and cross out what you don't like."
- Three: They are because I call them. This assumes a kind of reverse influence, one that would have delighted Borges and inflamed Harold Bloom. That the screenplay not only adapts the book, but in some sense changes it forever. Can one really read the pages of Harper Lee except through the spectacles of Horton Foote? As a thought

> experiment: close your eyes and say the words 'Atticus Finch.' Can you do that without seeing Gregory Peck?

This, then, is the paradox of adaptation. The adaptation leaves the book untouched: the copy of *Moby-Dick* on my nightstand written before the movies were invented, was widely read even as Ray Bradbury's adaptation was being filmed, and will exist when all the celluloid in the world has turned back into dust.

But the adaptation also transforms the book. Rips the binding, shreds the pages, pulps them, and by wild alchemy transforms them into light, flickering light. The adaptation can betray the book, but it can also bring it to life for audiences far larger than those who frequent libraries and bookstores. The adaptation can change peoples' lives – in a way that the best films, the best books, always have. The power to make us realize that the world is far more troubling, and far more beautiful, than is conventionally sold to us, is what books and films do best. And more: the great adaptation will often complete the circle — lead the viewer back to the book, make the introduction, and then gently close the door from the outside.

— Howard A. Rodman
President, Writers Guild of America West
Professor, School of Cinematic Arts, University of Southern California
Artistic Director, Sundance Screenwriting Labs

Preface

Adaptations have been my passion ever since childhood, first manifesting at the end of a graduate seminar on Dante's *The Divine Comedy* at Yale University. I was an undergraduate, over my head. I didn't think I could write papers in Italian (although I'd done just that at the University of Florence the year before), but I had the chutzpah to think I could turn it into a film, with each rung of hell shot on a different platform of the New York subways. Little did I know, I'd left the filter holder out of the Bolex camera when filming in the woods, streaking purgatory with a thick vertical stripe that didn't even match the tree trunks – although the storyline was still cohesive.

A dozen films later and finally in the Writers Guild, I've grown a bit more confident about both my filmmaking and my writing. Inspired by the passion for adaptations of master filmmakers like Truffaut and Kurosawa, I've shared the craft and alchemy of transforming literature into film and television with my students at California State University, Northridge for over twenty years. But while students from Australia, China, India, Japan, Mexico, Nigeria, Norway, Senegal, and Thailand have flocked to southern California eager for a break in Hollywood, there are actually more films made per year in India's Bollywood and Nigeria's Nollywood than what we make in the United States. And some of my international students – particularly from China, France, Japan, Mexico, South Korea, and Peru – study with the intent of bringing back our lessons to their home countries.

After traveling to film festivals in 25 countries with my last two films – both global in scope – I've learned to broaden my scope of how adaptations should be taught. But I grew up thinking that Hollywood was the center of the film world. Ford, Hawkes, and Welles were the canon, and if we wanted to go international, we could add Renoir. Whether the works of Western masters or the product of studios that we called "sausage factories," most of the films had storylines that borrowed from the plot summaries of tried and true literary and dramatic work from America and Europe, relying on Aristotle for structure.

By the time I started studying film in the late 1960s, my generation felt that experimental cinema was all that mattered, and that kowtowing to narrative formulas meant selling out. Our main role model for such endeavors was Jean-Luc Godard. As for Aristotle, as my feminist consciousness grew, I was surprised to discover that Aristotle thought of women as the flower pots in which male semen would bloom;[1] I couldn't help but also question whether his thinking about plots was also antiquated. But it wasn't until the 1980s, when I began to write and direct global documentaries, that I fully realized the provincialism of my Yale education.

"Global" means more than high-budget action films with mega-stars distributed in markets all over the world, or a way of raising funds from different countries for another blockbuster. It can also be an approach to international filmmaking honoring other cultures – not just as angry alternative cinema that screens in hip college courses, art houses, and festivals in Europe. For example, in *Caméra Arabe* (1987) Egyptian filmmaker Youssef Chahine says,

> For me, the Third World is England, France, the U.S. I'm the First World. I've been here for seven thousand years.[2]

While it can be fascinating to study the significance of trade routes of the Black Sea region dating back to the first millennium BC or earlier to the myth of Jason and the Argonauts, and to trace how that impacts the economics of action films distributed globally from Hollywood (and the international co-production financing currently behind it), what I find more pertinent to global study is the crisscrossing of other cultures and their potential for global resonance today. No longer can the one-size-fits-all "Hero's Journey" be the only template for storytelling. As Robert Cooper points out in his book *The Breaking of Nations*, "what we consider universal values are not so universal."[3]

Going back to Ancient Greece as the creative bedrock isn't far enough, knowing that tragedy may have made its way from Indonesia across the trade routes to Madagascar, and only later up to Aristotle's home turf. Trans-Pacific trade routes from Asia to the Americas also carried stories with them. The trade route across the Black Sea that gave rise to the story of Jason in search of the Golden Fleece,[4] which is a bedrock story of the "Hero's Journey," is just one of many trade routes that brought cultural, religious, and economic changes to various regions of the world, and along with them, more stories. But let's not call these "other" stories; we need to transcend being someone's "other" in today's world.

For example, Africans may have travelled to the Americas from the Mali Empire – whose Timbuktu was a major center of learning with 25,000 students at its height[5] – as early as the fourteenth century, two hundred years before Columbus.[6] Think of the ramifications of the African Ink Road, the Silk Road, and other trade routes to the underlying interconnectedness between countries and continents,[7] centuries before the instantaneous exchanges of the internet. The Indonesians are also thought to have sailed back and forth to South America many times between 5000 and 1500 BC, which has additional transcultural and transnational implications. Looking further back, recent anthropological discoveries trace the migration of East Africans to Europe, Asia, and the Americas, making our world far more "global" than ever before considered.

Both as a professor and as a writer, I take immense pleasure in stretching boundaries, whether they pertain to hybrid genres, or morphing from manga to feature, from feature to musical, or from television in one country to television in another, or digging into transnational influences. Boundary-stretching is a practice that has inspired many writers and is sometimes a factor of their universal appeal. For example, José Emilio Pacheco, the Mexican author who won the Cervantes Prize in Spain, wrote a poem in Spanish that included "American poet Ezra Pound's translation of Japanese version of an ancient Chinese poem," as well as contributing to the screenplay of the Mexican film, *El Lugar Sin Limites* (*Hell Without Borders,* Ripstein, 1987), based on José Donoso's novel, set in Chile. The poem, published in his collection *Miro la Tierra* (*I Look at the Earth*) was Pacheco's reaction to the Mexico City earthquake, universalizing a tragic theme.

By studying Bengali poets, novelists, and filmmakers recommended by Trina Lahiri, a screenwriter friend in Kolkata, the world of adaptation opened up, full of exciting transmigrations of influence. Knowing what to glean from your adventures in intertextuality and tapping into the myths and story-telling techniques that are the bedrock of a myriad of cultures are secrets to success in screenwriting for today's world.

This book exists to honor diverse cultures rather than to insist that there is only one way to approach storytelling – the overly formulaic Western way. And in the West, the storytelling contributions of women and minorities are enriching our perspective. By addressing the collective spirit of our times and the coexistence of globalization with national identities, I hope to show that adaptations have the power to ultimately contribute to world peace.

Los Angeles, California
March 10, 2017

Notes

1 Aristotle, *Generation of Animals,* trans. by Arthur Platt (London: Aeterna Press, 2015). As discussed in Caroline Whitbeck, "Theories of Sex Differences," in *Women and Philosophy* by Carol C. Gould and Marx W. Wartofsky (New York: G.P. Putnam's Sons, 1976).
2 Youssef Chahine, interview in "Caméra Arabe: The Young Arab Cinema," special features DVD, *Asfar al-sath Halfaouine: Child of the terraces,* directed by Ferid Boughedir (New York: Kino on Video, 2003).
3 Robert Cooper, quoted in Steven Erlanger, "Are Western Values Losing Their Sway?" *New York Times*, September 12, 2015.
4 Antoine Faivre, *The Golden Fleece and Alchemy* (Albany, NY: State University of New York Press, 1993).

5 "Lost Library of Timbuktu," Understanding Slavery Initiative, accessed Ma 30, 2017, www.understandingslavery.com/index.php?option=com_content &view=article&id=378&Itemid=233.

6 While many of Ivan Van Sertima's claims in *They Came Before Columbus: The African Presence in Ancient America* (New York: Random House Trade Paperbacks, 1976) have been contested, other sources discuss the possibility of Emperor Abukari II of Mali giving up his throne in order to lead an expedition across the Atlantic Ocean in the fourteenth century, such as: *The Legacy of Timbuktu: Wonders of the Written Word*, International Museum of Muslim Cultures in partnership with the Mamma Haidara Memorial Library, November 28, 2006.

7 Such as the "migration of myths between the Mediterranean and Indonesia by way of Arabia ... in the pre-Islamic period." Carl Kerenyi, *Eleusis: Archetypal Image of Mother and Daughter,* trans. by Ralph Manheim (Princeton, NJ: Princeton University Press, 1967), 136.

Acknowledgments

Writing this book would not have been possible without the support of California State University, Northridge, where I've taught screenplay adaptation and film as literature for over two decades, and my students, whose passion and scholarship challenged us all to expand our knowledge of this subject. My profound thanks to two of CSUN's Department of Cinema and Television Arts Chairs: Dr. John Schultheiss for helping me to make the transition from teaching film production (and screenwriting) to teaching media theory and criticism (and screenwriting), and Prof. Jon Stahl for encouraging me to experiment by adding television and new media studies during my recent years of teaching screenplay adaptation. Both Schultheiss and Stahl facilitated my travel to festivals and conferences around the world, which strongly strengthened my global approach to adaptation. A research fellowship from the Mike Curb College of Arts, Media and Communication enabled me to further expand my global exploration of adaptation, and a sabbatical from the university enabled me to complete the manuscript. Some of the many international film festivals which screened my film, *Women Behind the Camera*, also broadened my mind to films from other countries, particularly the International Film Festival of India (Goa), the Female Eye Film Festival (Toronto, Canada), and the Flying Broom International Film Festival (Ankara, Turkey).

I am grateful to Louise Hilton, Research Specialist, Margaret Herrick Library, Academy of Motion Picture Arts and Sciences; Dean Arnold, Music & Media Supervisor, and Lindsay Hansen, Music & Media Librarian, Oviatt Library, California State University, Northridge; Hilary Swett, Archivist, Shavelson-Webb Library, Writers Guild Foundation; and the many librarians at the Los Angeles Public Library for facilitating my research. A warm thanks to Michael C. Donaldson, Esq. for his input regarding the legalities of adaptations, and to my colleagues: Prof. Dianah Wynter, for our discussions of film as literature, which we both teach; Dr. Ah-Jeong Kim for introducing me to the Korean classic *Chunhyang* and its adaptations; Dr. Frances Gateward, for lending me her copies of *Chunhyang*'s adaptations; Dr. Jacob Enfield, for demonstrating how virtual reality adaptations work; Dr. Maria Elena de las Carreras, for introducing me to Argentinian adaptations; Dr. Hamidou Soumah for translating a French interview with Senegalese filmmaker Djibril Diop Mambéty; and Nancy Hendrickson Riley for her friendship and support. Special thanks also to Bond Emeruwa, former President of the Directors Guild of Nigeria, and film critic Shaibu Husseini for their assistance regarding Nigerian adaptations; to May Wu, for her research and translation of material regarding the Chinese screenwriter Lu Wei; and Rana Minakshi for her suggestions regarding adaptations from Assam.

More than a thousand CSUN students have studied adaptation and film as literature with me over the years. I am grateful for their inquisitive minds, their capacity for scholarship as well as creativity, and their many challenges to the status quo. Among the many who excelled in their contributions to our studies in adaptations are Jamie Burton-Oare, Ellen Chen, Danielle Foster, Josiah James, Tiffany Katz, and Frances Tull. Several research assistants and/or instructors' aides also stand out for their exceptional contributions: LaVeria Alexander, Lara Ameen, Mallory Fencil, Linda Fitak, Michael Gonzalez, Sarina Grant, Lori Harris, Andrea Harrity, Alli Hirshfield, Atesha Jones, Alexandra Karova, Katherine Moe, and Deborah Parsons. Robin Swicord (*The Curious Case of Benjamin Button*)'s visit to my adaptation class was deeply encouraging. I am especially grateful to my former students Tiago Augusto Souza Barreiro for his research in Brazilian adaptation; Rosalinda Galdamez for her Mexican and South American television research; Roberto Lazarte for his research in Peruvian film adaptations; Robert Taylor for his suggestions regarding Australian adaptations; and Gwen Alexis for her stimulating questions and her advocacy. I am also grateful to my son, Thomas Finney, for introducing me to additional films throughout the years – both the hero-driven action films that were so important to his childhood and adolescence, and the more obscure but inspiring classics of his young adulthood as a budding filmmaker and scholar, studying at the University of California, San Diego, and CalArts.

Special thanks to Trina Lahiri for her inspiring words of wisdom from Kolkata; to my friends Satene Cat, Kristin Glover, and Caroline Fitzgerald for their encouragement and support here in Los Angeles; to my friend and technical expert Reseda Mickey and CSUN's Equipment Systems Specialist Caleb Fahey for keeping my computers running; to Sheni Kruger, Emily McCloskey, and Simon Jacobs, my editors at Focal Press/Routledge; and to John Makowski, editorial assistant at Focal Press/Routledge.

Finally, I would like to thank Tery Lopez, Director of Diversity of the Writers Guild of America West, and the many hard-working members of WGA's diversity committees, especially those of which I am a member – the Committee of Women Writers and the Committee of Disabled Writers. It is their passion for change in an industry that has long discriminated against women and minorities that buttressed my resolve to write this book, in hopes that a sea change – at least in the world of adaptation – will be imminent.

Part I
Introducing Adaptation

Welcome to the world of adaptation! While the movie *Adaptation* (USA, 2002), written by Charlie Kaufman, refers to the Darwinian principle of adaptation as well as a screenwriter's struggles to write one, this book will focus on the writing process. It's not just about adapting novels or nonfiction to film, however: writers also work in television; we write webisodes and novelizations. For our source materials, we look at short stories, manga, comic strips, biographies, plays, and a variety of other media – sometimes more than one at a time. *Great Adaptations* includes both faithful and loose examples: Marielle Heller's *The Diary of a Teenage Girl* (USA, 2015), for example, not only faithfully renders most of the storyline of the original graphic novel, but animates the drawings of its teenage protagonist who is a would-be cartoonist. At the other end of the spectrum, the Coen Brothers were so loose with *O Brother, Where Art Thou?* (UK/France/UK, 2000) that they claimed not to have even read Homer's *Odyssey*. In between are all the gradations of the spectrum, from faithful biopics like Spike Lee's *Malcolm X* (USA/Japan, 1992) which combines some of the real-life characters for dramatic purposes to Gurinder Chadha's *Bride and Prejudice* (UK/USA/India, 2004), a loose adaptation that keeps Jane Austen's English storyline mostly intact, but sets it in a postcolonial jetsetter's world between Amritsar, Los Angeles, and London.

Because so many writers are influenced by other stories, including their own, even when primarily concerned with adapting one short story, play, or novel, *Great Adaptations* also explores the references to myths, fairy tales, biblical, classical plots and characters, popular culture, and personal history that give many adaptations their zing, whether it's Iago from Shakespeare's *Othello* giving another dimension to Sean Parker in *The Social Network* (USA, 2010), written by Aaron Sorkin, or the biblical references that help make the Wachowskis' *The Matrix* (USA, 1999) so memorable.

Part V, "Global Storytelling Revisited," explores regional and international storytelling in both recent films and classics. For example, in

Figure 1.1 Bride and Prejudice (UK/USA/India, 2004). Paul Mayeda Berges' and Gurinder Chadha's screenplay updates Jane Austen's 1813 novel without sacrificing its class issues. Image courtesy of Miramax. Produced by Pathé Pictures International (in association with UK Film Council, Kintop Pictures, Bend It Films, and Inside Track Films)

Japanese cinema, we examine how Kenji Mizoguchi based his cinematic masterpiece, *Ugetsu* (Japan, 1953), not only on ancient Chinese ghost stories, but on a French short story by de Maupassant, and how Akira Kurosawa strengthened his adaptation of *King Lear* by overlapping it with a legendary account of a Japanese feudal lord in the making of *Ran* (Japan, 1985). There are also twenty-seven adaptations of Murasaki Shikibu's great eleventh century novel, *The Tale of Genji*, ranging from anime television series, girl comics, and an all-female musical to a loosely adapted film set in Portugal. Some of the adaptations in this book are meant for international audiences and transcend boundaries, while others are meant to honor national literatures by those who are most familiar with its classics and best sellers.

When asked if he had a special feeling for books, critic-turned-filmmaker François Truffaut answered, "No. I love them and films equally, but how I love them!" As an example, Truffaut gave the example that his feeling of love for *Citizen Kane* (USA, 1941) "is expressed in that scene in *The 400 Blows* where Antoine lights a candle before the picture of Balzac."[1] My book lights candles for many of the great authors of this world: Chinua Achebe (Nigeria), Angela Carter (UK), Saratchandra Chattopadhyay (India), Janet Frame (New Zealand), Yu Hua (China), Stieg Larsson (Sweden), Clarice Lispector (Brazil), Mario Vargas Llosa (Peru), Naguib Mifouz (Egypt), Murasaki Shikibu (Japan), and Alice Walker (USA) – to name but a few. Furthermore, graphic novels, manga, musicals, television, webisodes, and even amusement park rides like *Pirates of the Caribbean* can inspire work in adaptation. Let's be open to learning from them all.

ONE

Creative Issues
Where Do Ideas Come From?

Sometimes ideas come from our real life experiences or other forms of creativity. For example, Robert James Waller's best-selling novel, *The Bridges of Madison County*, which later became a film (USA, 1995) and a Broadway musical (2014), may have begun with photographs of covered bridges that he shot while on leave from teaching business, coupled with a song he had written about a woman named Francesca, who would become the novel's protagonist.[2]

At other times, ideas pop into our heads while dreaming or meditating. Maybe that's because in those states we are relaxed and open enough to let our stories rise to the surface; we can train ourselves to be more receptive to these. Describing the Tibetan practice of lucid dreaming, Tenzin Wangyal Rinpoche states:[3]

> Some images or traces are burned deeply into us by powerful reactions while others, resulting from superficial experiences, leave only a faint residue. Our consciousness, like the light of a projector, illuminates the traces that have been stimulated and they manifest as the images and experiences of the dream. We string them together like a film, as this is the way our psyches work to make meaning, resulting in a narrative constructed from conditioned tendencies and habitual identities: the dream.

Whether we first identify ideas and storylines in our dreams or while wide awake, Jonathan Gottschall, author of *The Storytelling Animal: How Stories Make Us Human* claims that "the principles of good storytelling ... are coded in the DNA of our species and won't change until human nature does."[4]

Psychologist Carl Jung believed that archetypes are also inherited.[5] Perhaps in part that's why there are almost two thousand versions of "Cinderella," including European, African, Asian, and American variations complete with deceased mother, a slipper, and a fairy godmother (or magical animal) that helps Cinderella wed her prince. We will explore film adaptations of myths and fairy tales in Part IV; however, it is important to state up front that these stories which are so basic to our lives can, in fact, morph frequently to serve the moral imperatives of a given society or its counter-culture. If the idea for your film comes from a novel, play, manga, or other source, you are still likely to filter it through your own consciousness and filmic style if you live in a society that treasures individual perspective.

In West Africa griots – males and females – were the official storytellers. They told stories and fortunes, recited history, and played the bala; female griots also braided hair. These were not trivial pastimes: It was said that every time a griot died, a library died with him. To be a griot was an inherited position in society: you could not be a griot if your great-great-grandparent wasn't one. The griots of fifteenth-century Mali were so powerfully elite that the emperor could not kill a griot for giving him a less than favorable fortune. The griot tradition continues today in the form of African rock bands that are the current craze in Africa, Europe, and other continents; however, the griot rule of inheritance changed with Ousmane Sembène, the Senegalese novelist and filmmaker, known as the father of African cinema. Although his ancestors were fishermen, not griots, Sembène claimed that the new medium of film justified new storytellers, hence new griots.

Today it is possible for almost anyone in the U.S. to go to film school – although it can be prohibitively expensive for the poor without scholarships or bank loans, and it has become increasingly harder to get into classes in state universities. You may not learn to play the bala to accompany your story-telling, but you can learn Final Draft, digital cinematography, and Final Cut Pro to get your stories out. However, one of the ways that the griot tradition is extremely important to U.S. filmmaking is its emphasis on the oral tradition. Mark Twain, bidialectal because of his friendship with both white and black children when he was growing up, is widely considered as the first "real" American author, for writing stories based on his childhood experiences.[6] It's very possible that the griot tradition has in that way made a profound influence on American literature as a whole. Oral storytelling – or pitching – is also key to how film and television projects often get their financing.

To excel as an original filmmaker, the way in which ideas are translated to the screen must be invented anew. Senegalese writer/director Djibril Diop Mambéty's film *Hyenas* (*Hyènes*, Senegal/Switzerland/France, 1992) an adaptation of Friedrich Dürrenmatt's play *The Visit*, which was originally set in Switzerland,[7] satirizes consumerism in Africa. Mambéty credits his grandmother, and storytelling grandmothers in general, for the imperative to tell a story in a new and refreshing manner "for it to last forever":

> ...The grammar that wants you to tell things in this or that way: Grandma herself allows us to betray the grammar. That is, the ABC's

we learn in film school can be utterly transformed, and grandma wants us to always reinvent the grammar ... Like Don Gormas says in *Le Cid*: "Go, fly, and avenge me."[8]

One of the worst problems of adaptations is that they can be stifling. Contemplating film adaptations, Student Edward Bowden asked, "If one is not creating something new – a new way of looking at things, a new voice, new questions – is it really a creation?"[9] While creating adaptations is dependent on pre-existing work, we need to honor the spirit of that work, not just regurgitate its storyline and dialogue. That can require being less faithful than Francis Ford Coppola was when he adapted Fitzgerald's *The Great Gatsby* (USA, 1974): the dialogue, that flowed so beautifully on the pages of the novel, felt as long-winded and artificial as Robert Redford felt miscast. Adaptation calls for a close relationship with the original author, but you don't want to be slavishly married to the book. It may mean divorcing yourself from the material you're adapting in order to discover your own voice in the process; that fresh perspective can be the key towards involving your audience.

Gender and ethnicity can play into this process of self-discovery. As Hélène Cixous first stated in 1975:

> Every woman has known the torture of beginning to speak aloud, heart beating as if to break, occasionally falling into loss of language, ground and language slipping out from under her, because for woman speaking—even just opening her mouth—in public is something rash, a transgression.
>
> A double anguish, for even if she transgresses, her word almost always falls on the deaf, masculine ear, which can only hear language that speaks in the masculine.[10]

Although women screenwriters only accounted for 13 percent of all screenwriters working on the 250 top-grossing screenplays in 2016 ("even with the figure from 1998"[11]), more and more women are finding it possible to break new ground. Peruvian writer/director Claudia Llosa's Academy Award-nominated *The Milk of Sorrow* (*La Teta Asustada*, Spain/Peru, 2009), based on an account of women who suffered from mass rape during a time of terrorism between 1980 and 1992 in Peru,[12] features a female protagonist whose breakthrough involves discovering that her voice is of great value, even as her songs are stolen from her.

Life and art often intersect in the world of adaptations. Russell Means, the Oglala Lakota activist who co-founded the American Indian Movement, and later acted in *The Last of the Mohicans*, *Natural Born Killers* and other films, said of his year in prison, "The human being is a very special being because it can accommodate and adapt to just about anything. In many cases it may be a sad adaptation, but we can make it more beneficial than detrimental."[13] *The Last of the Mohicans* (USA, 1992) in which Means plays the Mohican chief, is a sprawling and romantic epic, one of several adaptations of the novel in film, television, radio, and opera. It would be interesting to see the application of Native American storytelling principles to future adaptations in which Native American characters and their issues are central, although *Smoke Signals* (Canada/USA, 1998), the adaptation of a short story from Sherman Alexie's *The Lone Ranger and Tonto Fistfight in Heaven* is an impressive start. As UCLA Professor of English, Paula Gunn Allen states in *The Sacred Hoop*, "the structure of American Indian literature ... does not rely on conflict, crisis, and resolution for organization."[14] With implications to plot, Allen describes the Native American way of "perceiving reality" as viewing "space as spherical and time as cyclical, whereas the non-Indian tends to view space as linear and time as sequential."[15] With implications to character development, the hierarchical protagonist surrounded by supporting characters and extras "is antithetical to tribal thought."[16]

Structure as well as content can benefit from thinking outside of the Hollywood box. For example, traditional Chinese medicine describes the human energy system as "a microcosm of the universal energy patterns that run like templates throughout nature and the cosmos, from the galactic and solar systems down to the cellular, molecular, and atomic levels of existence."[17] Try to imagine the sequence of influence coming from the universe (no, not just Universal Studios!) to the human experience of our sun and its planets to the acts, sequences, scenes, and words of our scripts. The interconnectedness of the five Taoist elements – wood, fire, earth, metal, and water – and their emotional attributes can also be used to rethink story structure and character relationship, as can the seven yogic chakras regarding characterization and character arc. For example, a character who is centered in the third chakra may be focused on personal power. What happens when he or she confronts a character guided by the love and compassion of the second chakra – or, as the progressive complications of the screenplay's second act unfold – uses the psychic perception of the sixth chakra to intuit what needs to be done to save the world?

In the workshop "Narrative Medicine: Extracting Nuance from Literature, Media, and Each Other," psychotherapist Shari Foos pointed out that our stories change in the process of their being told. Furthermore, "we change each other by neurobiology, as our brains do their work in sharing our stories – which changes us further."[18] Brian Boyd concludes his masterful study, *On the Origin of Stories*, with "We do not know what other purposes life may eventually generate, but creativity offers us our best chance of reaching them."[19] Is it overly optimistic to think that our world can change for the better by the intellectual and creative interaction between the writing of a novelist and the screenwriter who interprets his or her work? (Or have commercial media cheapened and flattened beyond recognition the deeper emotions that literature provides mankind?)

Even within the work – even within a predominantly violent work – it is possible to think in terms of healing and catharsis. Sometimes that means paying attention to other ways of shaping a story beyond what is suggested in the structure and content of the original source material. An interesting example of medical issues applied to character arc that can focus both on the traditional protagonist and on his or her relationships, is posttraumatic stress disorder or PTSD – one of many mental conditions or personality disorders that can be applied to your story's "person with a problem," whether you're writing an action film or a historical or personal drama.

Symptoms of PTSD include: "nightmares, insomnia, flashbacks of frightening event, avoiding scenes that remind one of it, startling easily, trouble concentrating, emotional numbness, irritability and aggression,"[20] and Dr. Kanan Khatau Chikhal, a clinical psychologist writing in the aftermath of the terror attack on Mumbai in 2008, added the following symptoms: "anxiety, guilt, depression and detachment; shying away from relationships, inability to deal with grief and anger."[21] What interesting character traits! Of course we don't want our friends, our loved ones, or ourselves to have to experience PTSD, but as screenwriters, this is a list made in heaven, perfect for dramatic conflict, flashbacks, and character development.

Apocalypse Now (USA, 1979), *Saving Private Ryan* (USA, 1998), and *The Hurt Locker* (USA, 2008) are some of the Hollywood films that incorporate PTSD. American television show adaptations that have depicted PTSD include: *Boardwalk Empire* (HBO, 2010), based on a non-fiction book; *Homeland* (Showtime, 2011), based on the Israeli television drama series, *Prisoners of War* (Keshet, 2010); the Spanish-language television series *Metástasis* (Sony Entertainment Television, 2014) set in Colombia is in turn based on the American television show *Breaking Bad*.[22]

Other war-related films which include PTSD are: the Bollywood blockbuster *Deewaar: Let's Bring Our Heroes Home* (India, 2004); *Persepolis* (France/USA, 2007), about the consequences of war in Iran to a young girl's life; and *Traffic* (USA/Germany, 2000), about the Mexican drug wars. Biyi Bandele's Nollywood film, *Half of a Yellow Sun* (Nigeria, 2013), based on Chimamanda Ngozi Adichie's book of the same title, is set at the outbreak of the Nigerian Civil War. Film critic Shaibu Husseini writes:

> Of course they depicted how the war turned people into refugees in their own country, how people were fleeing from town to town and how inadequate the refugee camp became for the amount of people trooping in there to seek refuge … and how people searched for their loved ones within the mass of people that were moving from town to town. … Even the lead characters had to find solace in the camp since they had to heal out of their homes as a result of the heavy bombing going on.[23]

The storyline of Jon Woo's *Red Cliff* (China/Hong Kong/Japan/Taiwan/South Korea, 2008–9) is structured around extensive battle sequences that

Figure 1.2 Half of a Yellow Sun, written and directed by Biyi Bandele (Nigeria, 2013), based on the novel by Chimanda Ngozi Adichie. Image courtesy of FilmOne Distribution. Produced by Slate Films, Shareman Media, British Film Institute, and Lipsync Productions

to the Western mind seem scripted by Machiavelli, but are more likely to have referenced the military strategies of Sun Tzu's fifth-century *The Art of War* in the creation of a plot that expands the legendary AD 208 Battle of Red Cliff described in part of Luo Guanzhong's 1522 novel, *Romance of the Three Kingdoms*. With its heavily orchestrated battle scenes trumping the on-screen emotions of its characters, *Red Cliff* may appeal more to military strategists and their followers.

If we look at the steps of what was first labeled by Chaim Satan as "post-Vietnam syndrome" before it became known as posttraumatic stress disorder,[24] it becomes clear how to apply these to Three-Act Structure in feature writing and/or a higher number of acts for television:

1 persistent guilt: desire to atone or to self-punish;
2 feelings of betrayal;
3 rage at society/individuals;
4 combat brutalization;
5 alienation from humanity and other human beings;
6 inability to love, trust, accept affection, or to be intimate.[25]

As an example of how this can be applied to screenwriting, in *Born on the Fourth of July* (USA, 1989) Oliver Stone and Ron Kovic, in adapting Kovic's autobiographical hero, create a protagonist whose journey we can identify with and follow in one clear arc. When Ron returns from Vietnam in Act I, his cheerful "It's really great to be home" is a part of his denial that anything has changed as a result of losing his ability to use his legs, echoed in his mother's initial lack of eye contact when she says, "It's good to have you home, Ronnie."[26] But by page 101, Ron's feelings of betrayal and rage – at his mother, his country, and God – have emerged, as he "sweeps all his baseball and wrestling trophies off the bookshelf" and screams "It's all a lie Mom. The whole thing's a lie!"[27] which escalates to:

```
                    RON:
The church blessed the war, they told
us to go, they blessed the burning
villages and the killing. Thou shalt
not kill Mom thou shall not kill
women and children Mom ... Remember
Mom you taught it to me ... but they're
the evil Mom, they're the ones we
should be fighting.[28]
```

But Mom, writhing in her own Supporting Character Arc, won't listen to what she feels is sacrilege. Instead of respecting her rules, Ron pushes forward to the end of the line, brandishing the family crucifix at her (Steps 2 and 3), then horrifying his parents even more by breaking his urine bag (Steps 1 and 3), which escalates still further in the movie where, in anguish, he screams the word "penis" at his mother – a penis that never made love to women, and now dangles from his permanently paralyzed body due to what happened in the war (Steps 4, 5, and 6). This is a Plot Point, as his mother no longer wants him in the house, and his father suggests that Ron take a trip to Mexico, which will become Act II's location of Ron's debauchery and alienation (Steps 1 and 5).[29]

What is our business as screenwriters, if not dealing with our protagonist's physical and emotional needs in answer to the events that he or she has experienced? We can choose to wake up humanity in reaction to the catharsis that tragedy provides, or we can provide solutions for the "Person with a Problem" with which we can identify. In *Born on the Fourth of July*, Ron's rage is transformed into collective action as he becomes a leader of the Vietnam Veterans Against the War, speaking out against the war at the Democratic National Convention at the end of Act III.

As we can see from the impact of Ron Kovic's PTSD on his mother and his fellow Vietnam vets, our supporting characters are also affected by the protagonist's PTSD. Barbara Sourkes, associate professor of pediatrics in Stanford University's School of Medicine states: "'There's no formula, and it'll change from person to person.' The only certainty is that traumatic events change relationships outside the family as well as within it."[30]

Posttraumatic stress disorder is something that happens to more people than just soldiers, and something that happens to men, women, and children on a daily basis, not just during wartime. Concentration camp survivors, earthquake, flood, and tornado victims, also suffer from long-term patterns of behavioral change and life disruption.[31] Violence and its effects are not only found on battlefields.

In China, Zhang Yimou's *Red Sorghum* (China, 1987), based on the novel by Nobel laureate Mo Yan, makes thematic metaphors between the violence experienced when the Japanese army invades, and domestic violence. *Red Sorghum* features a protagonist who faces life with courage despite her suffering from a tragic fate. Zhang Yimou writes:

> Chinese literature emphasizes female protagonists. What it's most adept at depicting is primarily women ... [W]omen in Chinese literature are a bit more complex than men. Writers all know that placing a figure in a complex environment full of obstacles makes depicting a plot relatively easy.[32]

Rape, abuse, even car accidents can cause PTSD.[33] Explaining her motivation for taking part in *The Birth of a Nation* (Canada/USA, 2016), loosely based on the story of Nat Turner's slave rebellion which features a rape, Gabrielle Union states, "Posttraumatic stress syndrome is very real and chips away at the soul and sanity of so many of us who have survived sexual violence."[34]

The New York Times reports that worldwide, women "ages 15 to 44 are more likely to die or be maimed as a result of male violence than as a consequence of war, cancer, malaria and traffic accidents combined."[35] Manju Borah's Assamese adaptation *Dau Huduni Methai* (*Song of the Horned Owl*, India, 2015), based on the novel *Dao Hudur Gaan* by Rashmirekha Bora, tells the story of separatist violence in the Bodo community after World War II from the perspective of a rape victim.

According to RAINN (Rape, Abuse and Incest National Network)'s website, one out of every six American women and about three percent of American men have been victims of rape.[36] Films like *Monster* (USA, 2003), an adaptation of the story of Aileen Wuornos, a prostitute-turned-serial-killer seeking revenge for a lifetime of abuse, certainly belong on our PTSD list. Sticking your thumb out to hitch a ride from strangers looking for sex can lead to just as much trauma as pointing a gun at the enemy on a front line.

Healing from what we now know as PTSD, Gerald Nicosia explains in his book, *Home to War,* is dependent on what Chaim Shatan called "society's 'moral acceptance,' ... an embracing of each veteran's physical and emotional needs" and "some form of political or moral activism."[37] Storytelling can play a big part in informing society of the truths that lead to social justice, whether or not your screenplay overtly addresses social activism. For example, the Academy Award-winning original screenplay for *The Hurt Locker* (USA, 2008) came into being because of Mark Boals' personal experiences working with a bomb squad in Iraq.[38] While *The Hurt Locker* isn't as political as *Born on the Fourth of July*, it gets the feelings that individual soldiers experience in Iraq out into the public awareness as much as the Dewey Canyon demonstration of 1971, where one Vietnam vet stood at the microphone and said, "I have only one thing to say to the Vietnamese people...Oh, God, God, I'm sorry."[39]

Samuel Beckett once wrote, "Every word is a stain upon silence." By breaking through silence and living to tell stories of those who have suffered PTSD, you are helping those people, their loved ones, their communities, our societies, our nations, our world, and our universe to heal.

There are six basic steps to healing from PTSD:

1 Exploring the impact: acknowledging that it happened and how it changed you.
2 Reducing self-blame (such as no longer believing that standing at a bus stop late at night in a short dress led to rape).
3 Changing the story – creating a new narrative with self as survivor rather than as victim. Re-examining the event in a very different way that is personal.
4 Reducing the biological response to having been terrified by talking/walking the event over and over until it loses its power. Re-teaching the body to calm down usually involves relaxation techniques such as meditation. Then one can deal with avoidance.
5 Talking to friends to understand the meaning and impact (part of processing).
6 Realizing a plateau of safety to open up about whatever happened.[40]

All of these steps (though not necessarily in a step-by-step order) are part of the process of catharsis and letting go.

In the following example, Step 3 is personified by the Mentor/Crone figure of a grandmother, giving advice to Marjane as they prepare for bed in the privacy of a house surrounded by the Iran–Iraqi War. The night before Marjane Satrapi's parents send her out of Iran for safe-keeping in Europe in Marjane Satrapi and Vincent Paronnaud's film *Persepolis*, her grandmother tells her, "Nothing ever comes of bitterness." The grandmother recognizes that Marjane, on the brink of puberty, may be leaving the bloodshed and gender oppression of her country behind, but is likely to face other obstacles in her journey through life, including heartache, illness, and discrimination.

Discussing *Persepolis*, based on her autobiographical graphic novel, Satrapi states:

> We didn't want the movie to become a political, or historical, or sociological statement; it was more a story of a person. So we tried to do it in a form; for example, anytime there was something about the history, we made it like a puppet scene. The politics are very much a puppet game to start with, but these scenes are also the visions of somebody who hears things, who imagines things ... It's a question of rhythm, of equilibrium, and of never forgetting the human aspect, because before everything, the story is the story of one person. That's why it becomes universal, because it's very easy to relate to one person, and it's impossible to relate to a nation.[41]

Falling asleep in the safety of one's grandmother's loving arms transcends national boundaries.

In the article "Following a Script to Escape a Nightmare," Sarah Kershaw interviews Dr. Barry Krakow, who founded the PTSD Sleep Clinic of the Maimonides Sleep Arts and Sciences Center. Dr. Krakow says the rate of adults reporting experiencing nightmares "is as high as 90 percent among groups like combat veterans and rape victims."[42] Using a technique called *scripting* to rewrite PTSD nightmares while awake, his patients come up with new dreams to replace the nightmares. Essentially, this is something that screenwriters can do to help societies to heal. Kershaw states, "Hollywood has even produced its own spin on the idea of controlling dreams ... with *Inception*, a thriller whose plot swirls through the darkest layers of the dream world."[43]

The centuries-old Tibetan practice of training the mind through lucid dreaming to make positive choices in life has many implications for the screenwriter seeking teachers and truths for guidance. As Tenzin Wangyal Rinpoche states, describing the yoga of dreaming:

> Dreams of clarity may occasionally arise for anyone, but they are not common until the practice is developed and stable. ... The dream of clarity includes more objective knowledge, which arises from collective karmic traces and is available to consciousness when it is not entangled in personal karmic traces. The consciousness is then not bound by space and time and personal history, and the dreamer can meet with real beings, receive teachings from real teachers, and find information helpful to others as well as to him or herself.[44]

Writing practice has a lot to learn from these methods of dream practice. By practicing your writing on a regular basis – which may include keeping a dream journal and developing lucid dreams as well as freewriting and learning the discipline of screenwriting craft and its necessary revisions – you are much more likely to become capable of writing with the clarity needed by your audiences for understanding the visions you are tackling. That lucidity is also needed if you want to use the writing process for healing.

Original Writing Versus Adaptation

Denise Levertov has compared the writing process to the labor of birthing, the consequences of conception, and the birth of the poet: out of her slides a poem, "the remote consequence of a dream of his, acted out nine months before, the rhythm that became words, the words that were spoken, written down," which the poet uses "to call out to the world with what he finds is his voice."[45] For screenwriters of adaptations, the process may be less painful in terms of conception and labor, but may carry all the stigma of step-parenting when it comes to bringing up the project so that it can go out into the world and survive its production and distribution.

Beginning with arguably the very first fiction film adaptation – Alice Guy-Blaché's *The Cabbage Fairy* (France, 1896), based on a French myth about babies brought to life by a fairy in a cabbage patch[46] – filmmakers have also addressed the issue of birthing in their films. Dutch-born screenwriter Menno Meyjes' adaptation of Alice Walker's Pulitzer Prize-winning novel, *The Color Purple* (USA, 1985) begins with the birth of a baby that is snatched away by her father, who had incestuously forced her to conceive it. Julie Dash's beautiful and original *Daughters of the Dust* (USA/UK, 1991), which preceded her novelization when the film became a classic, is narrated by Unborn Child, who cryptically says, "I am the silence that you cannot understand; I am the utterance of my name,"[47] in contrast to the talkative baby, who's funny both *in utero* and without, voiced by Bruce Willis in Amy Heckerling's blockbuster hit, *Look Who's Talking* (USA, 1989), which later inspired the ABC sitcom, *Baby Talk*, adapted by Ed Weinberger.[48] The baby *in utero* who narrates the opening of Volker Schlöndorff's *The Tin Drum* (*Die Brechtrommel*, West Germany/France/Poland/Yugoslavia, 1979), adapted from the Nobel Prize-winning novel by Günther Grass, is so horrified by the Nazi era into which he tumbles out of the uterus, that he refuses to grow up physically beyond the age of three, despite his high IQ. His consciousness and his drum allow this boyish-looking, heavy-hearted intellect to sound the alarm about the abuses of humanity surrounding him, which Schlöndorff and Grass so brilliantly portray through the visual setting and narrative.[49]

Compared to the short description of less than a page in Mary Shelley's early nineteenth-century novel, in which Dr. Frankenstein anxiously "collected the instruments of life around me, that I might infuse a spark of being into the lifeless thing that lay at my feet,"[50] then rushes out of the room in horror soon after seeing the monster move, Kenneth Branagh's birthing of the monster in *Mary Shelley's Frankenstein* (USA/Japan/UK, 1994) is a never-ending tour de force of technology combined with whirlwind performances by both doctor and monster. Extending the birth as a series of technological steps was already evident in James Whales' 1931 *Frankenstein*, starring Boris Karloff, which Mel Brooks made fun of in *Young Frankenstein* (USA, 1974); Tim Burton parodied the birth by making a nerdy science student patch together his dead dog to revive it with a lightning bolt in *Frankenweenie* (USA, 2012).[51] But where did Mary Shelley's idea come from? In this era of clones and test-tube babies, could these ideas be taken in new directions in future adaptations, instead of the conceptual rehash of films like *Victor Frankenstein* (USA/UK/Canada, 2015),[52] which teems with special effects but offers little substance?

Some of Mary Shelley's story was inspired by the ghost story-telling marathon that her husband, the great Romantic poet Percy Bysshe Shelley and their friend, the poet Lord Byron launched by the fireside during the summer nights of 1816, challenging her to top the German ghost stories they'd been telling.[53] These may have included *Vathek, an Arabian Tale*,

Figure 1.3 House of Frankenstein, directed by Erle C. Kenton, written by Edward T. Lowe Jr. (USA, 1944), based on Mary Shelley's *Frankenstein*; or, *The Modern Prometheus*. Image courtesy of Universal Pictures

an exotic story of a Caliph insatiable for knowledge beyond the humanly possible,[54] and *Der Golem*. In the Bible, the Golem is a shapeless mass of clay.[55] As the title of the first edition of Shelley's novel indicates – *Frankenstein; or, The Modern Prometheus*[56] – some of the story is based on the ancient Greek myth of Prometheus, the Titan who created mankind out of clay, as well.

According to Talmudic legend, "Adam is called 'golem,' meaning 'body without a soul' (Sanhedrin 38b) for the first 12 hours of his existence."[57] Versions of the story of the Golem date back as far as sixteenth-century Prague.[58] In recent years, the most famous retelling of "The Golem" in literature is that of Nobel Prize-winner Isaac Bashevis Singer, whose story was first published in Yiddish in 1969, with the English translation first appearing in 1982. In Singer's version, Rabbi Leib sculpts the golem out of clay, and brings it to life by engraving the Hebrew characters for the name of God on its forehead. Later, when the golem is helping the rabbi to save his people from being destroyed, he is sleepless with the fear that he has not deserved the "great power … granted to him from heaven."[59]

> He also felt a kind of compassion for the golem. The rabbi thought he saw an expression of perplexity in the golem's eyes. It seemed to the rabbi that his eyes were asking, "Who am I? Why am I here? What is the secret of my being?"[60]

The cemetery where the actual Rabbi Löw (1513–1609) is buried – which I filmed in Prague for a documentary about my roots[61] – was depicted in an early Golem film, Paul Wegener's *Der Golem* (Germany, 1915), based on Austrian author Gustav Meyrink's 1915 novel of the same name.[62] Wegener also made a 1917 film entitled *The Golem and the Dancing Girl.*

Wegener's third Golem film, *The Golem: How He Came Into the World* (Germany, 1920) was a big hit in New York, inspiring the making of James Whales' American blockbuster, *Frankenstein* (USA, 1931) (although Edison Studios had already released a short film, *Frankenstein,* in 1910). While in the ancient Greek myth Zeus punished Prometheus for giving the gift of fire to mankind, Whale's *Frankenstein* features a monster destroyed by a mob reminiscent of the pogroms of Europe (although the village in the 1931 *Frankenstein* is set in Switzerland, not Germany), or the lynch mobs of the American South. Ironically, the image of the Jewish star that ends Wegener's pro-Semitic film was later appropriated as the opening image of the Nazi propaganda film, *Jud Süss* (*Jew Süss,* Germany, 1940), "as if to present itself as a sequel."[63] In *Jud Süss*, however, the anti-Semitic and propagandistic storyline features Jews forced into exile, and Rabbi Löw is reduced to a vain stereotype.

There have been many other Golem-inspired stories and films, ranging from "The Sorcerer's Apprentice" in Disney's *Fantasia* (USA, 1940), although Mickey Mouse's chores undertaken by a broom which comes to life is more directly adapted from Goethe's poem "Der Zauberlehrling" ("The Sorcerer's Apprentice") than "The Golem," to more recently, videogames. In Amos Gitai's *Birth of a Golem* (*Naissance d'un golem: Carnet de notes,* France, 1990), the Golem, played by Annie Lennox of the Eurythmics, muses on "a film made like a Golem," making filmic creation an open question for filmmakers.[64]

Not only can we ask how stories like "The Golem" and "Prometheus" transform into new *Frankenstein*s and Frankenstein-related films like *Blade Runner* (USA, 1982) and *The Matrix* (USA/Australia, 1999), television programs, and virtual reality shows, but how can we apply the lessons of these stories to the problems of our world today? Isaac Bashevis Singer has stated, "I am not exaggerating when I say that the golem story appears less obsolete today than it seemed one hundred years ago. What are computers and robots of our time if not golems?"[65]

Quite possibly, the personal anguish that Mary Shelley felt from having recently suffered from the miscarriage of her third baby also made its way into the heartfelt sufferings of the monster that wasn't meant to live. According to Susan Tyler Hitchcock, the guilt of not giving her first baby a name before it died "was a major influence on the monster remaining nameless."[66] The fact that Mary Shelley was born to a mother who died from childbirth complications may have impelled her to deal with the idea of birth as a traumatic event. Her mother, Mary Wollstonecraft, author of *A Vindication of the Rights of Woman* (1792) and a novelist, also may have inspired her daughter, even from beyond the grave, with the legacies of creativity as well as cogent arguments for the civil rights of the Other.

Towards the end of Mary Shelley's novel, Dr. Frankenstein's friend Walton writes in a letter,

> Frankenstein discovered that I made notes concerning his history: he asked to see them, and then himself corrected and augmented them in many places; but principally in giving the life and spirit to the conversations he held with his enemy. "Since you have preserved my narration," said he, "I would note that a mutilated one should go down to posterity."

What would Victor Frankenstein and the monster he created have made of the many different *Frankenstein* adaptations and remakes that have become part and parcel of film history, and the test-tube babies, robots, and clones that are some of the newest creations of our technical era?

Writer as Character

Many adaptations have featured central characters for whom the creation of a literary career and/or writing itself is a central focus to their lives, including *Adaptation*, in which a screenwriter struggles to adapt an article about orchids from *The New Yorker* magazine;[67] *An Angel at My Table* (New Zealand/Australia/UK/USA, 1990), written by Australian screenwriter Laura Jones and based on the three autobiographies of New Zealand's best known author, Janet Frame; *The Basketball Diaries* (USA, 1995), about a writer struggling with heroin addiction; *Gone Girl* (USA, 2014), a thriller about a writer who concocts a "real-life" plot which fakes her suicide in order to frame her husband, who's also a writer; *Harriet the Spy* (USA, 1996), based on Louise Fitzhugh's classic children's novel;[68] *The Help* (USA/India/United Arab Emirates, 2011), which deals with the personal dangers and triumphs of writing about civil rights in Mississippi during the 1960s; *Midnight in Paris* (Spain/USA/France, 2011), an original story in which a screenwriter jumps back in time to the cultural mecca for American expatriates – such as F. Scott Fitzgerald, Ernest Hemingway, and Gertrude Stein – that was Paris in the 1920s; *Misery* (USA, 1990), about a writer struggling to survive his capture by a crazed fan; *Moulin Rouge!* (USA/Australia, 2001), about a young writer's love affair with a courtesan in the heart of a hedonistic Paris; *Mrs. Parker and the Vicious Circle* (USA/Canada, 1994), a biopic of Dorothy Parker, the wittiest writer of New York's Algonquin Round Table; *My Brilliant Career* (Australia, 1979), which tells the story of a young girl from the Outback of Australia who chooses getting her novel published over getting married in the Outback; *Il Postino* (Italy, 1994), a fictionalized episode in the life of the exiled Chilean poet, Pablo Neruda;[69] *Precious* (USA, 2009), in which the quest for literacy and self-expression in Harlem brings self-worth and personal empowerment; *Shakespeare in Love* (USA, 1998), in which a fictionalized Shakespeare comes up with the story of Romeo and Juliet; *Total Eclipse* (UK/France/Belgium, 1995), about the tempestuous relationship between the nineteenth-century French poets, Paul Verlaine and Arthur Rimbaud; and *Tune in Tomorrow* (USA, 1990), an adaptation of Peruvian Nobel Prize-winner Mario Vargas Llosa's novel, *Aunt Julia and the Scriptwriter*.

There's a monster in the psychological suspense thriller *Misery* (USA, 1990) – the writer's crazed fan, Annie Wilkes, played by Kathy Bates. The character of Annie was inspired in part when Stephen King was asked for his autograph by John Lennon's assassin, Mark Chapman, who told the author he was his "number one fan."[70] Unlike Frankenstein's monster, Annie is not the creation of King's fictional author/protagonist Paul Sheldon, who has created a series of romance novels that he finds monstrous enough in their superficiality that he longs to write something more realistic. Author Stephen King wasn't necessarily going for realism in creating Annie, however:

> I'm sitting at the word processor and I can remember so clearly, thinking, "OK, you set this up and sure she's nasty and she's unpleasant but she must have a good side because everybody has a good side." And then this voice rose up inside me and said, "Why does she have to have a good side? If she's crazy go ahead, make her a monster! She's a human being but let her be a monster if that's what she wants to be," and it was such a relief![71]

The monstrosity of Annie's character has been further developed by screenwriter William Goldman and director Rob Reiner to maximize the pathology, while at the same time making her seem like a normal person to maximize the moments of horror when she explodes into rage.[72] Goldman, who wrote the part of Annie specifically for actress Kathy Bates, also toned down the gore to make the film more palatable for audiences, as well as to emphasize the film's theme, which Reiner describes as "a man struggling to grow as an artist."[73] Reiner explains the scene in which Paul is hobbled in order to make it impossible for him to escape Annie's clutches:

> In the book, she hacks the foot off with an axe, and then cauterizes it with a blowtorch. Nice! But what I wanted to say in that scene was that in order to grow you have [to] go through pain. So we ended up using the ankle break, with the guy still going through a lot of pain but coming out whole in the end. Conceivably, more whole than when he went in.[74]

Additionally, actor Warren Beatty, who was interested in playing the part of the writer, worked with Goldman to make Paul's character less passive.[75] And, as Goldman explains, Castle Rock, Reiner's production company, sat with Reiner "for weeks talking about [the] screenplay, which very few directors and almost no executives will or can do. And I mean really going over it, sentence by sentence by sentence."[76] Goldman's script shared with its protagonist a formidable resilience.

Part of what drew Rob Reiner to undertake a second Stephen King adaptation after *Stand By Me* was his identification with *Misery*'s Paul Sheldon, a creative artist in need of a new challenge. This identification is something the original author felt deeply, too: as Reiner describes it, King was eager to take on a project that would allow him to be perceived by the masses as something other than "some schlocky horror writer."[77] Hollywood was pressuring Reiner to do another show just like Reiner's mega-successful hit, *All in the Family*. "That's what attracted me to *Misery*," said Reiner. "That terrible fear you have when you go through a change."[78]

But Stephen King lauds the film adaptation that resulted.

> If there's a flaw, it's that the movie never quite explains writer Paul Sheldon's salvation – his imagination. I got a peek at Goldman's original script, which would have allowed viewers to explore the writer's mind.[79]

In King's novel, we are treated to an interior monologue the voice-over adaptation of which would certainly slow down the tantalizing action, no matter how intrinsically compelling:

> Oh why in Christ's name are you doing this asshole Horatio-at-the-bridge act and who in Christ's name are you trying to impress? Do you think this is a movie or a TV show and you are getting graded by some audience on your bravery? You can do what she wants or you can hold out. If you hold out you'll die and then she'll burn the manuscript anyway. So what are you going to do, lie here and suffer for a book that would sell half as many copies as the least successful *Misery* book you ever wrote; and which Peter Prescott would shit upon in his finest genteel disparaging manner when he reviewed it for that great literary oracle, Newsweek?[80]

The novel can afford the luxury of extensive defiance, a chapter break to heighten the suspense, and even Paul's inability to light a match. Instead, in Goldman's script of *Misery*:

> For a moment – nothing – and then, KA-BOOM, the goddam thing practically explodes and[81]

... because a blockbuster hit demands quick action.

Baz Luhrmann's *Moulin Rouge!* (USA/Australia, 2001) provides a kaleidoscope of action and appropriation in its writing, dancing, and lovemaking scenes, fueled cinematically by the inspiration of Bollywood musical numbers. Addressing the musical genre, Luhrmann states,

> People want to see music and story work together ... and I think we've got the cinematic language. Music unites us. It transcends time and geography and unites us no matter what our backgrounds. Definitely, music has a power beyond our literal understanding. Now if you can collude that with the act of storytelling, it is a powerful and unstoppable force.[82]

Several *Moulin Rouge* movies were produced before Luhrmann's – one in the US (1934), one in France (1940), and two in the UK (1928 and 1952) – but those don't utilize mashups (such as "Diamonds Are a Girl's Best Friend," from the film *Gentlemen Prefer Blondes*, mashed with Madonna's "Material Girl")[83] or borrow its characters and plot elements from operas (Puccini's *La Bohème* and Verdi's *La Traviata*), let alone the ancient Greek myth of Orpheus and Eurydice.

Moulin Rouge! tells the story of a British writer in love with Satine, the beautiful but consumptive courtesan who presides at the Moulin Rouge nightclub in 1899 Paris. Luhrmann makes the most of an analogy between the avant-garde artists of the bohemian era such as Henri de Toulouse-Lautrec, and the pop culture of Andy Warhol's time, by juxtaposing turn-of-the-century French characters with late twentieth-century music from the US and UK. "[T]he whole idea of where we are today started to come from this extraordinary time and place," said Luhrmann. "So I had the desire to recapture that spirit."[84]

In a game of intertextual Scrabble, it is possible to take some of Luhrmann's sources into directions of their own. For example, *La Bohème*, the 1896 opera by Puccini which was in turn adapted from a loosely constructed novel, Henri Murger's *Scènes de la vie de bohème*,[85] – which Murger adapted with Théodore Barrière into a play in 1849 – provided Luhrmann with his poor, starving bohemian artist characters. *La Bohème* was also adapted several times in its own right, including the Broadway musical *Rent*, which updated tuberculosis into AIDS and reset the story in New York's East Village. The musical was in turn adapted into the film *Rent* (USA, 2005), although earlier adaptations of *La Bohème* had already been produced, including *La Bohème* (USA, 1926) starring Lillian Gish and *Mimi* (UK, 1935), both set in nineteenth-century Paris.

From *La Traviata* (*The Fallen Woman*), the 1853 opera by Giuseppe Verdi, co-screenwriters Baz Luhrmann and Craig Pearce took the storyline of the consumptive courtesan whose struggle to choose between a young bourgeois admirer and a rich, unfeeling Baron lead to her demise. In Act II, Scene 3, the Baron's rival Alfredo sings:

> I have called you here as witnesses that I have paid her all I owe. (With furious contempt, he throws a purse down at Violetta's feet. Violetta faints in the arms of Flora …)

Baz Luhrmann and Craig Pearce's homage to *La Traviata* manifests in their screenplay as:

```
CLOSE ON: Christian. Gazing down at the crumpled distraught
form of Satine he throws the money he still clutches at
her. His words are a simple cold whisper.
```

```
                CHRISTIAN (cont'd):
I have paid my debt. I owe you nothing
and you are nothing to me. Thank
you for curing me of my ridiculous
obsession with love.
```

But wait! *La Traviata* was itself an adaptation of a play written just one year earlier, that was based on the great French novelist Alexandre Dumas's semi-autobiographical *La Dame aux Camélias*.[86] The novel and play – about the tragic love of a consumptive courtesan – gave rise to a host of *Camille*'s (most notably the 1915 version adapted by Frances Marion and the 1936 version starring Greta Garbo) well before the opera itself was faithfully though subtly truncated into a film adaptation by the great Italian director, Franco Zeffirelli (Italy, 1983). Erich Segal's best-selling novel *Love Story* reset the story in contemporary New York; it became a blockbuster hit.[87]

In her novel, *The Art of Joy*, Goliarda Sapienza's protagonist writes about a "rat of aesthetics" that is ready to gnaw at her skeleton.

> just a few more instants of unawareness would have made me fall from reality into the grip of the "artist" drug – a drug more potent than morphine and religion.[88]

The tornado of contemporary mashups, operatic plot twists, the music of Orpheus from ancient Greece, musicals from Bollywood, and the bohemian lifestyle and artistic style of Toulouse-Lautrec, and his circle in turn-of-the-century Paris, would carry us away if it weren't for Luhrmann and Pearce's wannabe writer, Christian. His simplicity grounds us even when he himself is swept off his feet by love. Like the eye of a storm, however, this character is a bit empty, even if we can relate to Christian better than to the rats that we can imagine gnawing away in the shadows of his writer's garret.

Less likeable but more fascinating is the radio soap opera-writing character of Pedro Camacho in Nobel Prize-winner Mario Vargas Llosa's novel *Aunt Julia and the Scriptwriter*,[89] which turns the idea of soap opera writing by a Bolivian in Peru into a high comedic art form. The radio soap operas are made all the more absurd as Vargas Llosa alternates their synopses with a largely autobiographical love story about an aspiring young writer and his all-too-experienced aunt, whose romance Pedro mines for dialogue and storylines. As Pedro's plots become more and more fantastical and Pedro himself become more and more deranged, the protagonist of his soap operas morphs into an exterminator, literally beset by rats. Looking back at what drew him to his subject matter, Vargas Llosa writes:

> In spite of the fact that soap operas are such a distortion of real life, of reality, these melodramas have more influence in real life – at least more visible influence on the attitudes of the people – than

> creative literature. Radio and television serials have a tremendous impact on the way people think, act, and function in life. Therefore, it can be said in Latin America, in Peru, the literature that is most representative of real life, of real reality, is not creative literature – the great achievement of the intellect – but the popular genres.[90]

Less popular was the film adaptation of *Aunt Julia and the Scriptwriter*, known in the US as *Tune in Tomorrow* (USA, 1990). Resetting the story in New Orleans, screenwriter William Boyd lacked the courage to take the story to the end of the line, leaving Pedro's character, played by Peter Falk, amusingly multi-faceted yet superficial, without the degree of abandonment into insanity with which Vargas Llosa horrifies Marito, who considers Pedro Camacho to be the ultimate role model for a writer. Nevertheless, *Tune in Tomorrow*'s Pedro Carmichael does his best to encourage his mentee:

```
    PEDRO CARMICHAEL:(to Martin)
There's an army of them out there,
groping blindly, toiling in the
darkness, waiting. For what? For you.
For your incandescent, brilliant,
palpitating talent to light up their
miserable, impoverished, dull and
worthless lives.[91]
```

Embarrassingly enough, Boyd exchanges the intense rivalry between Latin American countries – Peru, where the novel is set; Bolivia, the homeland of the novel's soap opera writer; and Argentina, the country which fuels the soap opera writer's lurid hatred – by switching the object of Pedro's hatred to Albania. Albania is far too abstract for American audiences (although twenty years after the movie was made, there is now an active Albanian Mafia ripe for comedifying), and is far removed from the racism that white New Orleans of the 1950s would have displayed towards its black and Creole citizens in a more provocative adaptation. It's the "safe" choice, which makes it so forgettable.

The novel *Push* by Sapphire and its Academy Award-winning screenplay adaptation written by Geoffrey Fletcher, *Precious*, are more memorable for many reasons. One is the process by which the book came into being; another is its use of writing in the storyline – both in the protagonist's love of literature by Langston Hughes and Alice Walker, author of *The Color Purple*, and in Precious's quest for literacy and self-expression. *Push* and *The Color Purple* share similar storylines of an underage African-American girl considered ugly by her family, whose father makes her pregnant through incest, twice, and how this girl grows into adulthood and eventually heals. However, in the case of *Push*, while the protagonist heals emotionally and spiritually like Celie of *The Color Purple*, Precious is dying of AIDS.

Sapphire, the author of *Push*, interweaves African-American writers throughout this novel about learning to read and write for the sake of transformation and survival. Unlike Marito's imaginative, well-educated antics in *Aunt Julia and the Scriptwriter*, Precious starts her autobiographical account struggling to get Ebonics onto the page in order to write down her reality:

> Some people tell a story 'n it don't make no sense or be true. But I'm gonna try to make sense and tell the truth, else what's the fucking use? Ain' enough lies and shit out there already?[92]

Like Vargas Llosa's characters, however, Sapphire's Precious is also preoccupied by mass media, frequently referencing television commercials, movies, and stars. When Precious's father is raping her, she survives the ordeal by imagining she is somewhere else – walking the red carpet, bestowing autographs to adoring fans – instead of a dismal tenement in Harlem, her insides burning with pain mixed with pleasure. The film deletes the pleasure: so far, few Hollywood movies have catered to addressing women's sexual needs, which are especially complex in *Push*. She stares at the wall:

> till wall is a movie, Wizard of Oz, I can make that one play anytime. Michael Jackson, scarecrow. Then my body take me over again, like shocks after earthquake, shiver me, I come again. My body not mine, I hate it coming.[93]

Then afterwards, she takes out her father's razor and cuts her arm:

> trying to plug myself back in. I am a TV set wif no picture. I am broke wif no mind. No past or present time. Only the movies of being someone else. Someone not fat, dark skin, short hair, someone not fucked. A pink virgin girl. A girl like Janet Jackson, a sexy girl don't know one get to fuck. A girl for value.[94]

The movie makes a big deal of these fantasy scenes, relegating the reality of sexual abuse into short blurry shots that can bypass an "X"-rating, instead adding MTV-style obese-can-be-beautiful dance montages. At the same time, Fletcher's adaptation ignores other potential montage scenes, such as when Precious fantasizes about life with her children. But this is part of its commercial appeal to young girls who have been so brainwashed in our society to deal with lookism above all, and it does have its benefits in keeping the movie from being too bleak to hook mainstream audiences. It also deletes the colorism issue, in which Precious fantasizes that she has light skin, which makes her more beautiful. Only as the novel progresses do we see Precious coming to understand her own inner beauty, as she becomes better educated through reading Langston Hughes, Alice Walker, and other African-American writers. The protagonist's view of

Alice Walker is expressed several times, such as when Precious says, "I love *The Color Purple*, that book give me so much strength."[95]

The Color Purple not only gave the character of Precious her strength, it gave the author Sapphire the basic underpinnings of her novel *Push*: both the protagonists of *The Color Purple* and *Push* are underage girls who've had two children by her own father, and both are vilified by their mothers for this incest rather than offered commiseration, safety, or support. Both girls speak and write an Ebonics appropriate to their background, educational level, and predominantly black environments.

Both girls transform their lives through reading and writing. In the case of *The Color Purple*, Celie survives her isolation and abuse when her sister and children are wrenched away from her by writing letters to God. Eventually a heartfelt correspondence ensues between the two sisters – Celie in the rural South, and Nettie in Africa, where she has become a missionary. This storyline survives in Spielberg's Oscar-nominated film adaptation of *The Color Purple* written by Dutch-born screenwriter Menno Meyjes. In the case of *Push*, literacy is a monumental arc accomplished through Precious's writing journal full of poetry and self-discovery, and from reading *The Color Purple* itself. Precious is ecstatic with excitement when, after finding herself and her baby homeless, she spends "ONE NIGHT IN LANGSTON HUGHES' HOUSE HE USE TO LIVE IN. Me and Abdul in the Dream Keeper's house!"[96] This major literary event, in which Precious is saved from having to spend a night in the streets by an opportunity to stay in the great Harlem Renaissance writer's house – is changed in the film to a night in the guestroom of her teacher. But movies aren't literary shrines: by developing and dramatizing the teacher's loving relationship with another woman – one who doesn't exist in the book – Fletcher is able to address Precious's overcoming homophobia without having to mention a subplot of the book that focuses on Louis Farrakhan. Even though eventually Precious's arc takes her well beyond idolizing Farrakhan, Jews might have walked out, not waiting for the novel's equivalent of an Act III, where Precious's education has moved her beyond unquestioning devotion towards the anti-semitic, anti-gay leader.[97]

The novel *Push* ends with 35 pages of poems and journal entries by Precious' classmates, who have their own stories to share – some of which Fletcher morphs into supporting characters' events in his adaptation. Instead, Fletcher succeeds in bringing Precious's conflict with her mother over child support, welfare payments, and the backstory of her abuse to a head at the end of Act III. Although the film ends knowing that Precious has AIDS, she informs her social worker that she has also scored high enough on her tests in school that she will be headed to college. Precious has become firm in her feelings of self-worth and her ability to persevere as a result of her writing experiences.

Writing is also intrinsic to the characters of Gillian Flynn's novel and screenplay, *Gone Girl.*[98] In this he-said, she-said, and he-wrote, she-wrote thriller, the intertwining imaginations and realities of unemployed

Figure 1.4 In this scene from *Precious* (USA, 2009), winner of the 2010 Academy Award for Best Adapted Screenplay, Precious (played by Gabourey Sidibe) meets with her social worker, Ms. Weiss (played by Mariah Carey). Image courtesy of Lionsgate. Produced by Lionsgate

writers Nick and Amy wreak havoc with each other's lives. As in *Misery*, the screenplay leaves out some of the interior monologue reflections on writing, such as Nick's self-conscious thinking while choosing business-casual slacks to wear to the press conference to announce the disappearance of his wife:

> It would make an interesting essay, I thought, picking out appropriate clothes when a loved one goes missing. The greedy, angle-hungry writer in me, impossible to turn off.[99]

But being writers is also intrinsic to the plot. Nick losing his job as a writer in New York and Amy's trust fund from her parents' wildly successful children's books that rip off her childhood are what make it possible for them to get up and go when the inciting incident of Nick's mother getting cancer propels them on their journey. As Nick contemplates the bankrupt mall back in small-town Missouri, feeling emotionally bankrupt himself, he intellectualizes about our "ruinously derivative" society:

> I can't recall a single amazing thing I have seen firsthand that I didn't immediately reference to a movie or TV show ... You know the awful singsong of the blasé: Seeeen it. I've literally seen it all, and the worst thing, the thing that makes me want to blow my brains out, is: The secondhand experience is always better.[100]

A cynical thought for Flynn's character Nick, but one with a happy ending for Flynn herself, who had spent ten years reviewing television and films for *Entertainment Weekly* prior to becoming a novelist: the adaptation rights of her best-selling novel *Gone Girl* sold for $1.5 million.[101] Twentieth-Century Fox kept her aboard as sole screenwriter to a film that would go on to make over $300 million.[102]

Being writers is intrinsic to Flynn's characters Nick and Amy's conjoined plots. Amy has perfectly crafted a fictionalized diary in order to send her adulterous husband to the electric chair, and most of the film shows us its effects. Both husband and wife want to capitalize on their versions by the story's end; however Amy makes Nick delete his version from his laptop in order to perpetuate the illusion of a happy marriage and to hide her success as a murderer.

In contrast, the theme of writing that makes Brazilian writer Clarice Lispector's novel *A hora da estrela* (*Hour of the Star*) so aesthetically compelling and philosophically iridescent is entirely missing in its film adaptation. The story of Macabéa, a young woman from the poverty-ridden north-east of Brazil who makes her way to the slums of Rio de Janeiro in search of some kind of a life, is narrated by a character named Rodrigo S.M., who agonizes about how to tell Macabéa's story with meaning and integrity. Rather than hustle through the steps of her "Hero's Journey," Lispector, through the veil of Rodrigo, presents us with two sets of parentheses back to back:

> (I am having a hellish time with this story. May the Gods never decree that I should write about a leper, for then I should become covered in leprosy.) (I am delaying the events that I can vaguely foresee, simply because I need to make several portraits of this girl from Alagoas. Also because if anyone should read this story, I'd like them to absorb this young woman like a cloth soaked in water. The girl embodies a truth I was anxious to avoid. I don't know whom I can blame, but someone is to blame.)[103]

Later, when Macabéa's death is imminent – having been run over by a Mercedes – we feel that this protagonist has been betrayed, because earlier in the threadbare story, this simple, poverty-stricken character without any special features to commend her (not even the un-made-up beauty of Robert Bresson's *Mouchette* [France, 1967]) is set up as follows:

> The only thing she desired was to live. She could not explain, for she didn't probe her situation.[104]

As someone places a candle beside her body, the narrator comments, again parenthetically:

> (I give the bare essentials, enhancing them with pomp, jewels and splendour. Is this how one should write? No, not by accretion but rather by denudation. But I am frightened of nakedness, for that is the final word.)[105]

Suzana Amaral's film adaptation of *A hora da estrela* (Brazil, 1986) strips the story even further. There is no narrator and seemingly no writer, only a low budget, documentary-style rendition of Macabéa's story, underscoring the protagonist's poverty. Ironically, the story is told with perfect clarity, the camera replacing the narrator's doubts as to whether fiction is capable of truth-telling. Indeed, cinematographers' concerns also include storytelling. Writer/director Agnes Varda credits herself for the "cinécriture" of her films, working closely with her cinematographers and sometimes shooting scenes herself as a kind of film-writing.[106] Recently the cinematographer Jost Vacano, ASC, BVK, successfully fought in the German courts for greater recognition for his contributions to Wolfgang Petersen's *Das Boot* (Germany, 1981), opening up further prospects of "co-author recognition" to cinematographers in the future, especially as digital and special effects cinematography is on the increase.[107]

However, what is left out of the film of Lispector's novel is worthy of our exploration of what lies at the heart of adaptation. In *Light in the Dark* (*Luz en lo oscuro*), Gloria E. Anzaldúa writes about the role of the unconscious in reading and creating a work of art, claiming that "A good fiction or other creation takes her [the writer] out of herself, allowing her to 'forget' herself."[108]

> Creation is really a rereading and rewriting of reality—a rearrangement or reordering of preexisting elements.[109]

Furthermore, Anzaldúa states, in order to "decolonize reality,"

> We must empower the imagination to blur and transcend customary frameworks and conceptual categories reinforced by language and consensual reality. To explore the "cracks between the worlds" (rendijas, rents in the world), we must see through the holes in reality ("seeing" is another type of perception).[110]

In sync with Lispector's willingness to open up the text to everything from self-doubt to mystical dimensions, the implications of Anzaldúa's examination of the writing process has profound implications to the adaptation process. Imagine a collaboration in which the writer whose work is adapted and the writer who adapts the work serve as soul sisters ("comadres") or soul brothers, whether working at the computer, or in front of or behind the camera.

Notes

1 Charles Thomas Samuels, "Francois Truffaut," in *Encountering Directors*, Paris, September 1–3, 1970, accessed August 11, 2016, http://zakka.dk/euroscreenwriters/interviews/francois_truffaut_529.htm.

2 William Grimes, "Robert James Waller, Author of 'The Bridges of Madison County,' Dies at 77," *New York Times*, March 10, 2017, accessed March 12, 2017, https://nyti.ms/2mbUnil.

3 Tenzin Wangyal Rinpoche, *The Tibetan Yogas of Dream and Sleep* (Ithaca, NY: Snow Lion, 1998).
4 Jonathan Gottschall, "Story 2.0: The Surprising Thing About the Next Wave of Narrative," *Co-Create,* October 27, 2013, accessed August 21, 2017, www.fastcocreate.com/3020047/story-20-the-surprising-thing-about-the-next-wave-of-narrative.
5 Eleazar M. Meletinsky, *The Poetics of Myth*, trans. by Guy Lanoue and Alexandre Sadetsky (New York: Garland, 1998), 44.
6 Shelley Fisher Fishkin, *Was Huck Black? Mark Twain and African-American Voices* (Oxford: Oxford University Press, 1994).
7 Friedrich Dürrenmatt, *The Visit* (play) (New York: Grove Press, 1962), first produced in Germany in 1956.
8 Jean-Pierre Bekolo, *La grammaire de ma grand'mère.* Interview with writer/director Djibril Diop Mbéty on the DVD *Hyenas*, directed by Djibril Diop Mambéty (1992; New York: Kino Video, 1995), DVD; translated for *Great Adaptations* by Hamidou Soumah.
9 Edward Bowden, "Reaction to *Breathless*" (paper, California State University Northridge, Northridge, CA, May 26, 2004).
10 Hélène Cixous, *The Newly Born Woman* (Minneapolis, MN: University Minnesota Press, 1986), 92. Originally published as *La Jeune Née* (Paris: Union Générale d'Éditions, 1975).
11 Martha M. Lauzen, "The Celluloid Ceiling: Behind-the-Scenes Employment of Women on the Top 100, 250, and 500 Films of 2016," Center for the Study of Women in Television and Film, San Diego State University, San Diego, CA, 2016, accessed May 31, 2017, www.nywift.org/documents/2016_Celluloid_Ceiling_Report.pdf.
12 Kimberly Theidon, *Entre Prójimos: el conflicto armado interno y la política de la reconciliación en el Perú* (Lima, Peru: IEP Ediciones, 2004).
13 John Edgar Wideman, "Russell Means: The Profound and Outspoken Activist Shares Some of His Most Ardent Convictions," *Modern Maturity*, 38(5) (September–October, 1995), 79.
14 Paula Gunn Allen, *The Sacred Hoop: Recovering the Feminine in American Indian Traditions* (Boston, MA: Beacon Press, 1992), 59.
15 Gunn Allen, *The Sacred Hoop*, 59.
16 Gunn Allen, *The Sacred Hoop*, 59.
17 Daniel Reid, *The Shambala Guide to Traditional Chinese Medicine* (Boston, MA: Shambhala Publications, 1996), 22.
18 Shari Foos, lecture, "Narrative Medicine: Extracting Nuance from Literature, Media, and Each Other," PEN Center USA, Los Angeles, July 20, 2013.
19 Brian Boyd, *On the Origin of Stories: Evolution, Cognition, and Fiction* (Cambridge, MA: Belknap Press of Harvard University Press, 2009), 414.
20 Marilyn Elias, "Posttraumatic stress is a war within for military and civilians," *USA Today*, October 26, 2008, accessed August 16, 2016, 70, http://usatoday30.usatoday.com/news/health/2008-10-26-PTSD-main_N.htm.
21 Kanan Khatau Chikhal, "The Trauma of Terror: BT gives you some strategies to fight posttraumatic stress disorder experienced by many after the recent terror attacks," *Bombay Times*, *Times of India*, December 2, 2008, 5.
22 Patrick Hackeling, "The Evolution of Posttraumatic Stress Disorder in American Cinema and Culture," *Oak Tree*, December 23, 2013, accessed August 24, 2016, https://theoakwheel.wordpress.com/2013/12/23/the-evolution-of-posttraumatic-stress-disorder-in-american-cinema-and-culture/.
23 Shaibu Husseini, email to author, September 22, 2016.
24 Gerald Nicosia, *Home to War: A History of the Vietnam Veterans' Movement* (New York: Crown, 2001), 170.

25 Chaim Shatan, "The Grief of Soldiers," op-ed article, *New York Times*, May 6, 1972. Discussed in Gerald Nicosia, *Home to War: A History of the Vietnam Veterans' Movement* (New York: Crown, 2001), 170.
26 Ron Kovic and Oliver Stone, *Born on the Fourth of July*, film script (1989), 60.
27 Ron Kovic and Oliver Stone, *Born on the Fourth of July*, film script (first draft, 1987), 101.
28 Kovic and Stone, *Born on the Fourth of July* (first draft), 102–103.
29 Kovic and Stone, *Born on the Fourth of July* (first draft), 103–106.
30 Barbara Sourkes, quoted in Harriet Brown, "Coping With Crises Close to Someone Else's Heart," *New York Times*, August 16, 2010, accessed August 16, 2016, www.nytimes.com/2010/08/17/health/views/17essa.html?_r=0.
31 Nicosia, *Home to War*, 203.
32 Law Wai-Ming, "Zhang Yimou's Black Comedy: *The Story of Qiu Ju*." In Frances Gateward (ed.), *Zhang Yimou Interviews* (Jackson, MS: University Press of Mississippi, 2001), 28. First published in *City Entertainment: Film Biweekly*, 351 (September 17, 1992), trans. by Stephanie Deboer.
33 Marilyn Elias, "Posttraumatic Stress is a War within for Military and Civilians," *USA Today*, October 26, 2008, accessed August 16, 2016, 70, http://usatoday30.usatoday.com/news/health/2008-10-26-PTSD-main_N.htm.
34 Gabrielle Union, "'Birth of a Nation' actress Gabrille Union: I cannot take Nate Parker rape allegations lightly," op-ed, *Los Angeles Times*, September 3, 2016, accessed September 3, 2016, www.latimes.com/opinion/op-ed/la-oe-union-nate-parker-birth-nation-rape-allegation-20160902-snap-story.html.
35 Nicholas Kristof, "To End the Abuse, She Grabbed a Knife," *New York Times*, March 8, 2014, accessed September 22, 2016, www.nytimes.com/2014/03/09/oinion/sunday/kristof-t-end-the-abuse-she-grabbed-a=knife.html?emc=edit_nk_20160921&nl=nickkristof&nlid=59804432&te=1.
36 "Scope of the Problem: Statistics," RAINN (Rape, Abuse & Incest National Network), accessed August 16, 2016, www.rainn.org/statistics/scope-problem.
37 Nicosia, *Home to War*, 171.
38 Chris Abani, *Song for Night* (New York: Akashi Books, 2007). Nigerian novella about an Igbo child soldier who's a mine diffuser, is still waiting for an adaptation to film or television.
39 Nicosia, *Home to War*, 153.
40 The author is indebted to Alison Lewis, Clinical Social Worker/Therapist, for the ideas on this list.
41 Marjane Satrapi, quoted in Laurie Koh, "The Voice of Dissent: Marjane Satrapi Draws a Revolution in Persepolis," *Film Arts: The Magazine of the Independent Filmmaker* (March–April, 2008), 15–16.
42 Barry Krakow, quoted in Sarah Kershaw, "Following a Script to Escape a Nightmare," *New York Times*, July 27, 2010, www.nytimes.com/2010/07/27/health/27night.html?_r=0.
43 Krakow, 2.
44 Rinpoche, *The Tibetan Yogas of Dream and Sleep*, 49, 52.
45 Denise Levertov, *The Poet in the World* (New York: New Directions, 1960), 107.
46 Jule Selbo, "Alice Guy (1873–1968)." In Jill Nelmes and Jule Selbo (eds), *Women Screenwriters: An International Guide* (New York: Palgrave Macmillan, 2015), 323.
47 Julie Dash, *Daughters of the Dust*, directed by Julie Dash (Arlington, VA: PBS American Playhouse, 1991).

48 Amy Heckerling, *Look Who's Talking*, directed by Amy Heckerling (Culver City, CA: TriStar Pictures, 1989).
49 Jean-Claude Carrière, Volker Schlöndorff, and Franz Seitz, *Die Brechtrommel* [*The Tin Drum*], directed by Volker Schlöndorff. Produced by Franz Seitz Film, Bioskop Film, Artemis Film, Hallelujah Films, GGB-14, Argos Films, and co-produced by Jadran Film and Film Polski, 1979.
50 Mary Shelley, *Frankenstein* (Mineola, NY: Dover, 1994), 34–35.
51 John August, Tim Burton, and Leonard Ripps, *Frankenweenie*, directed by Tim Burton (Burbank, CA: Walt Disney Studios Motion Pictures, 2010).
52 Max Landis, *Victor Frankenstein*, directed by Paul McGuigan (Los Angeles, CA: Twentieth Century Fox Film, 2015).
53 Shelley, *Frankenstein*, pp. vi–vii.
54 William Beckford, *Vathek, an Arabian Tale* (1786).
55 *Psalms* 139:16.
56 Mary Shelley, *Frankenstein; or, The Modern Prometheus*, 1st edn (London: Lackington, Hughes, Haring, Mavor & Jones, 1818).
57 Alden Oreck, "Modern Jewish History: The Golem," *Jewish Virtual Reality,* accessed September 6, 2016, www.jewishvirtuallibrary.org/jsource/Judaism/Golem.html.
58 Isaac Bashevis Singer, "The Golem is a Myth for Our Time," *New York Times*, August 12, 1984, accessed September 15, 2016, www.nytimes.com/1984/08/12/theater/the-golem-is-a-myth-for-our-time.html.
59 Isaac Bashevis Singer, *The Golem* (New York: Farrar, Straus and Giroux, 1982), 37.
60 Singer, *The Golem*, 37–38.
61 Alexis Krasilovsky, *Exile* (USA: Rafael Film, 1984).
62 Henrik Galeen and Paul Wegener, *Der Golem* (*The Golem*, Babelsberg, Germany: Universum Film, 1920).
63 Cathy Gelbin, "Narratives of Transgression, from Jewish Folktales to German Cinema," *Kinoeye: New Perspectives on European Film*, 3(11), October 13, 2003, accessed September 15, 2016, www.kinoeye.org/03/11/gelbin11.php.
64 Amos Gitai, *Birth of a Golem*, directed by Amos Gitai (France: Facets Multimedia Distributions, 1990). Produced by Agav Films, Paris, France.
65 Singer, "The Golem is a Myth for Our Time."
66 Susan Tyler Hitchcock, *Frankenstein: A Cultural History* (New York: W.W. Norton, 2007), 19.
67 Susan Orlean, *The Orchid Thief* (New York: Ballantine Books, 1998).
68 Louise Fitzhugh, *Harriet the Spy* (New York: Harper & Row, 1964).
69 Based on the novel by Antonio Skarmeta, *Ardiente Paciencia* [*Burning Patience*], trans. by Katherine Silver (New York: Pantheon Books, 1987).
70 Nigel Floyd, "Reiner Reason," *Time Out* (May 1–8, 1991), 18.
71 Stephen King, quoted in Lynn Flewelling, "Interview with Stephen King," August 1990, accessed March 10, 2011, www.sff.net/people/lynn.flewelling/s.stephen.king.html. Special thanks to student Chris Manask for the "Screenplay Adaptation" essay, "Stephen King: Authors in Trouble" and to Rebecca Lombardi for her additional research.
72 Stephen King, 19.
73 Rob Reiner, quoted in Nigel Floyd, "Reiner Reason."
74 Reiner, quoted in Nigel Floyd, "Reiner Reason," 19.
75 Rob Reiner, quoted in Patrick Goldstein, "Rob Reiner Takes On 'Misery: The director follows his hit comedy 'When Harry Met Sally…' with a chiller, his second film taken from a Stephen King novel," *Los Angeles Times*, April 29, 1990, accessed September 24, 2016, http://articles.latimes.com/1990-04-29/entertainment/ca-538_1_harry-met-sally.
76 William Goldman, quoted in Sheila Johnston, "The Short Cuts to 'Misery'; Sheila Johnston talks to William Goldman about rewriting Stephen King's *Misery* for film," *Independent* (April 26, 1991), 1.

77 Rob Reiner, quoted in Betsy Sharkey, "'Misery's' Company Loves a Good Time," *New York Times* (June 17, 1990), 19.
78 Reiner, quoted in Goldstein, "Rob Reiner Takes On 'Misery," 21.
79 Stephen King, "The Reel Stephen King," *Entertainment Weekly*, 516 (December 10, 1999), 40.
80 Stephen King, *Misery* (New York: Signet, 1988), 44.
81 William Goldman, *Misery* (Beverly Hills, CA: Castle Rock Entertainment, 1991), 36.
82 Baz Luhrmann, quoted in Serena Donadoni, "Moulin Rouge: Writer/director Baz Luhrmann, actress Nicole Kidman, and production/costume designer Catherine Martin – Interview by Serena Donadoni," "The Cinema Girl," 2001, accessed March 11, 2014, www.thecinemagirl.com/text/l/luhrmann_rouge.htm.
83 Joe Burke, Victoria Garrity, and Cara McGonagle, "*Moulin Rouge!*, The Musical Genre: An Exploration of Integrated and Non-integrated Films in the Musical Genre" (blog), accessed September 25, 2016, https://themusicalgenre.wordpress.com/moulin-rouge/.
84 Luhrmann, quoted in Donadoni, "Moulin Rouge," 1.
85 Henri Murger, *Scènes de la vie de bohème* (Paris: Gallimard, 1988, originally published 1851).
86 Alexandre Dumas, *La Dame aux Camélias* (Paris: A Cadot, 1848).
87 *Love Story*, directed by Arthur Hiller (Los Angeles, CA: Paramount, 1970). Based on Erich Segal, *Love Story* (New York: Harper & Row, 1970).
88 Goliarda Sapienza, *The Art of Joy*, trans. by Anne Milano Appel (New York: Farrar, Straus and Giroux, 2013), 360.
89 Mario Vargas Llosa, *La tía Julia y el escribidor* (*Aunt Julia and the Scriptwriter*, Buenas Aires: Editorial Seix Barral, 1977).
90 Mario Vargas Llosa, *A Writer's Reality*, Byron I. Lichtblau (ed.) (Syracuse, NY: Syracuse University Press, 1991), 119.
91 Jon Amiel, *Tune in Tomorrow* (Dallas, TX: Odyssey, Polar Entertainment, 1990), transcript of the film, 31:31.
92 Sapphire, *Push* (New York: Vintage Contemporaries, 1997), 3–4.
93 Sapphire, *Push*, 111.
94 Sapphire, *Push*, 112.
95 Sapphire, *Push,* 82.
96 Sapphire, *Push,* 80.
97 Sapphire, *Push*, 81.
98 Gillian Flynn, *Gone Girl* (New York: Crown, 2012).
99 Flynn, *Gone Girl*, 58.
100 Flynn, *Gone Girl*, 72.
101 Christy Khosaba, "Hollywood Film Awards: 'Gone Girl' Brings Gillian Flynn New Accolades," *Los Angeles Times*, November 15, 2014, accessed October 20, 2016, www.latimes.com/entertainment/movies/moviesnow/la-et-mn-gone-girl-writer-gillian-flynn-hollywood-film-awards-20141115-story.html.
102 Mike Fleming Jr., "Gone Girl's Profit in 2014: Disciplined $61 Million Budget Pays Off," *Deadline Hollywood,* March 11, 2015, accessed October 20, 2016, http://deadline.com/2015/03/gone-girl-profit-box-office-2014-1201390479/.
103 Clarice Lispector, *The Hour of the Star*, trans. by Giovanni Pontiero (Manchester: Carcanet, 1986), 38–39. First published in Portuguese in 1977.
104 Lispector, *The Hour of the Star*, 27.
105 Lispector, *The Hour of the Star*, 81.
106 Sandy Flitterman-Lewis, *To Desire Differently: Feminism and the French Cinema* (New York: Columbia University Press, 1996), 219.

107 Yuri Neyman, "New Issues in Authorship: Recognition for Cinematographers," *Global Cinematography Institute Newsletter*, email, August 12, 2016.
108 Gloria E. Anzaldúa, *Light in the Dark: Luz en lo Oscuro: Rewriting Identity, Spirituality, Reality*, Analouise Keating (ed.) (Durham, NC: Duke University Press, 2015), 40.
109 Anzaldúa, *Light in the Dark*, 40.
110 Anzaldúa, *Light in the Dark*, 45.

TWO

Career Issues

Writers' and Producers' Standpoints

The concept of influence is an intriguing one. In adapting a screenplay, you are distilling the essence of a story and its characters, sometimes translating, sometimes transforming these into a film. Where it all starts is in rights acquisition, which sometimes varies country to country.

What Walt Disney did in negotiating with P.L. Travers in Hollywood, London and Australia for the rights to her best-selling *Mary Poppins* books and what the producers of *The Graduate* (USA, 1967) did in paying author Charles Webb a paltry $20,000 for his first novel,[1] enabling them to make a film that went on to earn an adjusted gross figure of $736,815,800[2] differ considerably from what Tarantino did in the making of *Reservoir Dogs*. Some viewers see Tarantino's *Reservoir Dogs* (USA, 1992) as an uncredited adaptation of Ringo Lam's *Lung fu fong wan* (*City on Fire*) (Hong Kong, 1987), while others see it as "more of a homage to Hong Kong cinema than it is a straight rip-off."[3] Ideas *per se* are not copyrightable, but the treatments, articles, books, screenplays, and films are.

The idea of "homage" instead of adaptation, remake, or plagiarism is a long-standing one among writers. As William S. Burroughs once wrote, "After all, the work of other writers is one of a writer's main sources of input, so don't hesitate to use it; just because somebody else has an idea doesn't mean you can't take that idea and develop a new twist for it. Adaptations may become quite legitimate adoptions."[4]

Thomas Wolfe, considered the genius of his generation of American novelists in the 1930s but largely abandoned in the last decade or so because of his racism, anti-Semitism, and sexism, adapted part of the Ancient Greek epic poem *The Odyssey* into a novel set in the American South, *Look Homeward, Angel* (later made into a forgettable television movie).[5] Wolfe compared his work to the great masterpiece of English literature, James Joyce's *Ulysses*, which re-sets Homer's story of Ulysses in early twentieth-century Dublin, Ireland:

> Like many another young man who came under the influence of that remarkable work, I wrote my "Ulysses" book and got it published too. That book, as you know, was *Look Homeward, Angel*. And now, I am finished with "Ulysses" and with Mr. Joyce, save that I am not an ingrate and will always, I hope, be able to remember a work that stirred me, that opened new vistas into writing, and to pay the tribute to a man of genius that is due him.
>
> However, I am now going to write my own "Ulysses" ... Like Mr. Joyce, I have at last discovered my own America. I believe I have found my language, I think I know my way. And I shall wreak out my vision of this life, this way, this world and this America, to the top of my bent, to the height of my ability, but with an unswerving devotion, integrity and purity of purpose that shall not be menaced, altered or weakened by any one.[6]

Thomas Wolfe's idealistic resolve, as well as his deep working relationship with his first editor, Maxwell Perkins, has itself become the subject of a contemporary film. In *Genius* (UK/USA, 2016), screenwriter John Logan in adapting a biography of Thomas Wolfe by A. Scott Berg, minimizes the impact of Wolfe's second and final editor, Edward Aswell, on Thomas Wolfe's short life. Logan also marginalizes Thomas Wolfe's mother – arguably a more potent central antagonist in Wolfe's real life as well as in his autobiographical fiction – and in the process, streamlines the story to bromantic fluff.

Not only do Western screenwriters tend to salivate at myths and legends of ancient Greece – which provide such easily accessible blockbuster material in public domain – but to Shakespeare, whose plays are themselves highly influenced by others' earlier stories. Shakespearean adaptations abound in all media and throughout the world. Among the more intriguing adaptations that take Shakespeare out of Europe are Kurosawa's *Ran* (Japan/France, 1985), based partly on *King Lear* but set in Japan, and O (USA, 2001), based on *Othello* but set in the US. *The Lion King* (USA, 1994) shows close resemblance in theme and dialogue to *Hamlet* Act I, Scene v., where Hamlet talks to his father's ghost. The Lion King's father says, "Simba, you have forgotten me. You have forgotten who you are and so forgotten me."

But there's more to *The Lion King's* influences than *Hamlet*. *Kimba, The White Lion* was created from a shōnen manga series by Osamu Tezuka which became Japan's first color animated television series (1965–1967). The Japanese company was at first flattered by being copied when they saw *The Lion King*. But ultimately they were upset at the lack of acknowledgement, as well as by the colossal box office figures in which they held no share. Yet they were unable to sue Disney with its legions of corporate lawyers due to financial considerations as Tezuka had died in 1989.[7] Ironically, Tezuka had licensed Disney's *Bambi* (USA, 1942) to make into a 1951 manga and credits Disney, whom he met at the 1964 New York World's Fair as a creative influence in his autobiography,[8] but in the case of *The Lion King*, Disney simply disregarded any connection to Tezuka's *Kimba, The White Lion*, claiming that *The Lion King* was only based on *Hamlet* – which was conveniently in public domain, so they didn't have to pay Shakespeare's heirs a dime.

Pirates of the Caribbean, the film series and franchise that, at over $4 billion as of mid-2017, is the ninth highest-grossing of all time,[9] started as a ride at Disneyland. Storyboard artist, Francis X. Atencio of Imagineer, had received a call from Disney asking him to write the script for the ride. He had never written a script before, but, Atencio says, "I got my pirate hat on and started researching."[10] The ride is tableau-driven, without much of a plot, protagonist, antagonist, or theme, but it does feature vivid locations, the idea of pirates, and their jargon, like "Yo ho, yo ho, a pirate's life for me!"[11]

Screenwriter Ted Elliott's childhood home was about fifteen minutes away, and he claims to have probably been on the ride "at least a hundred times" while growing up; his co-writer Terry Rossio said, "I'd been on it maybe a hundred or two hundred times before we even contemplated doing the movie."[12]

Ted Elliott and Terry Rossio originally tried to interest Disney in adapting the ride into a film in the early 1990s. But Disney's chair at the time, Jeffrey Katzenberg, wasn't interested. (Meanwhile, Stuart Beattie wrote a spec script on modern-day pirates, *Lord of the Seas*, which would help form the first draft, giving Beattie a screen story co-credit on *Pirates of the Caribbean: The Curse of the Black Pearl* (USA, 2003) along with Elliott and Rossio and a fourth screen story writer, Jay Wolpert.)[13]

When Elliott and Rossio got a call from Jerry Bruckheimer's company, whom Disney, under different management, had asked to take over development, Elliott explains:

Figure 2.1 Pirates of the Caribbean – The Ride

> We said, yeah, but only if we can incorporate supernatural elements from the ride. They liked the idea, and that's how the first movie came about ... As far as the sequels go: Terry and I made the decision that we couldn't use the Fountain of Youth or Blackbeard as story elements in a Pirates movie without making sure Tim [the novelist, Tim Powers][14] got some money – not because Disney necessarily needed the rights in Tim's novel to use either of 'em – but because if we did use either of 'em, it would pretty much eliminate any chance of another studio paying Tim for the film rights in his novel ... So we asked Disney to option Tim's book. After a little resistance ("The Fountain of Youth is public domain" that kind of thing), they did, in time for us to use the Fountain of Youth as an element in the final scene of P3.
>
> By optioning the book, it gave us the ability to use both the Fountain of Youth and Blackbeard as elements in the fourth movie, so we did.[15]

Let's explore the definitions and details of options and purchase agreements a little further. The rest of this section will do just that.

The Legalities of Adaptation

Have you discovered the perfect novel, short story, article, play, musical, or comic strip that will make an unforgettable movie or television series? It may behoove you to study some of the legal issues connected to the field of adaptation before plunging into a six- or seven-figure production, the distribution game, and the spin-offs that may be essential for success.

For writers and producers, the following six-point checklist can be helpful in your journey of adapting articles, short stories, plays, or novels to film or television. Of course, there are many fine points and additional considerations, so it is crucial to consult with an entertainment attorney who specializes in copyright issues. However, attorneys can be very expensive – $500 per hour is not unusual in the US – and therefore doing one's homework prior to your consultation can be a worthwhile investment.

Negotiators' Checklist for Film Adaptation[16]

1 Is the basic story under copyright?
2 Who owns the rights?
3 Have the rights been previously granted to a third party?
4 If in public domain, have other versions been previously made and released?
5 Monetary negotiation with owner or agent of copyrighted version.
6 Non-monetary negotiations (territory, script approval, sequel, credits, etc.).

1. Is the basic story under copyright?

Going through this list step by step, the first issue is whether the story is under copyright. You'll need to determine whether the story is new enough to require negotiating with the author, his or her family, or whoever owns his or her copyright. According to the US Copyright Act of 1976, that usually meant 75 years from the copyright date if before 1978, or fifty years from the author's death date, if the material was copyrighted after 1978. Now, as copyright attorney Michael Donaldson explains:

> The number is 95 years after publication if the author is a corporation. Seventy years from the death of an author. While fifty years after death is still the law in many countries, EU members and an increasing number of others have gone to seventy years after death which [is] increasingly becoming the international norm.[17]

However, these agreements can get tricky: Canada, Mexico, and the US have further developed their copyright relations under NAFTA, though NAFTA may change before this book is published. The People's Republic of China doesn't recognize the 1909 Copyright Act, which is basic to the US. As we have seen, there is also a lot of piracy between countries, which is often difficult to prosecute despite the laws. Furthermore, the US Copyright Office states:

> In certain cases, the United States may have had copyright relations with former territories or colonies of countries such as France, the Netherlands, Portugal, the Soviet Union, Spain, and the United Kingdom before those countries and their territories gained independence and joined international copyright treaties and conventions and bilateral agreements in their own right. The legal situations involved may be fact-specific, and the scope of copyright protection for U.S. works in such situations may be complex.[18]

Older material than the dates specified under the 1976 Copyright Act described above, the Berne Convention Implementation Act of 1988 (which covers almost 90 countries), the Copyright Renewal Act of 1992, and other national and international agreements is "public domain," which is an important consideration for first-time screenwriters and producers who may not have the trust funds or other resources to pay a hefty option for the material they'd love to adapt to the screen. However, if you're adapting something from another language, you also need to verify that the translation you are using is old enough to be in public domain, or either pay the owner of the current translation or hire an independent translator of your own.

Beyond the consideration of the timelines above, the best way to determine the availability of rights is to contact an author directly. The second-best bet is to contact the author's literary agent to set up a meeting with the author, but as Donaldson cautions, "Often an agent will want to extract deal terms as a condition of a meeting which is exactly what the adapter would not want to do."[19] Although the author's publisher may be contacted by the author to negotiate the rights, having the author on your side before that happens is a big plus. That is especially true if you're a screenwriter or producer with limited funds. In the case of *Smoke Signals* (USA/Canada, 1998), Chris Eyre was an impoverished grad student when he fell in love with Sherman Alexie's *The Lone Ranger and Tonto Fistfight in Heaven*. He was able to meet with Alexie and convince him to form a joint venture, with Eyre as director and Alexie as screenwriter/producer. They found feature funding on the basis of Alexie's script.[20]

On the road to a full-fledged agreement pertaining to an adaptation is the "option agreement," which gives you a time-limited opportunity to develop the screenplay, seek financing, and possibly scout for stars who are intrigued enough by the possible role in the film to become part of the package. The option is important so that you can control the rights, preventing someone else from going out and making a different version of the story while you control these rights, and enabling you to monetize the project. Realistically, you'll need between one and three years to make the option agreement a worthwhile gamble. This is how it works: You might pay $5,000 for the right to try to sell a novel to a Hollywood studio with a price tag of $100,000 for three years, for example; if you're successful in making the sale, "an additional $95,000 will be paid to the author."[21] Mark Litwak, Esq., points out that "options are often 10% of the full purchase price, but the amount is negotiable."[22] Price tags for theatrical rights are sometimes hefty, especially with best-sellers: for example, author E.L. James received $5 million from Universal Pictures and Focus Films for *Fifty Shades of Grey*.[23] Michael C. Donaldson and Lisa A. Callif's book, *Clearance & Copyright: Everything You Need to Know for Film and Television,* offers an entire section on option and purchase agreements and how to acquire the rights to fiction and nonfiction books, short stories, articles, newspaper stories, comic books, plays, and old movies.[24]

From the point of view of the original author, the meeting with the screenwriter is even more important than the contract. Donaldson advises:

> Sit down with him or her and be sure you understand what their take would be on the material. Don't accept a lot of conclusory enthusiasm such as 'we will take care of your material.' Or, 'I love the book. We plan to turn it into a film you will really be proud of.' Or get sucked into a conversation about an unrealistic list of stars who will appear in this relatively low-budget indie film. And find out about this person's plan for financing the film. It doesn't have to be specific, but assess the likelihood that this person will actually get the film made. Then check out everything the person tells you. Talk to people with whom the person has worked in the past. Do your homework. These are long-term relationships and should not be entered blindly.[25]

Key factors from the screenwriter's point of view for the best possible contract include making sure you "acquire the rights to all the characters in addition to the plot"; the ability to write "sequels if the movie is a hit, with the author of the underlying work receiving half of the original remuneration"; and "a holdback period of exclusivity and no licensing ever again of film rights if your film is actually produced."[26]

Basically, the producer wants the same thing as the screenwriter, according to Donaldson. However, in drawing up the contract, "he or she needs the right to replace the writer if the script doesn't turn out as hoped." Donaldson also cautions: "Be sure that the original author doesn't retain any veto power over the final script. Consultation is OK, even extensive, good faith consultation, but not approval."[27]

Some producers combine their identities with publishers, or vice versa. For example, Francis Ford Coppola, whose work as a director of adaptations includes *The Godfather* (USA, 1972), *Apocalypse Now* (USA, 1979), and *Bram Stoker's Dracula* (USA, 1992), also founded the short story magazine *Zoetrope: All-Story*, "and publication in its pages includes a one-year film option by Coppola's film company, American Zoetrope."[28] Dark Horse, which has been in the film business for about 30 years, and produced *Sin City* (USA, 2005), based on Frank Miller's graphic novel of the same title, "gives comic book creators the right to control their work." Mike Richardson, who runs Dark Horse Comics and Dark Horse Entertainment, states, "The reason we go[t] into the film business was this naïve idea that we could protect the writer by being a producer."[29]

In the US, the screenwriter is typically a "writer-for-hire," which means that the production company or studio owns the rights to his or her work and is legally considered to be the "author," in return for monetary gain. As Donaldson and Callif explain in their book *Clearance & Copyright*, if a studio or production company hires a writer to write the screenplay, "there is no point in time when the words belong to the person who typed them. The employer is the author for all purposes."[30] Donaldson and Callif's book includes a sample "Writer Agreement – Work for Hire" which spells out some of the details of services, compensation, credits, and foreseeable problems that should be discussed and negotiated in advance of agreeing to write for the studio or production company.[31]

Even if the writer writes a screenplay based on work in the public domain on spec and owns the copyright to his or her work at first, "it will almost invariably be required to be transferred to the production company or studio when the script itself is sold."[32] It would probably take an act of Congress to improve the lot of screenwriters in the US who would like to own their literary property, i.e. the script, in keeping with current practices "in many other countries including Canada and France where writers retain ownership in their scripts but producers are still able to exploit the works through licensing."[33]

In some cases, authors don't want to make the transition from writing fiction to working on the adaptation. According to Sara Paretsky, who let others write the adaptation of her mystery novels, *V.I. Warshawski* (USA,

1991) – which turned out to be a box-office bomb – the collaborative process feels much more invasive than the solitary act of novel-writing, and it can be humiliating to a novelist when your input is ignored by the producers:

> The more input you put in, and the more it's ignored, the more frustrated you get, and so better just to draw a line in the sand and stay on your side of it.[34]

It's a lesson in avoidance that's reinforced by studying the demise of John Scott Shepherd's adaptation of his novel *Life*, which sold for $1.1 million as a book, but bombed at the box office as *Life or Something Like It*. Shepherd himself wrote the first draft of the screenplay, though he said "My first rewrite was terrible, because I tried to please everybody."[35] Plagued by too many people giving him a baffling deluge of good, bad, and vacuous notes, along with likability issues, the vanishing character arc of the female lead, and the gulf between the author's perception of the male lead and what people in Hollywood thought he should be, and casting problems, Shepherd bemoaned the lack of "one strong voice in the script meeting ... who would arbitrate debates and keep the movie going in one consistent direction."[36]

John Briley, the American screenwriter who wrote *Gandhi* (UK/India/USA, 1982) bemoans the problem of screenwriters not owning their own copyrights to their screenplays in the US:

> If writers in America had retained the copyright, as they do in books or in the theater or anything but films, the situation that has grown up in Hollywood would not exist. It is totally different from the procedure in other countries, certainly industries that for their size produce marvelous films – not only in England and France and Italy, but Sweden and Czechoslovakia, Switzerland, Germany, Poland ... there's no such thing as these collective writing establishments and advisors to directors and producers who have anything like the power that these people have in the United States.[37]

However, Briley was writing in 1994; since then, certain American screenwriters have come up with some savvy ways to protect their original work, even though "Work-for-Hire" still stands as a major impediment to controlling one's material in most cases. For example, Joshuah Bearman was able to sell a 2007 story he had written about the hostage crisis in Iran, which, as a film school graduate, he had written and placed in *Wired* with the primary ambition of having some control over its film adaptation. Since then, Joshuah Bearman and Joshua Davis have started http://epicmagazine.com/, an online literary platform that commissions and publishes "big, non-fiction narratives that might also make good movies."[38] So far, according to Epic's website, they have optioned 25 articles to Hollywood. ePublishing can likewise involve putting one's novel up on amazon.com or similar platforms in order to attract the attention of studios and production companies, and to gain leverage as a screenwriter at getting a chance to be hired to write the adaptation. Some screenwriters have been turning to novelizations with this in mind, such as Rob Thomas, creator of *Veronica Mars*, to capitalize on successful TV series. Amazon.com describes his paperback novel, *The Thousand Dollar Tan Line*,.as:

> From Rob Thomas, the creator of the television series and movie phenomenon *Veronica Mars*, comes the first book in a thrilling mystery series that picks up where the feature film left off.[39]

Writers and producers for the media in other countries sometimes benefit commercially from other kinds of legal problems, such as censorship, although censorship can also crush the soul of a writer. (See Part IX – Censorship.) In China, the world's largest online streaming market, Chinese viewers were so obsessed with shows originating in South Korea, such as *My Love From Another Star* (South Korea, 2013–2014) that the government imposed regulations to limit foreign television content in order to promote Chinese product. That meant that to satisfy public demand, writers were employed to adapt South Korean variety and reality shows, and mini-series.

2. Who owns the rights?

Item #2 concerns the owner of the rights, which may be the author or the estate of the author, represented by a literary agent, or the publisher.

Publishing houses increasingly insist that subsidiary rights such as film and television rights be controlled by them, at least when it comes to negotiating adaptations with studios and producers. However, some authors have successfully maintained ownership of the screen rights to their books, like Scott Turow, author of *Presumed Innocent*, which was a box office hit (USA, 1990), and *The Burden of Proof*, which he sold as a mini-series (USA, 1992) as "he felt the story couldn't be adequately told in a standard two-hour movie."[40] Turow has enjoyed his involvement in picking screenwriters and directors for the adaptations of his books, although he cautions, "There's no guarantee that the people who buy these books and make movies out of them are going to be talented."[41]

On the other hand, Terry McMillan, the best-selling author of *Waiting to Exhale,* who had studied film at Columbia University, when considering her choices, asked Amy Tan about the process of adapting her novel, *The Joy Luck Club* (USA, 1993), with positive results. Amy Tan had co-written the script with Ron Bass, one of the most successful screenwriters in Hollywood, and when she heard how much Tan had enjoyed that co-writing experience, McMillan got Ron Bass to co-write *Waiting to Exhale* (USA, 1995) with her.

> I'd sit down and do the writing. Then Ron would come in and help me figure out what scenes to leave and what works and what doesn't. He's a good technician. When you've written the novel, it's hard to distance yourself from the work. Ron helped me connect the dots.[42]

3. Have the rights been previously granted to a third party?

Item #3 pertains to copyright clearance. You will need to find out whether screen rights have been previously granted to a third party, for how long, and in what form: feature film, television, video? Thinking ahead to distribution (as well as to the pre-sales that often finance films), you should find out whether existing rights are exclusive for particular countries, regions, or the world, and whether those rights have expired or are about to expire.[43]

It's highly unlikely that a screenwriter who has worked on a film for an American production company owns these rights. But whether it's the screenwriter, a movie studio, or another individual, known as a "third party," that person or entity can command long-term benefits that should not be ignored. Having a good lawyer can sometimes help the original author or his heirs' or successors, as well. In the case of *Rear Window* (USA, 1954), the film was an adaptation of a short story by Cornell Woolrich that had been published in *Dime Detective Magazine* in 1942. After Woolrich's death, his final "third party" copyright successor, literary agent Sheldon Abend, successfully asserted his rights under copyright law in a case that went all the way to the Supreme Court, to require further negotiation with the owner of the movie rights after the movie had shown on television, long after the film was released.[44]

Also connected to the third item on the checklist is the issue of titles: will using the same title as another work confuse the public? You'll want to identify the title of the work and determine whether title changes must be approved.[45] An example of legal obstruction with regards to the use of a title is the rapper 50 Cent's attempt to use the title *Things Fall Apart* for a film about a college football player. *Things Fall Apart* happens to be the title of the most widely read book in modern African literature, written by Chinua Achebe, the Nigerian novelist and man of letters, and winner of the 2007 Man Booker International Prize for lifetime achievement. Achebe's legal representatives said the rights to *Things Fall Apart* wouldn't be sold to 50 Cent "for even $1 billion,"[46] although the novel had been adapted by David Oriere under the same name in 1987 as a very successful mini-series funded by the Nigerian Television Authority, and as a feature in 1971, prior to the advent of Nollywood, by Hans Jürgen Pohland (Nigeria/Germany, 1971).[47] 50 Cent ended up using the title *All Things Fall Apart.*

4. If in public domain, have other versions been previously made and released?

Item #4 pertains to the complications of public domain. If another version or versions have been previously made and released, are they currently available, and if so, who owns them? You may need to negotiate with those owners to restrict their competition with your new film.[48] It's always a safer idea to go back to the original work that's in the public domain, when possible.

To the extent that real-life stories are comprised of facts, these are also in the public domain.[49] So restating factual news from the public record is OK, but those seeking to make an adaptation of a real-life story should exercise caution: journalists' phrases can be copyrighted. Furthermore, there are significant rights differences between telling the story of someone who's famous and someone who is not famous. You may need "a life story agreement" and "a release from the people involved"[50] – whether family, friends, neighbors, or co-workers, all of whom are harder to research than a famous person, and therefore more challenging[51] – in addition to a contract with the reporter the details of whose newspaper article made you envision the film in the first place.

5. Monetary negotiation with owner or agent of copyrighted version

Item #5 delves into the sums, percentages, and scheduling of payments to be negotiated with the owner or agent of the copyrighted material you wish to adapt. What is the flat sum you can pay? Can that payment be in installments at various stages of development? For example, after the option period, you may agree to pay a certain portion upon executing the contract, another portion when the budget has been substantially financed, another at the start of principal photography, another when the production wraps, and a final stage when the film is released – with additional stages including the date of first television airing, foreign distribution deals, and/or DVD or online streaming.

What if you don't have that kind of money? It's possible to negotiate a percentage of earnings in lieu of a fixed fee. In that case, you may be entering into the world of complex accounting terminology – "net earnings," "net profits," and "recoupable advances" – where, without a lawyer, you may never see a dime, even on a successful picture.[52]

6. Non-monetary negotiations (territory, script approval, sequel, credits, etc.)

Finally, Item #6 extends your negotiations to many issues that may not involve money up front but can be important to the author's desire for regional or international fame and the quality and longevity of the adaptation. These may include all or some of the following:

1 territory of rights granted plus options for further territories;
2 type of film rights granted (feature film, animation, documentary, etc.);
3 media rights granted (theatrical, festival only, television, etc., or "all media now or hereafter known");
4 script approval (absolute discretion, or reasonable approval? deadline?);

5 exclusivity of rights grants: lapse of rights for failure to complete and distribute film within time deadline;
6 limited grant of option, with specified dates by which stages towards active production must be achieved, or else rights lapse unless further option negotiated for extending time – which would require further payment of a second specified sum;
7 sequel rights; characters, and/or basic plot rights;
8 screen credits to author of story, size placement, and prominence.[53]

If you don't want to choose something to adapt that's in the public domain, such as *Beauty and the Beast* or *Alice in Wonderland*, whose authors died over a century ago, careful negotiations up front are crucial towards the long-term success of your project – and even then, the Disney Studio had teams of lawyers available to negotiate screenwriter Linda Woolverton's writer-for-hire contract on these films.[54] "[T]he *only* woman with sole writing credit on a billion-dollar movie (Burton's *Alice*),"[55] Woolverton continued on as screenwriter of *Alice through the Looking Glass* (USA/UK, 2016), a loose adaptation in which Alice doesn't just cross the brooks and streams that demarcate the chessboard of her fantastical journey, as in Lewis Carroll's novel, *Through the Looking Glass*, but crosses oceans the world over as a sea-captain. "I set her out on a bigger adventure to face reality," explains Woolverton, because Alice just couldn't fit into the tiny Victorian world.[56] Although Woolverton bristles at the number of writers called in for the sometimes obfuscating rewrites of her more recent of the two *Alice*'s, Disney was still obliged to grant her sole screen credit, as specified by her contract, because of "strong WGA obligations in addition to the agreement with the writer."[57]

Script approval is central to the dramatic conflict of the film *Saving Mr. Banks* (USA/UK/Australia, 2013), about Walt Disney's quest to obtain the rights to *Mary Poppins* from its ornery author, P.L. Travers.[58] Disney, the idealized hero, goes to great lengths to woo these rights, from having stuffed animals delivered to her lavish room in the Beverly Hills Hotel and sending the writers' room cutesy snacks including a Mickey Mouse face shaped from jello cubes, to agreeing – at first – to leave the color red and any songs out of the film, and ultimately, at the film's climax, flying to Australia to share with her the deep, compassionate insights he has had into their fathers' troubled backstories – which finally conquers her. As a film about the struggles involved in making a film adaptation, it fails to measure up to Charlie and Donald Kaufman's *Adaptation* (USA, 2002), which replaces the whitewashing and tedious sentimentality of *Saving Mr. Banks* with postmodern angst.

From the author's point of view, whether or not to grant a filmmaker the rights to your work can be a soul-searching ordeal. In her book *The Same River Twice*, Pulitzer Prize-winning author Alice Walker reexamines the process by which her novel, *The Color Purple*, was adapted into a film. The decision as to whether to turn her book over to director Steven Spielberg, to come out of her reclusive lifestyle to work with Spielberg

Figure 2.2 The Color Purple (USA, 1985), based on the Pulitzer Prize-winning novel by Alice Walker. Image courtesy of Warner Brothers. Produced by Amblin Entertainment, The Guber-Peters Company, and Warner Brothers

and screenwriter Menno Meyjes, and finally to take their film around a world that would sometimes meet their work with hostile criticism was a painful and sometimes even physically sickening experience. But Walker's experience was mixed with magic and affirmation. Quincy Jones, with whom she chose some of the music, "saw" what she was "as an artist and a person."[59] While her own script adaptation of *The Color Purple* was turned down and another writer was hired for its adaptation, producer Peter Guber acceded to Walker's condition "that she be involved, to the level of her interest, as a consultant," and that "half the people involved in the production, apart from the predominantly black cast, would be blacks, women and/or people of the Third World."[60] Spielberg, who frequently consulted with Walker on the set and on location, was ultimately able to bring *The Color Purple* into a wider world where people who were unable to read her book due to library censorship or illiteracy might still experience Celie's story in a movie theater. In assessing her decision to go with the opportunity presented with her, risking that it might be mangled by an insensitive, racist, and homophobic Hollywood, Walker writes:

> That I survived the stress of trusting two men I'd never met, with work filled with my own and my ancestors' spirits, is to me the miracle. What made this possible? Was it simply my delight in Steven's boyish chutzpah, which, given Jewish history, is so moving? "t makes this Jewish boy think he can direct a movie about black people?' critics fumed. Well, what did, exactly? It was this that I wanted to know. I

> thought it might be love. I thought it might be courage. I thought it might be the most wonderful thing of all: Steven had outgrown being a stranger ... I felt the same way about Quincy, and about Steven: that the Universe loves something in the spirits of these men, and for that reason has given each of them enormous power to shift reality in the world.[61]

Finally, with regards to "sequel rights" mentioned in the list above, these rights were crucial towards the mega-success of screenwriter Melissa Rosenberg. Unlike Catherine Hardwicke, the director of *Twilight* (USA, 2008), who was replaced by other directors on *Twilight – New Moon, Twilight – Eclipse,* and *Twilight – Breaking Dawn, Parts 1 & 2*, Rosenberg successfully managed to negotiate to keep sequel rights in her screenwriting contract, which not only meant screenwriting credits on all the other *Twilight* films, but also led to additional contracts for television series, making her one of the highest paid screenwriters in Hollywood.

Notes

1 Sam Kashner, "Here's to You, Mr. Nichols: The Making of *The Graduate*," *Vanity Fair*, February 25, 2008, accessed November 25, 2016, www.vanityfair.com/news/2008/03/graduate200803.
2 "All Time Box Office," *Box Office Mojo*, imdb.com, accessed November 25, 2016, www.boxofficemojo.com/alltime/adjusted.htm.
3 Kristof Boghe, "The Eastern Connection, Part I: *Reservoir Dogs* and *City on Fire*,"accessed November 25, 2016, www.easternkicks.com/features/the-eastern-connection-part-1-reservoir-dogs-and-city-on-fire.
4 Linda Hutcheon, *A Theory of Adaptation* (New York: Routledge, 2006), p. v.
5 Thomas Wolfe, *Look Homeward, Angel* (New York: Scribners, 1929).
6 Thomas Wolfe, quoted in Elizabeth Nowell, *Thomas Wolfe: A Biography* (Garden City, NY: Doubleday, 1960), 356.
7 Special thanks to Josiah James, CTVA 420, "Screenplay Adaptation" student at California State University, Northridge, Spring 2016, for researching the relationship between *The Lion King* and *Kimba, the White Lion*.
8 Bill Bradley, "Was *The Lion King* Copied From A Japanese Cartoon? Here's the Real Story," *Huffington Post*, January 27, 2015, accessed December 3, 2016, www.huffingtonpost.com/2015/01/27/lion-king-kimba_n_6272316.html. With regards to underlying influences concerning *Bambi* (USA, 1942) beyond Walt Disney's input in adapting the book, *Bambi: A Life in the Woods* by Felix Saten that was first published in 1923 in Austria, the inspirational sketch artist on that film, Cyrus Wong, invoked "the exquisite landscape paintings of the Song dynasty (AD 650–1279) to create the mood of the backgrounds." (Margalit Fox, "Cyrus Wong, 'Bambi' Artist Thwarted by Racial Bias, Dies at 106," *New York Times,* December 30, 2016, accessed January 17, 2017, http://nyti.ms/3iOjHsg, 6.)
9 "List of highest-grossing films," Wikipedia.org, accessed December 3, 2016, https://en.wikipedia.org/wiki/List_of_highest-grossing_films.
10 Francis X. Atencio, Imagineer, quoted from *Pirates of the Caribbean: The Lost Disc (Documentaries)* (DVD: Walt Disney Studios Home Entertainment, 2004); Tanaka Clark, "An Excerpt from *History of the Pirates of the Caribbean* for 'Disney Secrets Uncovered,'" July 17, 2016, accessed June 1, 2017, www.youtube.com/watch?v=DbxF6E7Z8sA.

11 Special thanks to Frannie Tull, student in the Spring 2016 class, CTVA 420 "Screenplay Adaptation," at California State University, Northridge for her research and Midterm Project Summary on the *Pirates of the Caribbean* ride and the film *Pirates of the Caribbean: The Curse of the Black Pearl*, April 4, 2016, 2.
12 Scott Halleran, "Ted Elliott & Terry Rossio On Pirates of the Caribbean," *Box Office Mojo*, July 8 2006, accessed November 30, 2016, 2, www.scottholleran.com/old/interviews/elliott-rossio-pirates-caribbean.htm.
13 Special thanks to Alexandra Neal, MFA Screenwriting Program student in the Fall 2011 class, CTVA 420 "Screenplay Adaptation" at California State University, Northridge, for her research and Midterm Presentation on the *Pirates of the Caribbean* screenplays.
14 Tim Powers, *On Stranger Tides* (Northridge, CA: Babbage Press, 1987).
15 Special thanks to Ted Elliott, my mentor at the Writers Guild of America, West, for providing me and MFA Screenwriting student Alexandra Neal and our CTVA 420, "Screenplay Adaptation" class at California State University, Northridge, with his explanation of how the *Pirates of Caribbean* came about in his email of October 23, 2011.
16 M. William Krasilovsky, Esq., "Negotiators' Checklist for Film Adaptation," fax to the author, May 29, 1997, 3. Special thanks to my father, M. William Krasilovsky, for providing this checklist.
17 Michael Donaldson, email interview with the author, December 12, 2016.
18 "Circular 38a: International Copyright Relations of the United States," U.S. Copyright Office, August 2016, accessed November 26, 2016, 13, www.copyright.gov/circs/circ38a.pdf.
19 Donaldson interview.
20 Joanna Sabal, "Great Adaptations," *Independent*, 21(7) (August/September, 1998), 34.
21 Sabal, "Great Adaptations," 33.
22 Mark Litwak, *Dealmaking in the Film and Television Industry: From Negotiations to Final Contracts* (Los Angeles, CA: Silman-James Press, 1994), 23.
23 Jeff Bercovici, "Women On The Rise Among The World's Top-Earning Authors," *Forbes,* August 9, 2012, accessed December 3, 2016, www.forbes.com/sites/jeffbercovici/2012/08/09/women-on-the-rise-among-the-worlds-top-earnings-authors/#47b23b4645cf.
24 Lisa A. Callif and Michael C. Donaldson, *Clearance & Copyright: Everything You Need to Know for Film and Television*, 4th edn. (Los Angeles, CA: Silman-James Press, 2014), 133–147.
25 Donaldson interview.
26 Donaldson interview.
27 Donaldson interview.
28 Stephanie Harrison, "You Ought to Be in Pictures: A Story Writer's Guide to Film Adaptation," *Poets & Writers* (September–October, 2006), 71.
29 Mike Richardson, quoted in Gregory Schmidt, "Indie Comic Book Publishers Make Moves Toward TV and Film," *New York Times,* October 4, 2015, accessed December 3, 2016, 2, http://nyti.ms/1iX90U3.
30 Callif and Donaldson, *Clearance & Copyright*, 65.
31 Callif and Donaldson, *Clearance & Copyright*, 164–187.
32 Lesley Ellen Harris, "Copyright," *Journal*, 6(6) (June, 1993), 23.
33 Harris, "Copyright," 24.
34 Sara Paretsky, quoted in Yardeba Arar, "Movie Success Not Always by the Book," *L.A. Life – Daily News,* February 16, 1992, 16.
35 John Scott Shepherd, quoted in Patrick Goldstein, "Dumbed Down by Committee," "The Big Picture," *Los Angeles Times*, May 7, 2002, accessed

May 9, 2002, 2, www.latimes.com/entertainment/printedition/calendar/la-000032232may07.story.
36 Goldstein, "Dumbed down by Committee," 2.
37 John Briley, "On *Gandhi* and *Cry Freedom*," *Creative Screenwriting*, 1(1) (Spring, 1994), 20.
38 David Carr, "Magazine Writing on the Web, for Film," *New York Times*, August 11, 2013, accessed August 12, 2013, www.nytimes.com/2013/08/12/business/media/magazine-writing-on-the-web-for-film.html.
39 "Veronica Mars: An Original Mystery by Rob Thomas: The Thousand Dollar Tan Line," Amazon.com, accessed December 3, 2016, www.amazon.com/Veronica-Mars-Original-Mystery-Thousand-Dollar/dp/0804170703.
40 Scott Turow, quoted in Yardena Arar, "Movie Success Not Always by the Book," L.A. Life: Arts & Entertainment, *Daily News*, February 16, 1992, 16.
41 Scott Turow, quoted in Arar, "Movie Success Not Always by the Book," 16.
42 Terry McMillan, quoted in Veronica Chambers, "Terry McMillan Goes to Hollywood: The Novelist Talks about Taking her Bestseller to the Screen," *Quarterly Black Review* (November, 1995), 2, www.bookwire.com/qbr/features/95-no/mcmillan.html.
43 McMillan, quoted in Chambers, "Terry McMillan Goes to Hollywood," 3.
44 McMillan, quoted in Chambers, "Terry McMillan Goes to Hollywood," 5.
45 Krasilovsky, "Negotiators' Checklist for Film Adaptation."
46 Sean Michaels, "Chinua Achebe Forces 50 Cent to Rename Movie," *Guardian*, September 14, 2011, accessed October 23, 2015, www.theguardian.com/music/2011/sep/14/chinua-achebe-50-cent.
47 Shaibu Husseini, "Notes on Nollywood and Nigerian Cinema," email to the author, September 21, 2016.
48 Husseini, "Notes on Nollywood and Nigerian Cinema."
49 Cf. Justice Sandra Day O'Connor, "Opinion of the Court," *Feist Publictions, Inc. v. Rural Telephone Services*, 499 U.S. 340 (1991), accessed November 26, 2016, www.law.cornell.edu/copyright/cases/499_US_340.htm.
50 Patricia V. Mayer and Jill Rubin, hand-out, "Women in Film: The Art of the Deal (Part 2)," Mitchell Silberberg & Knupp, LLP, July 27, 2010, 1.
51 Donaldson interview.
52 Donaldson interview.
53 Donaldson interview.
54 Linda Woolverton, *Beauty and the Beast*, directed by Gary Trousdale and Kirk Wise (Burbank, CA: Buena Vista Pictures, 1991), DVD; and Linda Woolverton, *Alice in Wonderland*, directed by Tim Burton (Burbank, CA: Walt Disney Studios Home Entertainment, 2010).
55 Max Nicholson, "Linda Woolverton on Adapting *Alice through the Looking Glass*, Live Action vs. Animation," *IGN*, May 26, 2016, accessed November 27, 2016, www.ign.com/articles/2016/05/26/linda-woolverton-on-adapting-alice-through-the-looking-glass-live-action-vs-animation.
56 Linda Woolverton, quoted from the Q&A following the screening of *Alice Through the Looking Glass* with Linda Woolverton, screenwriter, and moderator Valerie Alexander, WGA/w Theatre, June 11, 2016.
57 Donaldson interview.
58 Kelly Marcel and Sue Smith, *Saving Mr. Banks*, directed by John Lee Hancock (Burbank, CA: Walt Disney Studios, 2013); about securing the rights for the film *Mary Poppins*, directed by Robert Stevenson, written by Bill Walsh and Don DaGradi (Burbank, CA: Walt Disney Studios, 1964); based on P.L. Travers' *Mary Poppins* (London and New York: HarperCollins and Harcourt, Brace, 1934–1988).
59 Alice Walker, *The Same River Twice: Honoring the Difficult: A Meditation on Life, Spirit, Art, and the Making of the Film* The Color Purple *Ten Years Later* (New York: Scribner, 1996), 31.

60 Elena Featherston, "The Making of 'The Color Purple': An exclusive report from the set with Alice Walker, Steve Spielberg, Whoopi Goldberg, Danny Glover and Quincy Jones," *San Francisco Focus*, December 1985. In Walker, *The Same River Twice*, 183.
61 Walker, *The Same River Twice*, 284.

THREE

The Ethics and Aesthetics of Adaptation

Ethical questions often arrive when embarking on an adaptation. Why are you the one who can best retell this story? What are your motives? Will the work do justice to the original author, or to a discerning audience of a more demanding era?

Director/co-screenwriter Oliver Stone says that the influence he received from Hollywood film characters and actors to enlist in the military changed once he got to Vietnam and experienced war first-hand:

> I think the militaristic John Wayne stereotype influenced many young men to enlist in the military and support the war ... I was more influenced by Tarzan, Errol Flynn, and Clark Gable, and definitely Hemingway ... I loved the rectitude of male heroes that, in that era, was a dominating impulse ... But that kind of idealism and romance quickly burned away when I actually went into combat and saw how ugly war really was ... Anyone who knows better and makes of war stirring, moving experience has made a fraudulent movie.[1]

Questions also arise regarding aesthetic issues. What should you preserve from the original source material: its tone, its style, its characters, its setting, its structure? Is it too dialogue-driven? Too dated? Too arty? Too sketchy? Too much part of a cultural canon to revise?

Before Barry Jenkins adapted it into the Academy Award winner, *Moonlight* (USA, 2016), *In the Moonlight Black Boys Look Blue*, an unproduced piece by Tarell Alvin McCraney, a playwright and MacArthur Fellow, was not quite a play, in that it was written in "a very visual language" peppered with cinematic "CUT TOs."[2] McCraney had originally structured his personal project to follow three different characters simultaneously in a circular pattern through the different, specific days, tracking "the macro, micro, personal and even spiritual" as the characters were eventually shown to be the same person.[3] Jenkins molded McCraney's story into a more standard three-act structure, showing the protagonist as a child, an adolescent, and an adult in each consecutive act, and bringing the poverty-stricken world of Liberty City, Florida – which Jenkins and McCraney had both experienced in their youth – to life through the transcendent visual style of cinematographer James Laxton. So expressive is the *mise-en-scène* of *Moonlight* that substantial credit must be given to the original source writer, the cinematographer, and his crew, the production designer and the art director, while simultaneously acknowledging the orchestration of these facets of the production by Barry Jenkins as *auteur*.

"Writing" a film through its camera, lighting, and editing is a concept created by the French director/theorist Jean Epstein, who is especially celebrated for adapting Edgar Allen Poe's "The Fall of the House of Usher" (France, 1928). Epstein described cinema "as a language ... a form of ideographic writing ... [and later] with a grammar peculiar to itself."[4] By 1923, director/theorist Germaine Dulac was fighting for the title "auteur" of her films,[5] such as *La Souriante Madame Beudet (The Smiling Mme. Beudet,* France, 1923), adapted from a play by Denys Amiel and André Obey,[6] and which revolves cinematically around "La Mort des Amants" ("The Death of Lovers"), a poem by Baudelaire.[7]

For the camera to serve as a pen is a very different concept from the 1880s concept of the camera as gun, which had preceded it, although most filmmakers still say we're going to "shoot a film" more than we say we're going to gather images the way a writer gathers words to write a poem, a story, an essay, or a novel. Independent French filmmaker Agnès Varda, whom I interviewed for my documentary, *Women Behind the Camera* (USA, 2007) in her house on the rue Daguerre in Paris in 2005, prefers the terms "cinécriture" to Epstein's "cinégraphie." Instead of saying "Directed by Agnès Varda" in her credits, she says, "Cinécrit par Agnès Varda." But regardless of what term is used, there is often a fine line – or no line – between writer and director.

Senegalese novelist/director Ousmane Sembène (1912–2007) hoped that through literature, he could correct some of the prejudices held about Africans by Europeans. But after serving in the Free French Forces during World War II, and later returning to Africa to travel and write, he realized how limited the access was to his work, due to illiteracy. Of his many novels, novellas, and short stories, the most well-known is *Xala*,[8] which means "impotence" in his native language, Wolof, and which satirizes postcolonial government corruption in his country. Sembène believed that film could reach a wider audience, and after studying film at the Gorki Studio in Moscow, he returned to Senegal to work as a film director/screenwriter. The many films that he directed – including the adaptation of his novella *Black Girl* in 1966 and his novel *Xala* in 1975 – were well received; Sembène established his own film studio. He also initiated film tours that allowed him to travel to the villages in Senegal to show his movies, thus overcoming the problem of his country's lack of theaters and adequate distribution for African films and inspiring Sembène to create an African cinematic language.[9]

In an interview by Noureddine Ghali, Sembène said:

> In the Francophone countries south of the Sahara, we have a bourgeoisie whose official language is nothing but French. They only feel significant when they express themselves in French. They merely copy the West and western bourgeois culture. ... But when these types find themselves face-to-face with the people, they are often illiterate in the country's national language – they are alienated to such an extent, for inside themselves they are colonized. They are always the first to say people's mentalities have to be decolonized, but it is actually their mentality which has to be.[10]

Western literature has often taken a problematic stance when it comes to issues of colonization and other forms of repression, sometimes implicitly perpetuating the status quo, sometimes fighting for liberation with varying degrees of success. Commercial American adaptations have been particularly remiss by depoliticizing novelists' attempts to include social consciousness in their work. For example, New York's *Daily News* gushed about John Ford's *The Grapes of Wrath* (USA, 1940), written by Nunnally Johnson based on the novel by John Steinbeck as follows:

> It is the most daring picture that has ever come out of Hollywood, and it is one of the most important ... The adapter and director have made no compromise with their sense of integrity by softening conditions to appease the officials of the states of California and Oklahoma.[11]

But a closer look at 20th Century Fox's production correspondence suggests otherwise: even if conditions weren't softened for the sake of California and Oklahoma government officials, a three-page letter from Joseph I. Breen of the Motion Picture Producers and Distributors of America (MPPDA) regarding suggested corrections conforming to the provisions of the Production Code includes:

> The business of the fight between the deputies Casy [sic] and Tom should not be excessively brutal or gruesome, and even though it may be argued that Tom killed the deputy in self-defense, it might be better not to suggest such a thing.[12]

A more contemporary example, *The Help* (USA, 2011), has been widely criticized in the black community as a "white savior" film. Both the novel and the film feature as protagonist Eugenia "Skeeter" Phelan, a bright white ingénue. Skeeter (played by Emma Stone) helps black women tell their stories of injustice in the Deep South in an era when the publishers who would consider publishing black women writers other than Maya Angelou were few and far between.

From a social and literary perspective, it's ironic and denigrating that the word "help" is relegated to the profession of maids. Yet one of the factors that makes both Kathryn Stockett's novel and Tate Taylor's adaptation popular among female audiences is that the book and the film are among the only expressions in mass culture of the cooking, cleaning, and childcare that are so intrinsic to most women's day-to-day activities, whether we are home care providers, or professors like me – who still have to clean when we come home. *The Help* pays attention to the details of diaper-changing, cake-baking, and oven-cleaning, and even makes some of these plot points, turning Aibileen Clark (played by Viola Davis) and Minny Jackson (played by Octavia Spencer) into unforgettable characters beyond their mundane routines. Many of us are hearing the maids' perspectives on race, power, and day-to-day survival skills for the first time. How unfortunate, therefore, that *The Help* "distorts, ignores, and trivializes the experiences of black domestic workers," according to the Association of Black Women Historians.[13]

However, where are the portraits of black women who were active in the struggle for civil rights in the 1960s, and why have the studios neglected to tell their stories? The film industry still has far to go to make as many films about the Rosa Parks and Gwen Ifills of America as it has about its slaves, maids, butlers, and chauffeurs.

In regards to its white filter construction, *The Help* is almost as bad as *Cry Freedom* (UK/USA, 1987), in which the story of South African leader of the Black Consciousness Movement Steve Biko is told from the standpoint of a white journalist named Donald Woods, who is courageous enough to befriend Biko despite the 1970s strictures of apartheid. Steve Biko doesn't even get to be the protagonist of his own biopic: the studios were too scared to tell his story except through a white filter. John Briley, the screenwriter of *Cry Freedom*, ended up adapting Biko's story from two books written by Donald Woods. Briley recounts:

> No studio would back a film that simply told "the black South Africa story." They simply did not believe anyone in the world – particularly in America – would come to see such a picture.[14]
>
> Woods' book had told the story linearly ... It was a white man's story, a life that had been altered dramatically and irrevocably by this experience with a unique and powerful young Black, but throughout *his* story. I wanted it to be Biko's story – or a least Woods and Biko's story.[15]

But "Biko dies on page 61 of a 143 page script," although Woods constantly flashes back to key moments of Biko's life, his murder, and his funeral.[16] It was director Richard Attenborough and screenwriter John Briley's intention "to get more people to understand the way life was lived in South Africa" through a white perspective, but Briley admits

> My worst feeling about it was that by having Biko dead and buried less than half way through the script, you focused so much on the Wood's predicament that it made it seem as though, we, the filmmakers, were telling you that the peril of these middle-class whites was far more important than the tragedy of the black peoples of South Africa.[17]

As an adaptation, *The Help* also plays with point of view detrimentally, even though this film was made almost a quarter-century later. The novel opens with Aibileen narrating her own story that forcefully underscores just what it meant for an intelligent black woman with limited educational and career opportunities to have to toil for hostile white women in the racist South, raising white children during the pre-Civil Rights era. The first paragraph of Kathryn Stockett's novel includes:

> Mae Mobley was born on a early Sunday morning in August 1960. A church baby we like to call it. Taking care a white babies, that's what I do, along with al the cooking and the cleaning. I done raised seventeen kids in my lifetime. I know how to get them babies to sleep, stop crying, and go in the toilet bowl before they mamas even get out a bed in the morning.[18]

The emphasis, from the very first sentence, is already on someone white who will grow up to be more privileged than the person narrating her own story, a strong hint that the "person with a problem" who could turn the story will be deprived of that status. The screenplay, in contrast, is one degree more distancing: we see Aibileen, though not her interviewer, in a way that is awkwardly objectifying and invasive:

```
                    WOMAN (O.C.)
          Did you know as a girl, growing up,
          that one day you'd be a maid?

                    AIBILEEN
          Yes, m'am. I did.

                    WOMAN (O.C.)
          And you knew that because?

                    AIBILEEN
          My momma was a maid. My grandmomma
          was a house slave.

The woman repeats Aibileen's answer slowly as she writes.

                    WOMAN (O.C.)
          A … house … slave.

Aibileen looks to the floor for a moment.[19]
```

Using the interview approach works to provide a logical structure to the movie version of *The Help* as well as setting up a context before Aibileen's own storytelling, but there's more to the arts than mere logic. Once we're introduced to the protagonist Skeeter, who is interviewing maids in order to obtain her coming-of-age entrance into the world of professional writers, the maids are turned into objects as supporting characters, their lives largely limited to the flavorful, Southern-style dialogue which Skeeter appreciates but also exploits.

And yet, I can't help being deeply moved by both the novel and the film's provocative premise and unique portraiture, despite these misgivings. Maybe it's because of my backstory. I'm a white woman filmmaker who was hired in the mid-1970s in Memphis, Tennessee by a Southern producer who passed for white to interview black business people, churchgoers, musicians, gamblers, radio hosts, and photographers, some of whom had witnessed the last march of Martin Luther King on Beale Street. While I don't flatter myself as a "white savior," as a co-director of *Beale Street* (USA, 1978), I was trying to save a part of black history for which a black director wouldn't have been hired at that time (although a few years later I worked on *I Remember Beale Street* for PBS as Reginald Brown's Associate Producer and token white on an otherwise all-black crew, putting him in touch with many of the same interviewees). Is that transitional period best forgotten?

The protagonist of *The Help* gets to be a white woman whose "Heroine's Journey" is to obtain a New York publishing deal off of the black women's stories; the deal is her Jason's Golden Fleece. Nevertheless, it's a triumphant quest, which manages to shed light on important historical events in the background, such as the murder of civil rights activist Medgar Evers in 1963. Aibileen's initial response to the news of Evers' death in *The Help* is moving, but as dialogue it's flat and on the nose: "We living in hell! We trapped. Our kids is trapped."[20] The line itself isn't so different from Stockett's dialogue, but the context is angrier and more specific in the novel. Instead of tears and the generalized, off-camera "The MAYOR begins giving a statement over the radio,"[21] we hear the historical facts of "policemen everywhere, blocking the road,"[22] and other historical details. It's the reality of "white people with guns" that breaks one maid, while the other stands drenched with sweat in fear.

America has had to wait for over half a century since Medgar Evers' death: his biopic is finally due out in 2017. In the meantime, Tate Taylor's *The Help* tones down the ending to this pivotal scene involving Evers, with Aibileen and Minnie hugging in faux closure: "They laugh a little through the tears."[23]

Notes

1 Oliver Stone, "On Seven Films," in "Part III: Stone Responds." In Robert Brent Topli (ed.), *Oliver Stone's USA: Film, History, and Controversy* (Lawrence, KS: University Press of Kansas, 2000), 236.

2 Tarell Alvin McCraney, quoted in Mose Halperin, "Playwright Tarell Alvin McCraney Discusses the Piece That Inspired 'Moonlight'," *Flavorwire*, October 21, 2016, accessed February 18, 2017, http://flavorwire.com/592191/playwright-tarell-alvin-mccraney-discusses-the-pic.

3 McCraney quoted in Halperin "Playwright Tarell Alvin McCraney Discusses the Piece That Inspired 'Moonlight'".
4 Noël Burch, *Life to those Shadows,* trans. by B. Brewster (Berkeley, CA: Univeristy of California Press, 1990), 18–19; cited in T. Jefferson Kline, *Unraveling French Cinema* (Chichester: Wiley-Blackwell, 2001), 13.
5 Germaine Dulac, interviewed by Paul Desclaux, "Nos metteurs en scène: Germaine Dulac," *Mon Ciné*, 88 (October 25, 1923), 6–7.
6 Charles Musser, "The Clash Between Theatre and Film: Germaine Dulac, André Bazin and *La Souriante Madame Beudet,*" *New Review of Film and Television Studies,* 5(2) (2007), 118.
7 Charles Baudelaire, "La Mort des Amants" ("Death of Lovers"). In Joseph M. Bernstein (ed.), *Baudelaire, Rimbaud, Verlaine: Selected Verse and Prose Poems* (New York: Citadel Press, 1947), 9.
8 Ousmane Sembène, *Xala*. trans. by Clive Wake (New York: Lawrence Hill, 1983).
9 Soumaya, "Legendary African Filmmaker: Ousmane Sembene," *Discover African Cinema*, February 18, 2014, accessed April 10, 2017, www.discoverafricancinema.com/legendary-african-filmmakerousmane-sembene/4/.
10 Noureddine Ghali, "An Interview with Sembene Ousmane," *Cinema,* 76(209) (April, 1976), reprinted in John D. H. Downing (ed.), *Film and Politics in the Third World* (New York: Autonomedia, 1987), 42.
11 Kate Cameron, *Daily News*, quoted in "What the New York Critics say," *Citizen News*, January 31, 1930; in *The Grapes of Wrath* files, Margaret Herrick Library, Academy of Motion Picture Arts & Sciences, researched December 19, 2015.
12 Joseph I. Breen to Colonel Jason S. Joy, letter dated September 29, 1939, page 3, re Scenes 207–209; researched at Margaret Herrick Library, Academy of Motion Picture Arts & Sciences, December 19, 2015.
13 Ida E. Jones, "An Open Statement to the Fans of *The Help*," Association of Black Women Historians, retrieved November 1, 2011, quoted in "*The Help* (film)," Wikipedia.org, accessed April 10, 2017, https://en.wikipedia.org/wiki/The_Help_(film).
14 John Briley, "On 'Gandhi' and 'Cry Freedom,'" *Creative Screenwriting*, 1(1) (Spring, 1994), 8.
15 John Briley, "On 'Gandhi' and 'Cry Freedom,'" 9.
16 John Briley, "On 'Gandhi' and 'Cry Freedom,'" 9.
17 John Briley, "On 'Gandhi' and 'Cry Freedom,'" 10.
18 Kathryn Stockett, *The Help* (New York: Berkley Books, 2009), 1.
19 Tate Taylor, *The Help* (Universal City, CA: Dreamworks, 2011).
20 Tate Taylor, 93.
21 Tate Taylor, 93.
22 Stockett, *The Help*, 230.
23 Tate Taylor, op. cit., 94.

Part II

Applying Screenplay Principles to Adaptation

FOUR

Plot

When teaching screenwriting, instructors love using *Die Hard* (USA, 1988) as the great example of how to write plot. Gotham Writers' Workshop's Alexander Steele introduces *Die Hard* as a "classic action/adventure and a prime example of the big-budget Hollywood movie."[1] Writer Adam Sternbergh calls it "a bona fide masterpiece," and adds, "If you can't get behind *Die Hard* as a great American movie, then I'd argue that you hate greatness, movies and America."[2]

In mapping out the "how-to"s of plot in *Writing Movies: The Practical Guide to Creating Stellar Screenplays*, Daniel Noah charts the five major events in *Die Hard* as follows:

> *Inciting incident:* Terrorists storm the building
> *Plot point 1:* Terrorists kill the head of the corporation
> *Midpoint:* McClane captures attention of the cops
> *Plot point 2:* Terrorists open the vault
> *Climax:* McClane faces off with the terrorist leader[3]

Noah goes into great detail breaking down *Die Hard* to illustrate how its plot is constructed. What he leaves out, however, is how screenwriters Jeb Stuart and Steven de Souza arrived at each event in the script while adapting Roderick Thorp's novel, *Nothing Lasts Forever*, upon which *Die Hard* is based. For example, in the film, John McClane "has come to L.A. to visit his estranged wife,"[4] while Thorp has Leland – the novel's protagonist – visiting his daughter: Stephanie Gennaro is "assistant to the vice president for international sales, Klaxon Oil,"[5] a corporation that "has promised to supply the Chilean fascist military regime with millions upon millions in arms."[6] Steffie has divorced her husband while keeping his name and raising their two children on her own.[7] Instead of a wife, Leland's love interest is an off-duty flight attendant whom the protagonist met on the plane.[8]

In the film, McClane is a sympathetic cop; in the novel, he is a die-hard anti-terrorist by training:

> He had participated in the secret seminars and conferences that had developed the contingency plans of many of the nation's municipal police departments. This was the real, only and true reason for the creation of SWAT teams. The Symbionese Liberation Army shootout was a case in point. Ex-LAPD Chief Ed Davis had tipped the strategy completely with his so-called jocular response to the problem of air piracy: "Hang 'em at the airport."
>
> The strategy: Kill them all.[9]

As for Gruber, the suave and mysterious antagonist, Thorp spells out Gruber's political affiliation: "third generation Red Army Faction, West Germany," and digs deep into Gruber's backstory as the son of a Nazi officer to provide motives for his cruelty.[10]

The movie entertains us with pure, unadulterated action, mixed with exchanges between buddies that make for further bonding, whereas the novel indulges in all-round remorse, as the near-dead Leland's reflects on how his daughter has died in a shoot-out, leading him to further regrets:

> He turned the gun around and looked into the barrel, screaming – if she had done what he had told her to do, she would be alive, unharmed[11] ... Any cop would tell you, sooner or later you were aware of every mistake you had ever made ... The mistakes were as much a part of human nature as the situations that created them. Maybe Little Tony had had the time to realize what he had done wrong. Tony had known about the gun behind Leland's neck, but had died anyway. It was Steffie who had made it possible for Leland to put one bullet after another into him. She had been sorry for what had happened to her father. She had held herself responsible.[12]

Ah! A blame-the-victim moment! In the novel, Steffie is only one of six women victims – most of whose demises are gore-filled descriptions by Thorp, private detective-turned-novelist. At the end of the novel, because of Steffie's death, Mr. and Mrs. Gennaro are clearly unable to resume their marriage, whereas John McClane and his wife reunite at the end of the film. We do have the makings of the protagonist's final triumph, however, in which McClane kills Gruber and saves the building from being blown up.

We also have a subplot resolution, which Gotham Writers' Workshop instructor Helen Kaplan describes as LAPD Officer Powell getting "his moment of redemption at the end."[13] Thorp is very specific: "Leland saw Powell take careful aim and, with two clean shots, tear off the top of Karl's head in a sheet of brains and blood," followed by more than a page's worth of declarations of mutual admiration, a tourniquet for Leland's bleeding leg, and friendly advice between the men in their newly cemented friendship.[14]

Figure 4.1 Aristotle's Plot (*Le complot d'Aristote*, Zimbabwe/Cameroon, 1996), written and directed by Jean-Pierre Bekolo – an action film for contemporary Africans. Image courtesy of Films Distribution. Produced by JBA Production

As Adam Sternbergh points out, "The action film – like automobiles, televisions and team-oriented basketball – is an American invention that is now produced much better elsewhere in the world."[15] One of the more unusual action films from outside the US, *Aristotle's Plot* (*Le complot d'Aristote,* Zimbabwe/Cameroon, 1996) written and directed by Jean-Pierre Bekolo, is saturated with references to other action films, as described by African Film Festival New York:

> In a southern African town, a group of wannabe gangsters hang out at the Cinema Africa, subjecting themselves to mega-doses of the latest action-fest. They've even taken the names of their screen gods: Van Damme, Bruce Lee, and Nikita. Into this walks an earnest cineaste who wants to enlist the government's help in cleansing Cinema Africa of Hollywood imports, replacing Schwarzenegger with Sembène.[16]

Many screenwriting texts pay homage to Aristotle when discussing plot, such as *The Screenwriter's Bible*, which reminds us that "Aristotle wrote in his *Poetics* that all drama (and that includes comedy, since comedy is drama in disguise) has a beginning, a middle, and an end. You've heard this before."[17] Bekolo's *Aristotle's Plot*, according to Matthias de Groof, questions the "formal aspects of storytelling that go along with Western imagery … through the storytelling of the film itself."[18] As Michael Dembor suggests:

> He wants to make movies that reflect the hybrid reality of contemporary young urban Africans, for whom the struggle to find

> an identity IS their reality. He is not interested in telling dramatic stories? Like Aristotle, rather, he wants to make films that are self-reflexive subversions of the Aristotelian conventions of linear narrative, mimetic realism, conflict rising to a climax, and catharsis (the purging of inner emotions by means of identifying with fictional characters and eliciting feels of fear and pity).[19]

Bekolo asks:

> Does a story have to generate pity and fear also in Africa? Do I embrace this formula or do I interrogate it in order to redefine what cinema is?[20]

In adapting Patricia Highsmith's novel *Carol*, screenwriter Phyllis Nagy paid close attention to the rules of dramatic structure which she knew well as an award-winning playwright, but ultimately, she left the book behind after reading it repeatedly and internalizing the material to make her own organic structure for the film version (UK/USA/Australia, 2015). Nagy comments: "The plot is secondary to the character shifts, the mood, and the subject."[21]

In the People's Republic of China, screenwriter Lu Wei would probably agree that plot does not come first. When writing the screenplay to *Farewell, My Concubine* (China/Hong Kong, 1993) based on the novel by Lilian Lee, Lu Wei wrote character analyses for every character, a practice he considers a must for every script that he writes. "Only when you fully understand the characters, can you understand each and every one's special tone."[22] His list of screenwriters' duties are: "First, to grasp the main subject. Secondly, to set up the genre. Third is to understand the characters. And the fourth is to design the plot."[23] How different this is from the Hollywood studio system of the 1930s through the 1950s, when writers would often start their work by summarizing the plots of novels or parts thereof, such as *Wuthering Heights* (USA, 1939), for which Charles MacArthur and Ben Hecht won an Oscar nomination despite their lack of insight into the psyches of Catherine and Heathcliff that immortalized Emily Brontë's novel.

Plot Endings

A novel is not a Simplicity pattern. Although the novelist Rosalie Ham paints a vivid portrait of a small, backwards town in Australia, *The Dressmaker*'s story is fundamentally about its protagonist, who gets her revenge on the townspeople through needle and thread. It seems expedient to open up the novel's ending cinematically in Jocelyn Moorhouse and P.J. Hogan's screenplay for *The Dressmaker* (Australia, 2016), to show the wild action of the town ablaze and burning to the ground: flames are exciting and any development executive worth his or her salt is going to think this is an easy way to entertain us. However, that's only the most obvious solution. It's overkill, like a symphony with too many endings, half of which aren't in the protagonist's key. It's also uncomfortably stagey – there's no Alfonso Cuarón at the helm, and this is no *Children of Men* (USA/UK/Japan, 2006) storyboarded and shot in all of its complexity by Emmanuel Lubezki with an unlimited budget to burn down a realistic set of a town at the conclusion of the production. Instead we are treated to beautiful landscapes, costumes, and details of character admirably directed by Jocelyn Moorhouse, who is especially astute at combining comedy and drama. But Moorhouse's and P.J. Hogan's screenplay of Rosalie Ham's novel would have been more effective if it had not been so faithful in including the town's demise. It's a character-oriented film, and therefore it would make more sense to hold the ending as Kate Winslet's character rides away from Dungatar, her mission of revenge accomplished in putting to shame the people who had once ruined her life. Setting fire to her old decrepit home marks a ritual that allows her to move into the future – presumably back in Paris and its world of couture. But burning down the entire town of Dungatar takes too much screen time and the results are embarrassingly ineffective on a $12 million total budget: a poor choice for both the screenwriters and the producers.

The novel, at least, is impressively understated about the fire, devoting one sentence to the action of the flames fanning "across the dry weeks and stems to the brown grass, then down The Hill towards town."[24] We see the destruction from the point of view of Tilly's enemies, who have just returned from a humiliating attempt to stage a scene from Macbeth in a regional contest, wearing ludicrous costumes. Even more humiliating is coming home to discover their town almost completely razed out of revenge for having badly maligned Tilly in her youth.

> A few smouldering trees remained, and a telephone pole here, a brick chimney there. Anxious pet dogs sat where front gates once swung, and chooks scratched between the twisted water tanks and iron roofs littering the black landscape. The cast stood in the wafting smoke, hankies to their eyes and noses, trying to block out the smell of burned rubber, scorched timber, paint, cars and curtains.[25]

Obviously we're past the days of Smell-O-Rama. But trees, telephone poles, and scorched timber and curtain are not big budget items, the way that multi-camera coverage of a full set of pyrotechnics extending over several acres might be. More effective might be to accentuate the ironic use of Macbeth[26] that underscores the dressmaker's double job of couture and revenge, which Ham spells out for us, down to the theatrical lighting:

> Inside the police station, Banquo pondered his big scene, his tongue searching for the end of his nose. He too was haloed by a sun shaft which caught the sheen of the ornamental rose on his patent leather Baroque shoes. He clasped his sword handle as though to draw and bellowed,

> 'And when we have our naked frailties hid,
> That suffer in exposure, let us meet,
> And question this most bloody piece of work...'[27]

Plays within screenplays certainly worked in New Zealand with Jane Campion's *The Piano* (New Zealand, 1993), in which the Maori audience members are confounded by the locals' adaptation of the decapitations of Bluebeard's victims in silhouette behind a white sheet up on the stage, although portraying the Maori as so naïve that they would race up to save the actresses from their faux death is demeaning. Corporate powerhouse Gondo's son and his friend, the son of a chauffeur, play cowboys and Indians in Kurosawa's *High and Low* (Japan, 1963) more effectively, setting up the children's innocence as well as making the point that both boys are "somebody" on life's stage, until one of them is kidnapped.

When do you let the hem down on a dress? When do you shorten it, ending precisely at the knee? When is the décolletage too little, or too much? These are sewing questions for screenwriters working on the fabric of their plot. One thing that Jocelyn Moorhouse and P.J. Hogan excelled at in adapting *The Dressmaker* is the visual splendor and spectacle of the shimmering fabrics and elegant outfits her protagonist creates for the townspeople of Dungatar. She really made the most of it, taking "Gertrude Pratt strolled through the door, her cardigan hanging from her shoulders and her purse over her arm,"[28] intent on getting the town's most eligible bachelor to dance with her, and instead having the screenwriters Moorhouse and Hogan debut their protagonist Myrtle's first stunning outfit of the town on the just-waiting-to-be-draped body of Gertrude, making her not only a sight for sore eyes in the audience, but irresistible to William. Myrtle's power to transform the looks and sex appeal of the local women, but not their small-mindedness, holds universal appeal and poignancy.

An ending that "works" for both the male-dominated worlds of filmmaking and film criticism, but may give feminists pause, belongs to David Fincher's *Gone Girl* (USA, 2014). Gillian Flynn's novel, *Gone Girl*, ends with Amy's written words: "I don't have anything else to add. I just wanted to make sure I had the last word. I think I've earned that."[29] She hasn't earned Nick's love, but she has earned the right to the last word. Flynn's screenplay, however, ends almost identically with how the film began, with: NICK (O.S.) "What are you thinking? How are you feeling? What have we done to each other? What *will* we do?" Amy turns to him and smiles. It's a perfect set-up for a sequel.

Earlier in the film, just before Amy checks into a motel as part of her scheme of revenge against Nick, she defines herself as a "Cool Girl": "Cool Girl is game. Cool Girl is fun. Cool Girl never gets angry at her man." In the film adaptation of *Gone Girl*, structurally speaking, "Cool Girl" screenwriter Flynn always gives her guy equal screen time and the final word, even if in the novel, the final word is hers.

Notes

1 Alexander Steele (ed.), *Writing Movies: The Practical Guide to Creating Stellar Screenplays* (New York: Bloomsbury, 2006), 29.
2 Adam Sternbergh, "How the American Action Movie Went Kablooey," *New York Times*, Magazine, March 30, 2012, accessed April 10, 2017, www.nytimes.com/2012/04/01/magazine/how-the-american-action-movie-went-kablooey.html.
3 Daniel Noah, "Plot: The Path of Action," in Steele, *Writing Movies*, 66.
4 Noah "Plot," 66.
5 Roderick Thorp, *Nothing Lasts Forever* (Los Angeles, CA: Graymalkin Media, 1979), 25.
6 Thorp, *Nothing Lasts Forever*, 217.
7 Thorp, *Nothing Lasts Forever*, 34–35.
8 Thorp, *Nothing Lasts Forever*, 16.
9 Thorp, *Nothing Lasts Forever*, 50.
10 Thorp, *Nothing Lasts Forever*, 127, 133.
11 Thorp, *Nothing Lasts Forever*, 226.
12 Thorp, *Nothing Lasts Forever*, 229.
13 Helen Kaplan, "Subplots: A Side of Story," in Steele, *Writing Movies*, 224.
14 Thorp, *Nothing Lasts Forever*, 243–245.
15 Sternbergh, "How the American Action Movie Went Kablooey."
16 African Film Festival New York, 2011, accessed April 10, 2017, www.africanfilmny.org/BR/aristotle%e2%80%99s-plot/.
17 David Trottier, *The Screenwriter's Bible,* 5th edn. (Los Angeles, CA: Silman-James Press), 5.
18 Matthias de Groof, "Intriguing African Storytelling: On *Aristotle's Plot* by Jean-Pierre Bekolo." In Lina Khatib (ed.), *Storytelling in World Cinemas*, 1 – "Forms" (New York: Wallflower, Columbia University Press, 2012), 118.
19 Michael Dembor, "Aristotle's Plot," *AfricAvenir International*, accessed September 29, 2016, 8–9, www.africavenir.org/film-distribution/aristotles-plot.html.
20 Jean-Pierre Bekolo, 2006, quoted in Matthias de Groof, "Intriguing African Storytelling,"118.
21 Phyllis Nagy, quoted in Louise Farr, "The Courtship of Carol: Phyllis Nagy Survives 19 Years of Tweaks and a Broken Heart," *WGAw Written By*, 20(2) (February–March, 2016), 32.
22 Lu Wei, quoted in Lu Wei and Wang Tianbing, *The Secret of Screenwriting* (Shanghai: Shanghai Jiao Ton University Press, 2013), 93.
23 Lu quoted in Lu and Wang, *The Secret of Screenwriting*, 93.
24 Rosalie Ham, *The Dressmaker* (Potts Point, NSW Australia: Duffy & Snellgrove, 2000), 270.
25 Ham, 273.
26 William Shakespeare, *Macbeth*, Act II, Scene iii.
27 Ham, 267.
28 Ham, 79.
29 Gillian Flynn, *Gone Girl* (New York: Crown Publishers, 2012), 415.

FIVE

Setting

One of the main decisions a screenwriter must face in adapting a work is whether to be true to the setting. Sometimes the setting is intrinsic to the theme or characters being portrayed; in other cases, the theme or characters can find a newer, vibrant life through relocation, or a work from one time and place can simply be reworked to strengthen another story. Thus, Henrik Ibsen's 1882 Norwegian play *Enemy of the People* got a new turn in the sun by inspiring director Stephen Spielberg and screenwriter Carl Gottlieb's rewrite of Ibsen's play to *Jaws* (USA, 1975), which was officially an adaptation of Peter Benchley's novel, *Jaws,* although Spielberg and Gottlieb described it as "*Moby Dick* meets *Enemy of the People.*"[1] Joseph Gaï Ramaka's *Karmen Geï* (Senegal/France/Canada, 2001), reset Prosper Mérimée's novella *Carmen,* which takes place in southern Spain, in Senegal.[2] Mark Dornford-May's *U-Carmen E-Khayelitsha* (South Africa, 2005) reset Bizet's opera (similarly based on the novella *Carmen*), sung in Xhosa in a South African township.[3] Maria Giese reset *Hunger,* Nobel Laureate Knut Hamsun's 1890 novel about a starving Norwegian writer, in contemporary San Francisco, where starving writers also abound.[4] Spike Lee reset Aristophanes' fifth century BCE anti-war comedy *Lysistrata* as *Chi-Raq* (USA, 2015), focusing on inner city gun violence in Chicago.

Before *Moonlight* was shot in Liberty City, Florida, the Miami suburb where both Barry Jenkins and Tarell Alvin McCraney grew up, there was some talk of producing a film based on McCraney's *In the Moonlight Black Boys Look Blue* in Chicago. But McCraney responded, "'Nah, you're missing the whole point.' There's something really important to this being in Miami."[5] Similarly, it's hard to imagine *My Brilliant Career* (Australia, 1979) taking place anywhere other than Outback Australia, *Trainspotting* (UK, 1996) and *T2 Trainspotting* (UK, 2017) without Edinburgh, *The Milk of Sorrow* (Spain/Peru, 2009) in any place other than Peru, or *Wuthering Heights* (UK, 2011) outside of England – although Luis Buñuel's 1953 adaptation of *Wuthering Heights* takes place in Mexico, renamed *Abismos de Pasión.*

Setting is what makes *The Motorcycle Diaries* (Argentina/US/Chile, 2004), a road trip and a buddy movie rather than a political biopic. In the screenplay by Puerto Rican writer José Rivera, Che Guevara and his best friend Alberto Granado travel from Argentina to Peru on a clunky old motorcycle prone to breaking down for comic relief, which also serves the purpose of keeping us in particular milieus long enough for mischief to ensue or for occasional coming-of-age life lessons to be learned.

Carlos Diegues' *Orfeu* (Brazil, 1999) takes place in the slums of Rio de Janeiro called the Carioca Hills, during Carnaval. Eurydice, a naïve young woman from the boondocks of Brazil, emerges in the city after a cutaway of an airplane, which is embarrassingly on the nose. The haunting mysticism which made the ancient Greek myth so memorable evaporates in the face of *Orfeu*'s many mundane clichés. Sociologically, she could be a cousin of Macabéa from another Brazilian film, *A hora da estrela* (*Hour of the Star,* Brazil, 1986), another country girl trying to survive against the odds in big city Rio, except that Eurydice has stumbled upon Orfeu, the charismatic leader of the Carioca Samba School, instead of being run over by a tourist's BMW.

Some of my students snicker at the sentimentality and childlike simplicity of the lovers in the earlier adaptation of Vinicius de Moraes' play *Orfeu de Conceiçâo* (*Black Orpheus,* Brazil/France, 1959), which Barack Obama likewise criticized when he first saw the film with his mother in New York;[6] others, Obama's own mother included, are entranced by their beauty and purity and swept away by the foreground–background setting of the Orphic storyline during Carnaval. The dancing, costumes, and bossa nova music of *Black Orpheus* are as spell-bindingly Brazilian as the singing, sets, and costumes of the Peking Opera are rapturously Chinese in *Farewell, My Concubine* (China/Hong Kong, 1993), or have we been suckered by exoticism? When the sun rises over Guanabara Bay in Rio de Janiero, it is thanks to the magic of Orpheus' guitar that compels it to rise, now played by the children who will grow up to be the next Orpheus and Eurydice of the slums. The vision of a real dawn – not lights dimmed up on a stage – makes all the difference: I am caught between despair at the endless cycles of poverty and death which we have witnessed here in Rio, and a universal vision of hope that transcends both boundaries and time.

Nobel laureate Naguib Mafouz's novel, *Midaq Alley*,[7] takes place in a run-down alleyway in poverty-stricken Cairo, Egypt; Jorge Fons resets the story in his film *Midaq Alley* (*El Callejón de los Milagros*, Mexico, 1995), exploring the parallel lives of Mexican characters in a run-down alleyway in Mexico City. (The film, which 11 Ariel Awards in Mexico and dozens of international awards and nominations, is discussed further in Chapter 15, "Stories without Borders.")

Setting is also important in Zhang Yimou's *To Live* (China, 1994), based on the novel by the internationally acclaimed author Yu Hua about a southern Chinese aristocrat-turned-peasant. *To Live*'s screenwriter, Lu Wei, explains that since Zhang Yimou had just finished making "two movies about a farmer's life," and came from an urban background

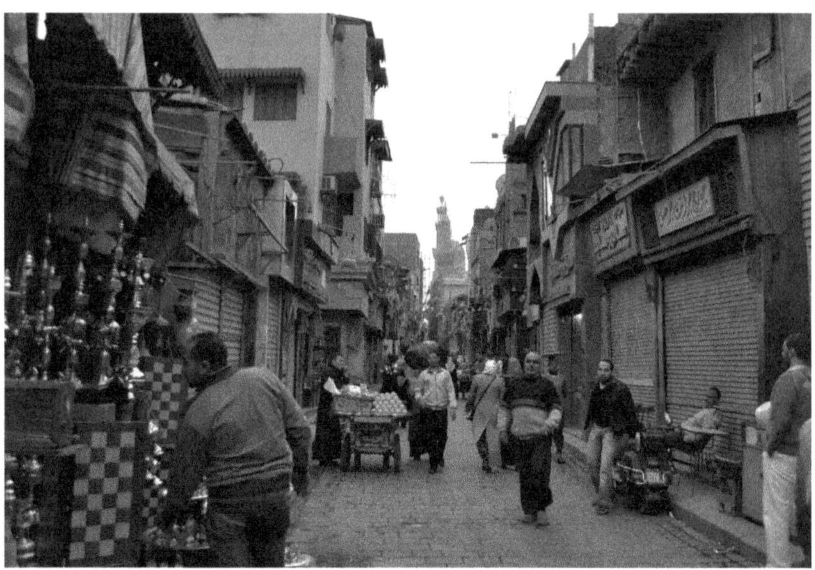

Figure 5.1 One of the Egyptian alleyways of Khan el-Khalili that inspired Naguib Mahfouz's novel *Midaq Alley*, later adapted into the film *El Callejón de los Milagros* (*Midaq Alley*, Mexico, 1995)

himself, the director "wanted this movie to explore average middle-class life in the city instead of a village for a change."[8] He also moved the story to northern China, a region he knew so much better than southern China.

On the other hand, being faithful to a unique setting can add both authenticity and uniqueness to a story based on real life. As Angela Workman, screenwriter of *The Zookeeper's Wife* (USA, 2017), explains, "Unlike other Holocaust movies, it's set in a zoo."[9] Workman's script was based on a non-fiction, "non-academic" book by Diane Ackerman which Workman describes as "colorful and alive,"[10] about a woman who saved the lives of hundreds of Jews during World War II in Warsaw, Poland by hiding them in a zoo which the Nazis had mostly destroyed. As Workman explains, the film metaphorically contrasts Antonina Źabińska's attempt to protect the natural world to the Nazis' attempt to control and exterminate its inhabitants. Setting also plays a role in whether or not Antonina and her husband can help more Jews escape from the Warsaw Ghetto, adding suspense. The close confines of the basement of the villa in the zoo where Antonina hides the Jews while increasingly despairing of carrying on a normal life upstairs adds intensity – a downstairs–upstairs twist much darker than *Downton Abbey*'s, though similar in intensity to Agnieszka Holland's *Angry Harvest* (Germany, 1985), based on a novel by Hermann H. Field and Stanislaw Mierzenski, in which a Jewish woman is hidden in a Silesian farmer's basement in exchange for sexual favors.

How does a screenwriter approach the text of a novel, line by line, in making the decisions about what details of a setting to keep, and what to discard? Here is one hypothetical example, based on the opening of Chapter 3 of Michael Punke's *The Revenant*, entitled "August 23, 1823":

> Hugh Glass stared down at the cloven tracks, the deep indentions clear as newsprint in the soft mud. Two distinct sets began at the river's edge, where the deer must have drunk, and then trailed into the heavy cover of the willows. The persistent work of a beaver had carved a trail, now trod by a variety of game. Dung lay piled next to the tracks, and Glass stooped to touch the pea-sized pellets—still warm.[11]

Well, this is a nice novelistic description, which Punke must have toiled long into the night to forge as an intro to the goings-on of Chapter 3. For a movie, however, we don't need conjecture unless it's a plot point in a thriller: better to see the deer and the beaver, except for that would be too cutesy, and detract from the impact of the more important animal that's so intrinsic to *The Revenant's* plot: the bear. Besides, how "clear as newsprint" will those cloven tracks appear onscreen, even if keeping Punke's lighting for roughly "three hours before sunset"? As for the pellets, the movie isn't being produced in Feel-O-Rama let alone Smell-O-Rama; if Glass's reaction to them aren't important, they don't belong in the movie. The key determination to the various details that are offered to the reader using all five senses is to provide authenticity of setting for the movie or television program that highlights the more unique and vibrant visuals and sounds, or occasionally the character's reaction to a smell or how something or someone feels, such as a woman's soft skin or a bear's sharp claws.

Much more of a keeper for scene description is the opening of the Chapter 23, entitled "March 6, 1824":

> The colors too were transformed. Stark daytime hues blended and blurred, softened by a gentle wash of ever darkening purples and blues.
>
> It was a moment for reflection in a space so vast it could only be divine.
>
> And if Glass believed in a god, surely it resided in this great western expanse. Not a physical presence, but an idea, something beyond man's ability to comprehend, something larger.[12]

This is something large-screen movies excel in: wide expanses of nature, providing a transcendent moment not only to the protagonist on screen, but to the audience members, cocooned in the dark auditorium yet transported to the magnificence of natural environments and the magic passage of time between day and night, which Glass "held as sacred as Sabbath."[13] In real life, western snows proved so elusive due to global warming that the director had to fly the cast and crew to South America to include shots of snow-capped mountains. But within the time and space of the novel's adaptation, we can still honor a story in which the protagonist, having survived mighty battles against man and beast, reflects on the mountainous "source of the waters" and "at the stars and the heavens, comforted by their vastness against his own small place in the world."[14]

Notes

1 Carl Gottlieb, in Brendon Connelly, "The Rewriting of Jaws – Carl Gottlieb Tells Bleeding Cool How It Came to Be, What It All Means," *Bleeding Cool*, September 5, 2012, accessed March 3, 2017, www.bleedingcool.com/2012/09/05/the-rewriting-of-jaws-carl-gottlieb-tells-bleeding-cool-how-it-came-to-be-what-it-all-means/.

2 Anjali Prabhu, *Contemporary Cinema of Africa and the Diaspora* (Chichester: Wiley Blackwell, 2014), 84.

3 Prabhu, *Contemporary Cinema of Africa and the Diaspora*, 92.

4 Maria Giese, Director/Screenwriter, *Hunger* (USA, 2001, released 2007), based on the novel *Hunger* by Knut Hamsun, 1890.

5 Tarell Alvin McCraney, quoted in E. Alex Jung, "*Moonlight*'s Tarell Alvin McCraney on Writing the Original Source Material, Taking Inspiration From Myths, and Creating Heroes With Black Skin," November 29, 2016, accessed February 18, 2017, www.vulture.com/2016/11/tarell-alvin-mccraney-on-writing-moonlight.html.

6 Barack Obama, excerpt from his memoir, *Dreams from My Father* (New York: Crown, 2004), accessed November 20, 2016, www.arraynow.com/our-blog-archive/2015/8/13/president-barack-obama-on-black-orpheus.

7 Naguib Mahfouz, *Midaq Alley: A New Translation*, trans. by Humphrey Davies (New York: American University in Cairo Press, 2011).

8 Lu Wei, quoted in Lu Wei and Wang Tianbing, *The Secret of Screenwriting* (Shanghai: Shanghai Jiao Tong University Press, 2013), 81. Translation provided by May Wu.

9 Diane Ackerman, Q&A moderated by Chuck Rose at the screening of *The Zookeeper's Wife*, Writers Guild Theater, Beverly Hills, California, March 25, 2017.

10 Ackerman, Q&A, *The Zookeper's Wife*.

11 Michael Punke, *The Revenant: A Novel of Revenge* (New York: Picador, 2002), 21.

12 Punke, *The Revenant*, 211.

13 Punke, *The Revenant*, 211.

14 Punke, *The Revenant*, 249.

SIX

Characters and Character Relationships

Ligiah Villalobos, writer/producer of the independent feature *La Misma Luna* (*Under the Same Moon,* Mexico/USA, 2007) – which was shot for $1.9 million and went on to make over $23 million worldwide – also worked as screenwriter on a Latino adaptation of an Israeli film. Speaking about *Homeland* (Showtime, 2011) and *In Treatment* (HBO, 2008–2010), which were adapted in the US from Israeli television shows, Villalobos says:

> What I like about the Israeli films and TV shows I've watched, is that they tend to focus on character and story. So many American shows nowadays focus on procedural or a high concept. At the core, I am still a character-driven and story-driven writer. So I enjoy getting in deep into the characters and the story. ... But much of television here in the States is about characters serving the plot – I would say most procedural shows are that way (copy, medical, legal shows). Or big concept TV. So I think maybe because other countries may not have the kind of budgets that we have here in the States, they still focus on story and character – not explosions or big set pieces.[1]

Zhang Yimou, director of *To Live* (China/Hong Kong, 1994), was drawn to the original source material, a novel by Yu Hua, [2] because of its characters:

> Yu Hua is very famous in China; he is an avant-garde writer, but *To Live*, his first realist novel, was not very successful. ... I loved the story because it talked about simple people, a very ordinary Chinese family, and their relationships. ... History was secondary while the individual and the family were in the first plan.[3]

To Live's screenwriter, Lu Wei, adds that the writer and director also put their own experiences into the adaptation:

> When we were shooting the movie *To Live*, Zhang Yimou and I were both 43. We both had a lot of life experiences, so we were able to write about them and then shoot it. It might seem impossible for a guy in his 20s to shoot this kind of movie because he does not have that much of life experience on his own.[4]

Although screenwriter Aaron Sorkin admits to not having had much computer experience, let alone knowledge of Facebook, when he started work on *The Social Network* (USA, 2010), "research assistant and UCLA computer science major Ian Reichbach, whom Sorkin praises extravagantly," was hired to provide all of the computer details in the film.[5] But to create dramatic characters beyond what was in the official adaptation source – Ben Mezrich's book, *The Accidental Billionaires: The Founding of Facebook: A Tale of Sex, Money, Genius and Betrayal* – Sorkin turned to Shakespeare for help.

It's not that far from the log-line for *Othello* in J.M. Evenson's book *Shakespeare for Screenwriters* – "Cold-hearted Iago befriends Othello, a powerful black military leader, only to prey on Othello's jealousy and drive him to murder his beloved wife, Desdemona"[6] – to one of the major subplots for *The Social Network*. As Joyce Britton points out, Mark Zuckerberg, as a "victim of his own jealousy," is Othello; "Saverin is Desdemona – innocent and pure, but steadfastly blind to Othello's fury"; and Sean Parker is Iago – "power-hungry and ambitious, determined to manipulate Othello at will, even if it means destroying the friendship between Zuckerberg and his only true friend, Saverin."[7] We can do the

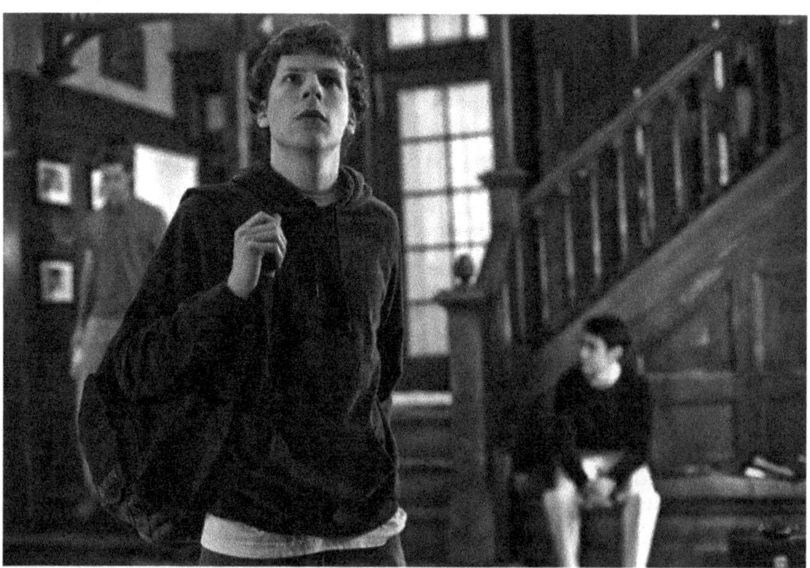

Figure 6.1 Facebook creator Mark Zuckerberg (played by Jesse Eisenberg) in *The Social Network* (USA, 2010), written by Aaron Sorkin. Image courtesy of Columbia Pictures. Produced by Columbia Pictures in association with Relativity Media

same thing with Shakespeare's *Macbeth*: Mark Zuckerberg is driven to take over Facebook the way Macbeth is willing to do anything to take over the throne of Scotland. In "*The Social Network:* Modern Day Shakespeare?", "Zuckerberg has an inordinate ambition that makes screwing Saverin over seem to be a lesser evil than failing to achieve his vision of Facebook," and "Sean Parker is Lady Macbeth."[8]

Ensemble Character Relationships

Chinua Achebe, the Nigerian novelist and critic whose book *Things Fall Apart* sold eight million copies and was adapted into a Nigerian television show directed by David Oriere, *Things Fall Apart* (Nigeria/Germany, 1971), wrote:

> If the philosophical dictum of Descartes, "I think, therefore I am" represents a European individualistic ideal, the Bantu declaration "Umuntu ngumuntu ngabantu" represents an Africa communal aspiration: "A human is human because of other humans."[9]

The relationships between characters in films with ensemble casts hold universal power, whether in Kurosawa's *The Lower Depths* (Japan, 1957), based on Gorky's play, or *The Best Exotic Marigold Hotel* (UK/USA/United Arab Emirates, 2011), set in Jaipur, India.

For the most part, Jorge Fons' *Midaq Alley* (Mexico, 1995) stays true to the characters in Naguib Mahfouz's novel and their problems in life, although they are no longer Muslim or Arabic, but Mexican. The 1947 novel *Midaq Alley* interweaves several characters' stories in a manner that Kurosawa would use three years later in constructing his now-classic film, *Rashomon* (Japan, 1950). Among the characters in the novel – all of whom live or work in the same lower-class alley in Cairo, Egypt, are: Hamida, the beautiful young woman who will turn sex worker to get what she thinks she wants (renamed Alma in the film); Abbas, the barber who's in love with her (Abel in the film); Radwan Hussainy, a Moslem scholar, who becomes Ubaldo, a Mexican bookseller; Kirsha, a café owner who prefers chasing after a young boy to celebrating his anniversary with his wife (the film's Rutilio, who suffers from machismo).

Of these characters, Hamida is used by Mahfouz symbolically to represent an Egypt that is exploited by Western forces. This is something that Fons does, too, except that he substitutes the contemporary quest for crossing the border into the U.S. for the British forces that were associated with Egypt in the 1940s.

However, by 1995, something else was happening to women in Mexico who, like Alma (played by Salma Hayek), strive to escape the poverty of *Midaq Alley*. Salma Hayek is as beautiful as the Egyptian character, brushing her long, silky black hair in Mahfouz' novel while contemplating whether or not to give her body away to the highest bidder. But for deeper insights into the problems of women today, there are other places to turn in addition to novels and films. For example, in 2016, UCLA's Global Media Center for Social Impact and The Hidden Tears Project co-sponsored a 2016 Writers Guild event featuring panelist Maria Suarez, advocate for victims of modern-day slavery in Los Angeles and Mexico. And Egyptian feminist Nawal El Saadawi's book, *The Hidden Face of Eve: Women in the Arab World*, takes the concerns of Arab women – including sexual relationships and prostitution – further than male writers and filmmakers such as Mahfouz and Fons could envision in their time. These concerns, in turn, can make their way into future novels and adaptations.

The Joy Luck Club (USA/China, 1993), co-written by Ron Bass and Amy Tan, based Amy Tan's 1989 novel, tells the stories of four sets of Chinese-American mothers and daughters. For such a complex assortment of characters, there are additional time-tested ways of structuring stories than following Robert McKee's three-act paradigm, Chris Vogler's 12-Step "The Hero's Journey," Eric Edson's "23 Steps All Great Heroes Must Take,"[10] Kim Hudson's 13-Step "The Virgin's Promise," or Jane Alexander's "The Heroine's Journey." Director Wayne Wang admits that "how to get into the stories in an elegant and simple way ... was the major part of the first step in the scripting process."[11] In an interview in *Literature Film Quarterly*, Wang states:

> [D]on't forget there are not just eight characters telling a story, but that each story has its own past and present. Sixteen stories! At first I was very worried about that, that it was very complicated; that it would be very tough to pull off. But we also connected up with a very experienced screenwriter, Ron Bass, who won an Academy Award for *Rain Man*, and he came in and had good ideas about how it would work: Using the simple structure of a dinner party to see one of the daughters off to China to visit her twin sisters. Using that to introduce all the mothers and daughters.[12]

It is also possible that Amy Tan's story was inspired in part by Chinese structural concepts. The number 6 (2 characters (mother/daughter) × 3 acts) brings to mind the hexagrams of the Taoist *I Ching: The Book of Changes*, in which three coins are thrown six times, resulting in a hexagram that tells one of 64 possible fortunes, changing into another hexagram with a different fortune depending on whether the coins land heads or tails. If we throw in the number of mother/daughter sets, we have another multiple of 6: 2 characters (mother/daughter) × 4 (sets of mothers/daughters) × 3 acts = 24. According to Jung, the interpretation of the 64 hexagrams "are equivalent to causal explanations";[13] studying the *I Ching* may be a powerful way for a writer to orchestrate connections between characters' fates.

Multiple characters are even more prevalent in television writing. In reviewing *Orange Is the New Black*, based on the memoir by Piper Kerman, and other TV series featuring women, Lili Loofbourow writes:

> Ostensibly about a women's prison or friendship disfigured by Hollywood or a geriatric ward or a trans woman transitioning late in life, these stories almost immediately defy their synopses. The spotlight is shared among characters in a way that avoids heroes, antiheroes or other familiar devices for generating dramatic crisis.[14]

The American TV series *Girls* (USA, 2012–2017) created by Lena Dunham, "comes directly and unapologetically from the life of Lena Dunham ... [and] just as directly and unapologetically from Dunham's obsession with *Sex in the City*, the HBO series about four stylish, affluent women living glamourous lives of cultural and sexual liberation."[15] Alexandra Karova describes both shows' stars as "sexually adventurous, autobiographical writers," and points out that since *Sex in the City* (USA, 1998–2004) is "an adaptation of *Pride and Prejudice* ... by default *Girls* is also a *Pride and Prejudice* adaptation."[16] Despite sharing "Jane Austen's DNA," Karova claims, *Girls* is "a pivotal change in verisimilitude of female protagonist and their love interests, including taboo sexual desires without slut shaming."[17]

It will be interesting to see how female characters like these continue to evolve in other television series and films. As Jessica Chastain stated at the 2017 Cannes Film Festival, "I do hope that when we include more female storytellers we will have more of the women I recognize in my day to day life, those who are proactive, have their own agency, don't just react to the men around them, they have their own point of view."[18]

Notes

1 Ligiah Villalobos, interviewed via email by author, September 9, 2016.
2 Yu Hua, *To Live,* trans. by Michael Berry (New York: Anchor Books, 2003). First published in China in 1992.
3 Zhang Yimou quoted in interview with Hubert Niogret, 1994. In Frances Gateward (ed.), *Zhang Yimou Interviews* (Jackson, MS: University of Mississippi Press, 2001), 57.
4 Lu Wei, quoted in Lu Wei and Wang Tianbing, *The Secret of Screenwriting* (in Chinese, translated by May Gu), 81–93.
5 Bob Verini, "The Truth (?) About facebook," *Script*, 16(5) (September/October, 2010), 54.
6 J.M. Evenson, *Shakespeare for Screenwriters* (Los Angeles, CA: Michael Wiese, 2013), 132.
7 Joyce Britton, midterm presentation on *The Social Network,* CTVA 420, "Screenplay Adaptation," Department of Cinema and Television Arts, California State University, Northridge, Spring 2011. Student research.
8 "*The Social Network*: Modern Day Shakespeare?" *Clapperbored*, October 24, 2010, accessed April 11, 2017, www.theclapperbored.com/2010/10/24/is-the-social-network-modern-day-shakespeare/.
9 Chinua Achebe, *The Education of a British-Protected Child* (New York: Anchor Books, 2009), 166.
10 Eric Edson, *The Story Solution: 23 Steps All Great Heroes Must Take* (Los Angeles, CA: Michael Wiese, 2012).
11 Wayne Wang, quoted in John C. Tibbetts, "A Delicate Balance: An Interview with Wayne Wang about *The Joy Luck Club*," *Literature Film Quarterly*, 22(1) (1994), 4.

12 Wang in Tibetts "A Delicate Balance," 4.
13 C.G. Jung, "Foreword," *The I Ching or Book of Changes*, trans. by Richard Wilhelm (Princeton, NJ: Princeton University Press, 1950, 1967), xxv.
14 Lili Loofbourow, "TV's New Girls' Club," *New York Times Magazine*. January 16, 2015.
15 David Hinckley, "Lena Dunham's 'Girls' Looks at 'Sex and the City' World Through Young Working-class Eyes," *New York Daily News,* April 12, 2012.
16 Alexandra Karova, *Girls* research, Department of Cinema and Television Arts, California State University, Northridge, October, 2015.
17 Karova, *Girls* research. Student research.
18 Jessica Chastain, quoted in Sharon Waxman, "Jessica Chastain Finds 'Disturbing' How Women Were Portrayed in Cannes Movies," May 9, 2014, accessed June 11, 2017, www.thewrap.com/jessica-chastain-finds-disturbing-women-portrayed-cannes-movies/.

SEVEN

Dialogue

Globally homogenized films often utilize that personable yet condescending news announcer lingo so cutesified by the prose stylists of *Time* magazine. It uncomfortably echoes something that's imposed from without and dead, like the Roman Empire. In contrast, regional dialect weds characters to their setting. The sounds – whether of tsunamis or trickling brooks – mixed in with the dialogue can make words come as alive as the flora and fauna that the cinematographer dangles in front of our eyes. Different uses of regional dialect can also personalize the characters.

In *O Brother Where Art Thou?* (USA, 2000), Ulysses Everett McGill takes pride in his high-fallutin' vocabulary, as he and his surviving buddy Delmar ride in the back of hay wagon, discussing their buddy Pete, whom they think has been lynched. In contrast to Ulysses' speechifyin', Delmar is a man of few but heartfelt words, creating a balance of opposites.

ULYSSES

Believe me, Delmar, he would have wanted us to press on. Pete, rest his soul, was one sour ass son of a bitch and not given to acts of pointless sentimentality.

DELMAR

It just don't seem right diggin' up the treasure without him.

ULYSSES

Maybe it's for the best he was squished. Why, he was barely a sentient being and … Well, as soon as we get ourselves cleaned up and get a little smellum in our hair,

```
why, we're gonna feel one hundred
percent better about ourselves and
about ... (He looks at the chain gang
as they pass on the back of the hay
wagon) ... life in general.¹
```

Notice, too, how *O Brother Where Art Thou* manages to slip history (i.e. Reconstruction), political attitude and a homage to the Dozens (an African-American game of exchanging insults) into its dialogue in one fell swoop, when one of the chain gang leaders barks out the order, "Talk, you unreconstructed whelp of a whore. Where they headed?" It's very effective regional dialogue constructing the poor white South out of an ancient Greek myth while at the same time paying homage to serfs of Russia, potato farmers of Ireland, or any other place where the poor have had to rely on their wits, resorting to fast talk and tall tales to survive.

More problematic is the screenplay of *Fences* (USA, 2016), written by the revered playwright August Wilson. The film serves an important function as a museum piece, preserving Wilson's dramaturgy for many generations to come, as well as giving us a chance to witness the superb acting skills of Denzel Washington and Viola Davis. But with little or no change in location, the film appears top-heavy with dialogue. Even worse is Jose Rivera's well-meaning adaptation of Jack Kerouac's *On the Road* (France/USA/UK/Brazil/Canada/Argentina, 2012). Adapting Kerouac, the poetic yet realistic-sounding all-American master of all-American mid-twentieth-century prose demands an understanding of the minutiae of poetic syntax, an ear for adrenalinated rhythm, and a first-hand knowledge of the subtext in Beat American slang. The dialogue of *On the Road* just doesn't sound authentic, though it may work as subtitles in a foreign language.

Sometimes the power of dialogue can extend beyond translations and subtitles, though in my opinion, it's a white-collar crime to add a cheap hack-job of inaccurate subtitles to a film that is otherwise a masterpiece. An example of dialogue that transcends its regional borders is that of Fausta in *The Milk of Sorrow* (Peru, 2009). She barely talks, but when she does, her words convey tremendous courage. In Andrea Arnold's *Wuthering Heights* (UK, 2011), the lovers' silence – which allows us to hear their anger and passion as wind whips across the moors – is what gives Arnold's adaptation its power, as much as Catherine's intermittent phrases in a Yorkshire accent convey the pathos of an uneducated, orphaned damsel who is bound to make poor choices for herself in life.

The Creature played by Robert DeNiro in *Mary Shelley's Frankenstein* (USA/Japan/UK, 1994) is also a man of few words (er, a monster, that is ...), stammering as he tries to speak. But somewhere behind his scarred, stitched-together face is a brain full of erudition: Unlike the low-IQ one in James Whale's earlier adaptation, *Frankenstein* (USA, 1931), this Creature has read at least some of the works of Milton, Plutarch, and Goethe that Mary Shelley mentions as his reading list in her novel.[2]

The Role of Silence in Dialogue

Keeping characters from excessive verbiage is a powerful and lucrative tool for transcending borders in general. Action with minimal dialogue can sell millions more movie tickets. What a relief for the semi-literate, not to have subtitles competing with visual effects on-screen! Whether it's James Bond, a man of few words, whose actions and occasional bons mots make us admire him, or Celie in *The Color Purple*, whose fear of expressing herself lest Mister beat her for it, strengthens our sympathy for her, silence is as an important component of powerful dialogue for writers as it is for avant-garde musicians and composers like John Cage.

While a line of dialogue such as "Rosebud" (*Citizen Kane,* USA, 1941) or "She's my sister AND my daughter!" (*Chinatown,* USA, 1974) can be the greatest revealer of the truth, a film often needs to rely on silence, subtext, or the subtleties of expression in an actor's face to convey unspoken truths, whether because of censorship, aesthetic taste, or the decency not to spoon-feed an intelligent audience. A theatrical adaptation – relying on dialogue, not close-ups – may take a different approach. For example, in adapting *The Talented Mr. Ripley* for the British stage, Phyllis Nagy commented:

> I was thrilled to do it for theater because I knew that I could structurally and theatrically make the creepy subtextual metaphor about Ripley's unspoken sexuality really very powerful on stage as opposed to film. Ripley would never, ever, ever admit to being gay, and that's my abiding problem with any adaptation that literalizes or makes him cognizant of his sexuality. It's the thing that makes him murder. You verbalize it and you lose the psychopathy, in a way.[3]

Silence is also a powerful tool in writer/director Barry Jenkins' Oscar award-winning *Moonlight* (USA, 2016), which explores the sexuality and coming of age of a largely inarticulate young man. The film is based on *In the Moonlight Black Boys Look Blue* by playwright Tarell Alvin McCraney, who claims that "it was never a play form. I never tried to produce or publish it because it wasn't meant for that. It's written in a very visual language."[4]

Film has an ability to let us be immersed in a world in a way that's different from books and plays. Of the recent film adaptations he has seen, McCraney cites *The Talented Mr. Ripley* (USA, 1999) by writer/director Anthony Minghella as his favorite, explaining that "[t]he intense wordplay going on in Patricia Highsmith's book is not the beauty that we were going to see in Matt Damon and Jude Law sitting in the bathtub."[5]

The painfully awkward silences of *Moonlight*'s three-part structure – first those of the shy, fearful child, then the secretive and poorly educated adolescent, then the man masked in toughness – too proud to admit his vulnerability as a gay man in love – take on a powerful universality that on-the-nose dialogue might have cheapened. Instead, Jenkins often relies on his actors' expressions and the nuances of his cinematographer's lighting and framing to convey the protagonist's powerful emotions.

Silence becomes a survival tool for the maids in Kathryn Stockett's *The Help* (USA/India/United Arab Emirates), working for Southern white women with entrenched racist attitudes, like Miss Leefolt, who has had a special toilet installed in her garage in order to avoid having her maid use the guest bathroom in the house. As soon as the new one is constructed, Miss Leefolt suggests that Aibileen use it, but Aibileen doesn't need to, doesn't want to, and has to concentrate on not talking back to her employer.

> I put the iron down real slow, feel that bitter seed grow in my chest, the one planted after Treelore [her only son] died. My face goes hot, my tongue twitchy. I don't know what to say to her. All I know is, I ain't saying it. And I know she ain't saying what she want a say either and it's a strange thing happenin here cause nobody saying nothing and we still managing to have us a conversation.[6]

The adaptation loses this degree of Aibileen's silence, so pregnant with conflict. It also dispenses with Minny's wonderful interior monologue, such as "Don't go ruirning [sic] this now, she offering you a jay-o-bee."[7] Tate's screenplay keeps only Minny's warning to her daughter (who is about to become a maid herself in order to help pay the bills): "No sass-mouthin'," a line which Minny repeats to herself as she approaches the huge mansion for a job interview, having been fired from her previous position on trumped-up charges.[8] Tate replaces the maids' silences with whatever they're allowed to say to their white employers, whatever they feel like saying among themselves, and ultimately, the stories they dare to express during Skeeter's interviews with them, which will contribute to tearing down some of the racist policies of the Civil Rights era. In short, dialogue is made into a component of the personal and collective heroism expressed in their character arcs.

In contrast, *12 Years a Slave* (USA/UK, 2013), written by Oscar-winning John Ridley, tells Solomon Northrup's historical story[9] with as few words as possible – showing us, not telling us, about his mistreatment as he falls into slavery. The silence as Solomon brings up the letter he had written, hoping for it to be delivered to those who could free him, is more deafening than if we heard an extensive voice-over about the family he longs to see alive. The practice of self-restraint by the screenwriter contributes to the brilliance of the visual storytelling; the practice of self-restraint by the character contributes to his survival.

The Power of Repetition

The screenplay to Kaige Chen's *Farewell, My Concubine* (China/Hong Kong, 1993) was written by Lilian Lee (also known as Li Bai and Pik Wah Lee), who also wrote the novel on which it is based, and Lu Wei.

When a young male actor playing the role of a female concubine recites the line, "I am by nature a boy, not a girl," on the eve of the Cultural Revolution, the line is drawn between artifice and reality. There are tragic consequences to failing to recite the line as it is written (i.e., "I am by nature a girl, not a boy), due to Douzi's confusion about the gender role he is forced to perform, both in the Peking Opera, and off-stage in the apartment of a lecherous patron.

As a student and later a star of the Peking Opera, the lines "My king has been trapped. How can I hope to live?" are also repeated many times in different circumstances, building in their obsessive power: Will the acting students learn their lines, or endure brutal beatings until they do? Will the performances of these lines make them famous? Will the lines of this traditional art form incite riots in a political upheaval that is purging everything that hints of elegance and wealth of a decadent past? Will the friends' love for one another survive when they are no longer allowed to recite these lines? The constant repetition of key dialogue throughout the movie gives these lines the monumental power of a mantra, and conveys just how meaningful a role the arts play in keeping humanity alive, especially in the clutches of ruthless historical forces.

Notes

1 Ethan and Joel Coen, *O Brother Where Art Thou?* directed by Joel Coen (Burbank, CA and Universal City, CA: Touchstone and Universal, 2000).
2 *Paradise Lost*, a volume of Plutarch's *Lives*, and the *Sorrows of Young Werther*. In Mary Shelley, *Frankenstein* (New York: Dover Publications, 1994), 91; first published in 1831.
3 Louise Farr, "The Courtship of Carol: Phyllis Nagy Survives 19 Years of Tweaks and a Broken Heart," *WGAw Written By*, 20(2) (February–March, 2016), 32.
4 Tarell Alvin McCraney, quoted in Moze Halperin, "Playwright Tarell Alvin McCraney Discusses the Piece That Inspired *Moonlight*," *Flavorwire*, October 21, 2016, accessed February 18, 2017, http://flavorwire.com/592191/playwright-arell-alvin-mccraney-discusses-the-pie.
5 McCraney in Halperin,"Playwright Tarell Alvin McCraney Discusses the Piece That Inspired *Moonlight*."
6 Kathryn Stockett, *The Help* (New York: Berkeley Books, 2009), 34.
7 Stockett, *The Help*, 42.
8 Tate Taylor, *The Help* (Universal City, CA: Dreamworks, 2011), 56–57.
9 Solomon Northup, *12 Years a Slave* (New York: Penguin, 2013); first published in the US by Derby and Miler, 1853.

EIGHT

Structure
Heroes and Heroines – Where Are We Going?

The Hero's Journey: Traveling in Disguise

In *The Hero with a Thousand Faces*, anthropologist Joseph Campbell described the eighteen stages of a journey that a hero like Jason must take to retrieve the Golden Fleece.[1] Theories abound as to what the fleece symbolize; according to Antoine Faivre's esoteric study of alchemy, the fleece may have been a parchment-like ram's skin on which was written the secret of transforming a base metal like mercury into gold.[2] Christopher Vogler applied these hero's journey stages to screenwriting structure in his famous book, *The Writer's Journey*, which has become the template for a great many Hollywood films, especially the ones on which he's served as a studio VP or story consultant, including adaptations such as *Fight Club* (USA/Germany, 1999) and *The Lion King* (USA, 1994).[3]

In introducing how the "Hero's Journey" works, Vogler includes examples of plot elements of several films that can be considered adaptations, including *The Wizard of Oz* (USA, 1939) and *Star Wars* (USA, 1977). *The Wizard of Oz* is an adaptation of Frank Baum's 1900 novel, *The Wonderful Wizard of Oz*, which had already been adapted several times, including an adaptation by Baum himself produced by the Oz Film Manufacturing Company. Briefly, the twelve stages of the "Hero's Journey" (which Vogler claims work equally well for male and female characters) for the 1939 version go like this:

1. "The Ordinary World": Dorothy is stuck on the farm in Kansas where she doesn't fit in anymore.[4]
2. "Call to Adventure": Dorothy runs away from home.[5]
3. "Refusal of the Call": Professor Marvel convinces Dorothy that it's too dangerous on the open road, and to return home.[6]
4. "Meeting with the Mentor": After a tornado carries Dorothy to the land of Oz, a new mentor – Glinda, the Good Witch – will give her a pair of magical ruby slippers.[7]

5 "Crossing the First Threshold": The tornado swoops up Dorothy and puts her in a new place, where she finds yet another threshold, following the Yellow Brick Road. (Vogler's stages sometimes vary from follow-the-dot order.)[8]
6 "Tests, Allies, Enemies": Dorothy meets up with her allies, the Scarecrow, the Tin Woodman, and the Cowardly Lion, who are put to the tests by her enemy, the Wicked Witch.[9]
7 "Approach to the Inmost Cave": It's "Dorothy being kidnapped to the Wicked Witch's baleful castle, and her companions slipping in to save her."[10]
8 "The Supreme Ordeal": "Dorothy and her friends are trapped by the Wicked Witch, and it looks like there's no way out."[11]
9 "Reward": "Dorothy escapes from the Wicked Witch's castle with the Witch's broomstick and the ruby slippers, keys to getting back home."[12]
10 "The Road Back": Dorothy is all set to take a hot-air balloon back to Kansas, but the Wizard takes off in it instead, leaving her behind to find another solution.[13]
11 "Resurrection": With the help of the Good Witch, Dorothy learns that she has the power to return home – which she finally perceives to be a place of "happiness and completion" – if she clicks her ruby slippers.[14]
12 "Return with the Elixir": "Dorothy returns to Kansas with the knowledge that she is loved, and that 'There's no place like home.'"[15]

The novelist Salman Rushdie, who was studying *The Wizard of Oz* while living a life in exile from his home in Mumbai, points out that according to a studio memo, the associate producer Arthur Freed may have come up with the "cutesy slogan":[16] "There's no place like home." Hiding from the fatwa that threatened his life after the publication of Rushdie's *The Satanic Verses* enabled him to see through the movie's "cloying ending":[17]

> the real secret of the ruby slippers is not that "there's no place like home," but rather that there is no longer any such place as home: except, of course, for the home we make, or the homes that are made for us, in Oz: which is anywhere, and everywhere, except the place from which we began.[18]

Of course, in 1939, a film about a runaway girl had to have a happy ending.

Whether *Star Wars* is simply heavily influenced by Kurosawa's *The Hidden Fortress* (Japan, 1958), as George Lucas claims, or is an actual adaptation or remake is a debate that Vogler doesn't pursue. However, examining the *mise-en-scène* of both films, it's clear that Step One, "The Ordinary World," are almost identical, although *The Hidden Fortress* is a samurai film set in sixteenth-century Japan, and *Star Wars* is a sci fi film set in outer space. The overall plots remain the same. As Michael Kaminski explains:

> Without the advantage of home video, Lucas relied on a plot summary of Kurosawa's film, copying entire passages from Hidden Fortress' synopsis in Donald Richie's authoritative book, *The Films of Akira Kurosawa,* first published in 1965.[19]

What makes *The Hidden Fortress* such a wonderful choice from a screenwriting perspective is that screenwriter Ryuz Kikushima was as influenced by American westerns as by Japanese battle history and traditional Noh dramas, strengthening the universality that is at the heart of Campbell's and Vogler's pursuits as well as Lucas' filmmaking.[20]

The "Hero's Journey" has worked magnificently with hero-driven stories like *Star Wars, An Officer and a Gentleman* (USA, 1982) and *Raiders of the Lost Ark* (USA, 1981), and provides a helpful template when writing adaptations of novels whose heroes may be mired in introspection, or adaptations of short stories, where plots may need to be expanded or restructured. For example, the protagonist of Vikas Swarup's *Q&A,* [21] a collection of short stories, may have answered all the questions on India's biggest quiz show, "Who Wants to Win a Billion?", but the twelve short stories don't automatically fit the twelve stages of the "Hero's Journey." Simon Beaufoy, the screenwriter of *Slumdog Millionaire* (UK/France/USA, 2008), kept the Indian setting and premise but tossed out "most of the novel's material in order to create his own story," exploring the slums of Mumbai on his own.[22] "[I]n a film you need a very dynamic, straightforward spine," says Beaufoy,[23] and the "Hero's Journey" has provided the vertebral disks in that spine for writers around the world, with the exception, perhaps, of Australia and Germany, which Vogler claims are "herophobic cultures."[24]

The "Hero's Journey" has served a valuable purpose, but has been squandered on increasingly formulaic blockbusters whose special effects only sometimes save them at the box office. In reducing Campbell's eighteen stages to twelve screenwriting steps, Vogler condensed "The Meeting with the Goddess" with other steps in Campbell's Act II, "Initiation," demoting the Goddess to supporting character status in his Step 6, "Tests, Allies and Enemies," and perpetuating a concept of journey that critic Manohla Dargis calls "unequivocally male."[25]

While the "Hero's Journey" has been an effective template for storytelling for men and women alike, even before screenwriters came into existence, it offers a male-biased way of telling stories, disguised as gender-free. A male perspective has been practical through most of the history of filmmaking, as most movies' stories have been men's stories; women screenwriters were shafted out of Hollywood once the studio system fell into place in the late 1920s, and most producers green-light men's films over women's.

Dr. Martha Lauzen's report, "The Celluloid Ceiling," shows that the number of female screenwriters making a living in 2016 was the same as in 1998: 13 percent of the 250 top-grossing features.[26] In indie films with a female director screened at US festivals in 2015–2016, "female screenwriters "comprised 77 percent of writers versus 6 percent on films directed exclusively by men."[27] Women comprised 29 percent of television writers of broadcast network programs during the 2015–2016 season, "an increase of 9 percent from1997–98."[28] Seventy-six percent of cable/streaming programs in 2015–2016 had no women writers.[29]

The "Hero's Journey" fits certain women's stories like a glove: *Pretty Woman* (USA, 1990), and *Erin Brockovich* (USA, 2000). It certainly worked for Shakespeare's women – smart, adventurous, and outspoken (like Rosalind in "As You Like It" and Viola in "Twelfth Night") – to embark on their journeys in disguise as men, back in the days when a "good" woman was a silent woman. If traditional Hollywood-style filmmaking were still the only game on the planet, there would be no need to go further in applying women's poetics to screenwriting. Ironically, for those who believe that films can profoundly impact society, applying women's poetics may be important for the longevity of the planet. If women are given more opportunities to write for film and television in the future, which already happens more often when women are serving as executive producers, must we follow male templates when structuring our stories, and will those helming the productions back our choices?

This chapter of *Great Adaptations* will serve to examine and restore the significance of the Goddess to story structure as an underlying template to the novels, short stories, or biographies that screenwriters may be adapting.

The Heroine's Journey

Recently some of us have been looking for new ways to structure our stories, not just come up with a feisty new line that fits the old shoe. It makes sense to do so, whether or not we're talking glass slippers. Movie-ticket revenue in the US used to be controlled by the male youth market. But as one executive told TheWrap ,[30] these "[y]oung men ... are toast ... You know what they're all doing right now? They're all playing 'Modern Warfare 3.'"[31] The people who remain in the audience are also demanding more significant female characters, if the $228 million global debut of *Wonder Woman* (USA/China/Hong Kong, 2017) is any indication.[32]

While Vogler's *The Writer's Journey* is compelling and has served many females as well as countless male screenwriters, Joseph Campbell's "The Hero's Journey" on which it is based is not the only way – and perhaps not the most compelling way – for screenwriters to examine women's lives.

Family therapist and educational consultant Maureen Murdock's 1990 book, *The Heroine's Journey*, provided a valiant first step towards providing an alternative for women's stories to Joseph Campbell's "The Hero's Journey." Murdock explains her quest in personal terms:

> My desire to understand how the woman's journey relates to the journey of the hero first led me to talk with Joseph Campbell in 1981. I knew that the stages of the heroine's journey incorporated aspects

> of the journey of the hero, but I felt that the focus of female spiritual development was to heal the internal split between woman and her feminine nature. I wanted to hear Campbell's views. I was surprised when he responded that women don't need to make the journey. "In the whole mythological tradition the woman is there. All she has to do is to realize that she's in the place that people are trying to get to. When a woman realizes what her wonderful character is, she's not going to get messed up with the notion of being pseudo-male."[33]

Murdock was deeply disappointed by Campbell's views on women, in which she could not recognize herself or the women she knew:

> They do not want to be handmaidens of the dominant male culture, giving service to the gods. They do not want to follow the advice of fundamentalist preachers and return to the home. They need a new model that understands who and what a woman is.[34]

Working as a therapist, often with women who were dissatisfied with what professional careers had had to offer them, Murdock came up with a 10-step "Heroine's Journey":

1. Separation from the feminine
2. Identification with the masculine and gathering of allies
3. Road of trials: meeting ogres and dragons
4. Finding the boon of success
5. Awakening to feelings of spiritual aridity: death
6. Initiation and descent to the Goddess
7. Urgent yearning to reconnect with the feminine
8. Healing the mother/daughter split
9. Healing the wounded masculine
10. Integration of masculine and feminine
    (and the cycle repeats: Separation from the feminine, etc.)[35]

Over two decades later, with new templates for women's "success" in journeying, and revised definitions of feminine and masculine in a LGBTQIA world, Murdock's template seems to be a product of its age. But it also serves as a timeless homage to the Goddess stories of Inanna's descent and Demeter's quest for Persephone that inspired her, which we will explore more fully later in this chapter.

Jane Alexander Stewart's lecture on what she called "The Heroic Journey of the Feminine," entitled "The Emerging Feminine Hero" at the Los Angeles County Museum of Art in 1998, provided further insights toward providing an alternative structure to the male-focused "Hero's Journey," using a Jungian approach.[36] In her second of two presentations (the first being Jane Campion's *The Piano* (New Zealand/Australia/France, 1993)) she utilized Clarice Starling's journey in *The Silence of the Lambs* (USA, 1991) to underscore her points:

"Hero's Journey" (Christopher Vogler)		*"Heroine's Journey" (Jane Alexander Stewart)*	
Act I		*Act I*	
1.	Ordinary World	1.	Ordinary World
2.	Call to Adventure	2.	The Break
3.	Refusal of the Call		
4.	Meeting with the Mentor		(There is no mentor.)
5.	Crossing the First Threshold		
Act II		*Act II*	
6.	Tests, Allies, Enemies	3.	Descent (meeting Lector in his cell)
7.	Approach to the Inmost Cave	4.	Initiation (Meeting with goddess – Campbell)
8.	The Supreme Ordeal	5.	Penetration
9.	Reward		
Act III		*Act III*	
10.	The Road Back		
11.	Resurrection		("Master of Two Worlds" – Campbell)
12.	Return with the Elixir	6.	Return to Reality

The descent can be a literal or symbolic descent: In the Oscar-winning adaptation, *The Silence of the Lambs*,[37] Clarice Starling descends to the hell of Hannibal Lector's prison cell. In *The Piano*, it's a land down under: New Zealand. In *Beauty and the Beast* (USA, 1991 and USA/UK, 2017), Belle's life descends to imprisonment in a castle. In *The Wizard of Oz*, it's Dorothy's split consciousness in Munchkinland, while her dreamer's body remains in Kansas.

Several women have applied the "Heroine's Journey" specifically to screenwriting beyond Jane Alexander Stewart's analyses of films with female protagonists. For over twenty years,[38] I've lectured on remodelling story through the model of Eleusis (the center of the ancient Greek cult that lasted for two thousand years) in my screenplay adaptation and advanced screenwriting courses; in her 2009 book *The Virgin's Promise*, Kim Hudson questioned whether Vogler's template spoke to all female protagonists' journeys; in 2015, Dara Marks and Deb Norton gave writing workshops entitled "Engaging the Feminine Heroic" in London, Montreal, and the US;[39] and Pamela Jaye Smith, founder of Mythworks, has offered seminars in "Alpha Babes: Women of Mythic Significance."[40] British story consultant Helen Jacey has also applied these issues to screenwriting in her book *The Woman in the Story*, exploring what she calls "The Real Heroine's Journey," which encourages us to have fun with the changing phases of female characters' identities.[41]

The Virgin's Promise: Another Alternative … Dot by Dot

Kim Hudson's *The Virgin's Promise: Writing Stories of Feminine Creative, Spiritual and Sexual Awakening*, not only provides an excellent summary of the "Hero's Journey," but offers a way of approaching a young "Heroine's Journey" as well.[42]

Basically, Hudson's 13-step journey goes like this: The young heroine is stuck in a *Dependent World* (Step 1), dependent on others for material survival. She maintains living there for the *Price of Conformity* (Step 2), suppressing her true self by "sleeping through her life." But something happens giving her the *Opportunity to Shine* (3) – the action that leads to the first expression of "[her]potential … reveal[ing] her talent, her dream, or her true nature." Accordingly, she *Dresses the Part* (Step 4), "providing the viewer with a fun and pleasurable sense that perhaps dreams can come true and life is meant to have joy in it." But it's not just an outward show; the Virgin creates a *Secret World* in which she can thrive (Step 5). As a result of trying to juggle these two worlds – the dependent world and the secret world – she discovers she *No Longer Fits Her World* (Step 6), and reality hits "when the two worlds collide": "The Virgin often finds herself punished, shamed or exiled" in Step 7, called "*Caught Shining*." Finally there's a major turning point in the psychological growth of the Virgin: Step 8, *Gives Up What Kept Her Stuck*, whether that's an outmoded faith, a relationship, or "'an imminent death that is a metaphor for the death that must occur' in order for the Virgin to move forward."[43] Step 9 is "*Kingdom in Chaos*," in Step 10, the Virgin "*Wanders in the Wilderness*," waffling between returning to her earlier, confining world or taking the bull by the horns with enough self-esteem to make it in a new world, until Step 11, she *Chooses Her Light*. But she is not alone in doing so: By Step 12, someone from her community helps her with some kind of a *Rescue*. By challenging the kingdom and throwing it into chaos, making it accommodate "her authentic nature or her dream" … "[w]hen the dust settles, the kingdom comes to realize that it is better off for having gone through this experience with the Virgin, for it was in need of change, and now *The Kingdom Is Brighter* (final Step 13).[44]

By "Virgin," Hudson is in sync with Esther Harding's definition which "has nothing to do with the modern association of sexual chastity." Instead, Harding defines Virgin as "a woman who acts independently of others, who refuses to conform to the demands of others, and who does not try to seek the approval of or exert power over others."[45] Elsewhere, Esther Harding and Patricia Reis also remind us

> that virginity is a process of being true to oneself, and, most significantly if we have not been true (as many of us have not for many reasons), our virginity is renewable. This is incredibly important for a woman to know. Many women who have been used and abused sexually, or misused their sexuality, need to know that, like Aphrodite, we may, through various rituals and ceremonies, renew our sense of intactness and integrity – our virginity.[46]

Nice to know there's something renewable besides library books!

While Hudson's theory seems more derivative of Vogler, Campbell, Jung, and Bettelheim than feminist theorists, she provides examples of contemporary films that make her work lively and useful. For example, in *Legally Blonde* (USA, 2001), based on the book by Amanda Brown,[47] Elle Woods grows in her journey from being Daddy's little rich girl in a "Dependent World" to class valedictorian at the male bastion of academia, Harvard University, where she has made the "Kingdom… Brighter."[48]

Co-screenwriters Karen McCullah Lutz and Kirsten Smith, who adapted Shakespeare's *The Taming of the Shrew*[49] for the screen prior to tackling *Legally Blonde,* joke about having bonded as writers at their first meeting over seven margaritas, followed by "literary sex," and affirm the theme of Elle's journey by stating that *Legally Blonde* is about "women who are underestimated."[50]

Kim Hudson has clearly done her homework in delineating the thirteen steps of Elle's journey to fit her template, although Smith and Lutz do not mention these steps or the "Virgin Archetypal Journey" when discussing their screenplay for *Legally Blonde*. Hudson's steps are as follows:[51]

1 Dependent World: "Elle Woods is Daddy's little rich girl who has found the man of her dreams, Warner, and believes he will propose, completing the plan for her perfect life."
2 Price of Conformity: "Warner, however, explains they have had loads of fun but he needs to marry someone serious because he plans to be a senator someday."
3 Opportunity to Shine: "But Elle Woods is no pushover. She gets accepted to Harvard Law School so Warner will see that she can be serious (anti-3)."
4 Dresses the Part: "In front of her mirror, on her first day at law school, Elle puts on a pair of horn-rimmed glasses."
5 Secret World "weakly developed/ back and forth element": "One day, Elle puts on her glasses (3) to impersonate a lawyer and help her friend get back her dog (5). She really likes the feeling of being taken seriously and helping people. Elle gets an internship to help defend a fitness guru, Brooke, accused of murdering her husband (5)."
6 No longer fits her world: "[After Warner's fiancée causes her to get kicked out of class] Elle phones her friends in California for support but they care only about getting married and their hair (6)."
7 Caught shining: "Just when she believes the worlds sees she has serious potential, her law professor/boss makes a pass at her (7)."
8 Gives up what kept her stuck: "Elle gives up trying to get married and applies herself to law school (8)." [Note: This, too, is out of sequence. This occurs *before* she gets the internship and her boss makes a pass at her.]

9 Kingdom in chaos: "Meanwhile [as Elle has quit the firm and is packing to go back to California], Brooke [the fitness guru] is in real trouble."
10 Wanders in the wilderness: "During the court case, [A]t first Elle asks stupid questions and the team starts to lose faith in her (10), but then... [See 13]"
11 Chooses her light: "Elle dresses as herself, pretty in pink (4), and steps up to the challenge (11) [of being Brooke's lawyer with the support of Emmett]."
12 Re-Ordering (Rescue): "Emmett, a lawyer who is rooting for Elle to channel her power as a blond towards the greater good, comes up with a plan (12)."
13 The Kingdom is Brighter: (A:) "...Elle's knowledge of perms reveals the witness is lying and she proves Brooke's innocence (13). (B:) Two years later, Elle is class valedictorian. She is a shining example of the importance of looking beyond first impressions, having passion in the law, and always having faith in yourself (13)."

I don't know if Kim Hudson's journey goes far enough. Although she uses the definition of "Virgin" as someone who's whole unto herself, empowered into making her own choices, I feel uncomfortable with that word, coming from a generation of women for whom choice includes choices for sexual fulfillment, career, and whether to have children, and if so, how many. And once she's past her childbearing years and no longer the sexually enticing Beauty that dominates Hollywood's portrayals of females, will she turn into a Beast?

In many cultures, "Virgin" implies a character that is valued and desired by men. For example, the Iranian writer Azar Nafisi quotes one of her students, who has arrived at their clandestine women's class hidden under a chador, ready to discuss *Pride and Prejudice*. Referring to the opening of the English novel and applying it to a repressive Iran, the student Yassi quips:

> It is a truth universally acknowledged that a Muslim man, regardless of his fortune, must be in want of a nine-year-old virgin wife.[52]

... to which another student, Azin replies sarcastically:

> The Islamic Republic has taken us back to Jane Austen's times. God bless the arranged marriage![53]

Girls who are virgins in cultures where virginity is central to their value also deserve stories. In the US, we have the television series *Jane the Virgin* (2014–), loosely based on the Venezuelan telenovela *Juana la Virgen* created in 2002 by Perla Farias in a country with strict abortion laws. A remake of *Juana la Virgen* entitled *La Virgen de la Calle* (*Street's Virgin*) was produced for Colombian release in 2013, and release in Panama and the US in 2014, prior to the release of *Jane the Virgin.* Rodolfo Hoyos, producer at RTI Colombia, describes the origins of the show as

> an interesting story about a seventeen-year-old adolescent who is a virgin. Juana becomes pregnant due to an error made by a gynecologist who mistakenly artificially inseminates her. She gets pregnant unintentionally and unknowingly. Also it is a story about a girl who becomes a woman because she is transitioning from being a seventeen-year-old girl to becoming an eighteen-year-old woman who has to face this unwanted pregnancy. She becomes somewhat of a historical virgin that grows up in a tough, urban neighborhood, full of the marginal problems that all cities in Latin America face.[54]

Virgins' stories can tell of empowerment, healing, and rites of passage into adulthood, but can also be tragedies of persecution – botched cliterectomies, death by stoning, child brides, the sex trafficking of girls, journeys in search of transgender. Hudson's book is a good beginning, but we can go even further.

We can also create stories that explore women's journeys where their value is determined by themselves and other women: sisterhood stories that don't necessarily duplicate buddy stories; mother and daughter stories that are far more complex than the nice, white middle-class suburban stay-at-home mothers we've traditionally seen on screen; and stories of girls and older women outside the age bracket of the virgin ingénue. Instead of virgins, whores, and other stereotypes outfitted as archetypes, we may think of ourselves as girls and women deserving of rituals that celebrate or heal different stages of our lives. These may include menstruation, sexual exploration, childbirth, miscarriage or abortion, marriage, divorce, conquering or succumbing to slut-shaming, disease or disability, coming into one's own in terms of creativity or spiritual transformation, or reaching (or tragically being denied) a level of power – whether military, economic, or sexual.

Films with female protagonists or revolving around female archetypes should not be marginalized as "chick flicks." As Audrey Wells, screenwriter/director of the adaptation, *Under the Tuscan Sun* (USA/Italy, 2003) protested,

> If that story is told by a woman, does that automatically make it a chick flick? … I don't feel that I need to defend against that … [F]or me, it's about what happens between the day you wish you were dead and the day you're glad you're alive again. What's that journey all about? And I don't think that's just a woman's journey.[55]

We can also choose to face the fascinating dark side of women, as in *Les Diaboliques* (France, 1955), *Batman Returns* (USA, 1992), *Maleficent* (USA/UK, 2014), or in contemporary psychological thrillers such as *Gone*

Girl (USA, 2014) and *The Housemaid* (Korea, 2010, based on an even more terrifying adaptation with the same name, written and directed by Kim Ki-young in 1960). There are also traditional stories featuring "good girl, bad girl" dichotomies which focus on purity and shame, such as Ingmar Bergman's *The Virgin Spring* (Sweden, 1960), adapted by novelist Ulla Isaksson from a thirteenth-century Swedish ballad. Can some of these be reworked from a non-racist, feminist standpoint?

Both Kim Hudson's *The Virgin's Promise* and Helen Jacey's *The Woman in the Story* credit Maureen Murdock's *The Heroine's Journey* as providing material that screenwriters can use in developing female characters' stories. But the discussions of the goddess that their theories rest on remain limited in scope. Beyond the cult of the individual beckon Demeter and Persephone, the Double Goddesses. We can use the "Virgin's Promise" steps for Persephone's journey to the underworld, into the arms of Hades; equally, we can use the "Heroine's Journey" to tell the story from the intertwined perspectives of mother and daughter.

While Demeter and Persephone – as well as the story of Dionysus – offer important alternatives from ancient cultures to the story of Jason and the Argonauts, what about the goddesses of non-Western cultures, like Durga, the Hindu Mother Goddess who is also the Destroyer? What about Amaterasu, Brigit, Coatlicue, Freya, Isis, Ishtar, and Kuan Yin ... all the way through Xi Wang Mu, Yemonja, and Zarya? Female goddesses from different cultures the world over undergo a variety of archetypal journeys which we can follow.

For example, there is the Hindu goddess, Kali. Appearing in Tantric texts by the eleventh century,[56] Kali is "the black Goddess of death, who decapitates her enemies and hangs their body parts from her neck and around her waist, [yet] would become the embodiment of motherly compassion and kindness."[57] Pretty awesome, huh? What if Kali meets up with Echidna, half-woman half-serpent from ancient Greek mythology described in *My Monster Notebook* as "very beautiful from the waist up; below ... a terrible serpent ... (She's a Beauty and the Beast.)"[58] Do Echidna and Kali get along? Do they fight? Over what or whom? Or you may want to put Echidna into the throes of labor with one of her babies, who tend to be monsters. Who midwifes her? Or is Kali busy with the corpse of Shiva while Echidna is bringing new life into the world? Or maybe Echidna is jealous of Kali, and fights over her with Argus – the giant with the hundred eyes – who then plots to kill Echidna. Do Kali and Argus end up together in this hybrid between East and West, or is that disrespectful, particularly to Hindus for whom Kali is part of an on-going religion? (Remember the kitsch of Cecil B. DeMille's biblical adaptation, *The Ten Commandments* [USA, 1956]?) I'll let you decide.

Multiplied by myths, legends, and religious figures of other cultures around the world, our choices in approaching underlying structure to adaptation are myriad. Goddesses from other cultures are also explored in Valerie Frankel's *From Girl to Goddess*, including South Africa's Armless Maiden, Russia's Baba Yaga, the Navaho's Changing Woman, and others.

She organizes their tales according to Campbell's "Hero's Journey," adding a section on female archetypes whose stories fit the phases of the moon, such as China's Golden Lotus as an example of the Rising Moon ("Maiden"), Mexico's La Llorona at the Full Moon ("Mother"), the wife of Hassan in Persia at the Waning Moon ("Crone"), and Iceland's "The Witch in the Stone Boat" at the New Moon ("Spirit Guardian").[59] Arranging goddesses and fairy tale heroines to the phases of the moon is an intriguing answer as to how to feminize the 28 incarnations of William Butler Yeats' moon-based system. In *A Vision,* the great Irish poet, working with his wife's automatic writing, attributed specific personality traits (mostly male, other than Queen Victoria and Lady Gregory) to the 28 phases of the moon.[60] While Helen Jacey's "Heroine's Journey" also uses a "Phase Approach,"[61] Valerie Frankel provides specific female character examples from myths and legends for each phase. Many of these stories from around the world can inform new adaptations.

Filmmakers are lagging behind contemporary fiction practices: it's about time we apply to screenwriting what Lidia Curti observes as already being applied in women's literature: "Theories and narratives arise from hybrid voices, standing on the borders between different, sometime multiple cultures, backgrounds and languages, both within Europe and across continents."[62] We can extrapolate new aesthetics for film, television, and new media from what Lidia Curti describes as "[t]emporal and spatial dislocations, non-corporeal connections, fantastic forms of narration even outside science fiction proper become essential narrative tools in contemporary women's fiction."[63] Even if the film and television industries remain essentially patriarchal, they too will benefit from how women perceive our world. This is something that we have known for a long time. Arthur Rimbaud wrote in 1871:

> Woman will discover the unknown. Will her world be different from ours? She will discover strange, unfathomable things, repulsive, delicious. We shall take them, we shall understand them.[64]

Appropriated or not, Patricia Reis reminds us:

> Patriarchal imagination operates as the myth-making, fantasy-producing, and interpretive aspect of the patriarchal mind. As such, it reflects and supports only patriarchal social structures and concerns. Patriarchal imagination has created and interpreted most of our existing mythologies. For any of us who works with mythological material, particularly as it relates to the female psyche, it is very important that the ideological foundations of the myth be exposed to critical examination.[65]

Diane Purkiss also comments:

> Ever since myths came into existence, women have been involved in writing and rewriting them. In many cultures, women are story-

> tellers; it is misleading to speak solely of women's "rewriting" of myth, since the term implies that man was its prime maker.[66]

One can examine the myth that follows, "The Descent of Inanna," in terms of the rhythms of creation, which Reis describes as "the great cycle of fragmentation, death and burial, self-seeding, and regeneration."[67] By undergoing this creative initiation, which begins with "a period of destructuring and dismemberment" (like the breaking of a ceramic pot, or the shedding of the menstrual lining of the uterus) and continues through "all the phases of her mysteries,"[68]

> we are given our creative divinity in her image; we come the self-creating Goddess.[69]

According to Reis, "[t]his ancient Great Goddess is literally the ground, the foundation, upon which our western culture has been built."[70]

Inanna's Descent to the Underworld

Written in about 2300 BCE by the first woman writer, Enheduanna in Mesopotamia (the land of modern-day Iraq), "The Descent of Inanna to the Underworld" tells the story of the Lady of Largest Heart, Queen of Heaven and Earth – the most powerful goddess for a period of 5,000 years.[71]

In the story of Inanna, the goddess leaves her throne, dressed in power, to visit her sister Erishkigal, who, raped by the gods, is moaning in childbirth. No sooner than Inanna arrives, her sister has her stripped of all her civilized qualities. Stark naked, she is beaten to death and left on a meat hook to rot. Two creatures – neither male nor female, made of the dirt underneath the God Enki's fingernail – are sent to retrieve Inanna's body, and bring her back to her upper world, where she is revived. The Passion of Christ and his Resurrection are similar, but in this case, it's the story of two female goddesses, and the tormentor is the source of her sister's resurrection: Inanna comes back to life with a new way of seeing that is holistic. "Now she is both a caring goddess ... and a goddess who has the capacity to stare with the eye of death."[72]

Once Inanna is back on earth, however, she discovers that her consort Dumuzi has taken over her throne. In punishment, he is sent to the underworld, but she mourns the loss of her love. Geshtinanna, Dumuzi's sister, hears her lament, and empathizes, as she is mourning the loss of her brother. She offers to share Dumuzi's sentence in the underworld, each spending six months below and six months above.

Inanna is all that we value in the upper world – but was disconnected from the realities of the natural world of death, etc. Her character arc is that she becomes a different, wiser person, with knowledge of the forces of nature, including her own nature, vis-à-vis her shadow side – her sister. Her relationship to Geshtinanna, whom Murdock claims "has much to teach the modern-day heroine" for experiencing "the full cycle of her feminine nature" is also an important part of the myth of transformation.[73]

Looked at from this perspective, *The Wonderful Wizard of Oz* might take a very different approach than that chosen by screenwriters Noel Langley, Florence Ryerson, and Edgar Allan Woolf (and 15 uncredited writers – all male) in their 1939 screenplay for *The Wizard of Oz,* with its Erishkigal-like witches, its Geshtinanna-like fairy godmother, and its Oz as the great underground "Other." It also has implications for fairy tales like *Frozen* (USA, 2013), in which the underground is replaced by an icy kingdom with which the sisters must come to terms. Another adaptation of a story that revolves around the intense power relationship between two friends is Kutluğ Ataman's award-winning film, *2 Girls (2 Genç Kız*, Turkey, 2005), based on Turkish author Perihan Mağden's novel, *2 Girls (İki Genç Kızın Romanı)* in which one puts the other through a psychological hell of lust and insane jealousy. So far, I haven't seen a full-length narrative feature adapting the myth of Inanna per se, although *SPLit* (USA, 2017), an indie film by writer/director Deborah Kampeier that references the myth with a protagonist named Inanna has just been released. *Monster* (USA, 2003), Patty Jenkins's adaption of the story of real-life serial killer Aileen Wuornos, also suggests an Inanna-like structure, exploring the physical and psychological hell of rape and prostitution that Aileen recounts to her sister-like lover Selby, which helps Selby in her ultimate choice to grow up from a rebellious teen into a woman.

Hopefully the Inanna myth can serve as a useful alternative to the ancient Greek myth of Jason and his Golden Fleece in giving narrative films both character development and structure both now and in the future.

Inanna is just one powerful choice: Heroine's journeys can be structured around a vast variety of women's experiences, be they menstrual cycles, which are celebrated in the Women's Room of the Temple of Inanna, where women come to self-knowledge in seclusion from men, or multiple orgasms instead of one crisis, climax and resurrection, or multiple pregnancies, miscarriages, childbirths, and the return to one-ness following menopause. In Mesopotamia, there was a Goddess of Birth, a Goddess of the Beginning of Labor, a Goddess of After Miscarriage. There was a strong relationship between early culture and menstruation: Women's bodies and women's bodily functions were the basis for creativity – both for the fertility of the people as well as the fertility of their crops. What were their stories, and what can we glean from them?

The Story of Demeter and Persephone

Roughly a thousand years after the story of Inanna and her sister, the ancient Greek story of Demeter and Persephone echoed Inanna's five thousand-year reign. Like Inanna, it was a story with long-lasting spiritual dimensions. Murdock writes:

Figure 8.1 Frozen (USA, 2013). The screenplay by Jennifer Lee keeps the Scandinavian setting but changes most of the story elements originally intended as an adaptation of Hans Christian Andersen's "The Snow Queen," focusing instead on the relationship between two sisters. Image courtesy of Walt Disney Studios Motion Pictures. Produced by Walt Disney Pictures

> The worship of Demeter was well established at Mycenae in the thirteenth century BC and continued throughout Greece for approximately two thousand years, to then be replaced by the worship of Mithras and later of Christ. Her temple at Eleusis, one of the greatest shrines in Greece, became the center of an elaborate mystery-religion. Demeter was worshipped as "The Goddess" at Eleusis by Greek peasants throughout the Middle Ages, even up to the nineteenth century.[74]

In the mother–daughter story of the goddess Demeter and her daughter, the young maiden Persephone is out picking flowers when the ground suddenly splits open and Hades emerges from the depths of the earth, grabbing her and taking her down to the underworld. She screams for help and though Zeus, Persephone's father, hears her, he doesn't offer to help. Demeter searches land and sea for her missing daughter, but it takes till dawn on the tenth day for Hecate, the goddess of the dark moon, to tell Demeter that Persephone has been kidnapped. Apparently, the abduction and rape has been sanctioned by Zeus, who was Hades' brother.

Demeter, enraged by Zeus' betrayal, leaves Mt. Olympus disguised as an old woman, grieving to such an extent that the land – her land, as Earth Goddess of grain – grows completely barren. She wanders to Eleusis, where she works as a nursemaid in disguise as an old woman, until, while babysitting, she puts the baby in the fire to make him immortal, horrifying the mother who catches her in the act – making her reveal herself as a goddess. Demeter commands that a temple be built for her, where she can sit "alone with her grief for Persephone."[75] As the famine spreads (perfect for our age of environmental concerns), the gods begin to implore Demeter to give back the crops. But Demeter refuses, until she can see Persephone again.

According to Clarissa Pinkola Estés, it is the goddess Baubo who pulls Demeter out of her depression in Eleusis. Baubo (also known as Iambe) is one of the "archetypal wild Goddess of sacred sexuality and life/death/life fertility," specializing in obscenity.[76] When Baubo arrives, her off-color jokes are stimulating enough for Demeter to take action to recover her daughter from the clutches of Hades – which is not that different than Melissa McCarthy's character, Megan, pulling Annie out of her depression in time to save her lifelong friend Lillian from a deadbeat life in *Bridesmaids* (USA, 2011).

Finally Zeus sends Hermes to send Persephone back to Demeter so that fertility can return to the earth. But before leaving Persephone is tricked into eating Hades' pomegranate seeds, which means she will have to return to the underworld for a third of each year – winter on earth. Once Persephone comes back to Demeter, Spring returns to the earth. But meanwhile, Demeter has taken an inward journey, confronted with the loss of her daughter and her youth. Both women have gone through profound character arcs: in the case of Persephone, she has gone from being an innocent maiden, who was raped, then forcibly married to the King of the Underworld, to becoming a Queen of the Underworld and an equal companion to her mother, the goddess Demeter.

Furthermore, if we make Persephone the protagonist rather than Hades, the typical action hero, that's only her Plot Point Two. As Tamara Agha-Jaffar points out in *Demeter and Persephone: Lessons from a Myth*:

> Victims are not responsible for their victimization; however, they are responsible for turning that victimization into something constructive that can strengthen and empower them and empower others by example. By eating the pomegranate seed, Persephone does just that. She exercises agency. She defines herself. She moves beyond her abduction, betrayal, and rape. She transcends her victim status and becomes the powerful and empowered queen of the underworld – a "kick ass" survivor.[77]

Erich Neumann, in his essay, "The Woman's Experience of Herself and the Eleusinian Mysteries," lists the "great motifs underlying the Eleusinian mysteries" as "Abduction, rape, marriage of death, and separation,"[78] stating: "The unity of Demeter and Kore [another name for Persephone] is the central content of the Eleusinian mysteries."[79]

According to Patricia Reis, this unity was split during the late Neolithic era, with the Great Mother simultaneously reduced and divided into good mother and bad mother. We all know the archetypes and stereotypes of good mother (the Virgin Mary) and bad mother (not only Eve, but Nurse Ratchet as a kind of Devouring Mother Goddess in *One Flew Over the Cuckoo's Nest* (USA, 1975)). Reis states: "It is this divided Goddess who reigns in the patriarchal imagination's myth of matriarchy."[80]

It is possible to simply squeeze the archetypal story of Demeter and Persephone into the classic "Hero's Journey," without acknowledging the splitting of the protagonist's role between Demeter and her daughter Persephone. Using Agha-Jaffer's outline of the Homeric hymn to Demeter and Persephone as his source,[81] Robert Taylor explains:

> The myth contains many elements familiar to the screenwriter: protagonist (Demeter or Persephone depending on perspective), antagonist (Hades), conflict and rising conflict, a structured plot, cause/effect momentum, climax and resolution. The hymn is a prime example of Vogler's mythic structure. It uses archetypal figures: Demeter is the archetypal Earth Mother, Hermes is an ally, Hekate the mentor and so on. Stages of the Heroic Journey are clearly marked: mother and daughter's idyllic Ordinary World; the abduction is Demeter's Call to Adventure or the Inciting Incident; Demeter's wandering is the Refusal of the Call, etc.[82]

In this story, rape plays a role that is perhaps difficult to understand in today's world, one that was acceptable to the patriarchy of that time. Does that mean it must remain acceptable to Hollywood's? If we think of the "Hero's Journey" in terms of power over women, then a young woman like Persephone, abducted and raped by Hades, is perceived primarily as his victim. However, as Amit Taneja points out in "From Oppressor to Activist: Reflections of a Feminist Journey,"[83] men can transcend their stereotypical roles as oppressors, and rethink their power. "As a poor, immigrant, big-boned, non-Christian, gay person of color who happens to be working in a country where Others are feared, some people would say that I have a lot going against me," he writes. "However, despite all that works against me, I still feel that I have power." Taneja goes on to say, "I have come to a place of questioning, resisting, and actively changing the tape ... I have come to fight the sexist messages that I was raised with, and, more importantly, to duck and cover from, deflect, and strike back against the thousands of similar messages that come my way on a daily basis."[84]

In *El Lugar Sin Límites* (*The Place without Limits*, also released as *Hell without Limits*, Mexico, 1978),[85] a film based on Chilean author José Donoso's novel of the same title, reset in Mexico, director Arturo Ripstein addresses both violent machismo and homophobia. The script was written by Donoso, Ripstein, and José Emilio Pacheco, one of Mexico's most important poets. Additional, uncredited screenwriters included Argentinian novelist Manuel Puig, who provided the structure that Ripstein used in the film as well as the dialogue during male transvestite La Manuela's seduction of the macho, homophobic Pancho, which Puig considered to be a "'rehearsal' for the adaptation of the novel *Kiss of the Spider Woman*" (Brazil/USA, 1985).[86]

In "Hombres y Machos," Alfredo Mirandé researched Latino men in the context of a rich and complex culture:

> I found in a roundabout way that contrary to what many scholars claim, negative machismo, or exaggerated masculinity, was neither a response to the Conquest nor an extension of pre-Columbia warring Aztec society. Instead, like Catholicism and many deadly diseases, negative machismo was imported and imposed on the indigenous population via the Conquest.[87]

As the "Heroine's Journey" is re-examined, so can the "Hero's Journey" take other paths, equally rich and complex in their cultural underpinnings.

For example, it is not necessary for all male- or female-oriented stories to be protagonist-driven. We are reminded of Mary Dalton's statement in "Conquer or Connect: Power, Patterns, and the Gendered Narrative," "independence evokes conquest, whereas interdependence evokes connection." [88]

Furthermore, Dalton continues:

> Simply put, stories told in a conventional, masculine form are generally linear, hero-driven tales about conquest, whereas stories told with a more circular and sometimes collective feminine structure are often about overcoming obstacles in order to find connection. That connection may be internal, may involve other individuals or groups, or may even relate to larger communities.[89]

Of course, men might tell some stories with a feminine structure, and women working in commercial Hollywood most often tell conventionally masculine stories. But for women writing from the inside out, taking a linear approach is clearly not the only way to structure a story.

Carol P. Christ, in her essay, "Learning from My Mother Dying," writes:

> Now I begin to understand that the union, separation, and re-union depicted in the myth [of Demeter and Persephone] are not poles in relation of mother and daughter. Each is a point in the circle whose center is "the flow of energy between two biologically alike bodies, one of which has lain in amniotic bliss inside the other, one of which has labored to give birth to the other." In this highly charged circle, the bond between mother and daughter is woven of love, admiration, and delight, but also, because none of us loves the self or the other perfectly, with fear, jealousy, and shame ... From every point in the circle, the bond remains, as mothers and daughters continually measure the self against the other.[90]

Circularly structured stories are also found in Native American cultures pertaining to both male and female characters; novelist Vladimir Nabokov describes "the prison of time" as spherical in writing about his own writing,[91] although Stanley Kubrick's adaptation of Nabokov's *Lolita* (UK/USA, 1962) pays little heed to this approach.

In his book *Rewrite*, screenwriter Paul Chitlik applies "Central Emotional Relationships," or "CERs," to the B-line of a story, the A-line being more akin to the beginning, middle, and end of a "Hero's Journey," complete with all its plot points. He uses as an example the 2012 film, *Argo*, in which six Americans hiding in the residence of the Canadian ambassador to Iran, whom Tony Mendez (played by Ben Affleck) must convince to trust him so he can help them escape them from Tehran.

Chitlik explains:

> The film's A story is the process by which he is recruited, creates a plan, enters the country, and prepares the group to escape. The B story is his developing a relationship with the group – not any specific individual – so that they trust him to accomplish his mission.[92]

However, what if the entire story down to its premise were rethought, putting the relationship first? Would the six individuals of the group become more memorable? Would the relationship of the people of Tehran and its government have been fleshed out more as well, instead of seeing a few vendors and passers-by in the streets? Knowing how rich Iranian cinema itself has been in portraying Persian culture, what seems to have been a mere afterthought – a "C" story at best – might have provided greater opportunities for character portrayal and conflict.

In the story of Demeter and Persephone, the "A" story could be hero's journey, as Persephone journeys to the underworld and reemerges as Queen of the Underworld, as powerful a goddess as her mother. Or it could be Demeter's heroic journey to save her daughter from the clutches of Hades. Using Chitlik's idea of CERs, the relationship between them is the B-line. But the story takes on a greater power if the relationship between mother and daughter is primary, like the double spirals that inform the structure of Iñárritu's *Biutiful* (Mexico/Spain, 2010), or the husbands and wives of Woody Allen's *Husbands and Wives* (USA, 1992). In the case of *Biutiful,* Uxbal's life spins out of control while his consciousness spirals inward, intensifying spiritually. In *Husbands and Wives*, two married couples' circumstances change in opposite directions, intersecting with one another. The structure of both of these films evokes the double spirals of Yeats' *A Vision*, which can similarly be utilized as a structural template for the major plot points of an adaptation. A double spiral of intertwining character relationships is a far cry from the classic male story template that Eric Leed calls "a spermatic journey."[93]

Novelist/screenwriter Gillian Flynn provides a gender twist to the double spiral, laced with the cynicism that a husband and wife feel on their fifth anniversary, in *Gone Girl*.[94] Both Flynn's novel and her film adaptation provide witty examples of the "flat cold inner remove" that critic Vivian Gornick's *The End of the Novel of Love* explored in the "remarkable novels ... where, at the exact moment the woman should melt, her heart unexpectedly hardens."[95] Flynn further dimensionalizes this tack by constructing a he-said, she-said alternating structure between Nick the Hero and Amy the Heroine's points of view. Flynn mines, explodes, then turns upside down and backwards the fears of Americanhood. As Gretchen Carlson, veteran Fox News broadcast journalist, has stated:

> [O]ne of our greatest fears is that we won't be believed. "He said, she said" is still a convenient phrase that equates victims with harassers. It trivializes workplace harassment and has become synonymous with "Don't take that risk; they won't believe you anyway."[96]

By bringing the issue of victimhood into the home instead of the workplace, Flynn's thriller is made that much scarier. Or does the double perspective simply make it light-hearted and entertaining? Nick-and-Amy's story is so self-referential that the structure is even labeled as such at the end of the novel, when the love is off (except to the media circus outside their blood-stained home, eager for their reconciliation and a happy ending), but the book deal is on, and Amy can finally gloat:

> I have a book deal: I am officially in control of our story. It feels wonderfully symbolic. Isn't that what every marriage is, anyway? Just a lengthy game of he-said, she-said? Well, she is saying, and the world will listen, and Nick will have to smile and agree.[97]

Nick maintains his own version of the story throughout the 400+ pages of the novel, but by the end, his wife has managed to blackmail him into deleting his version from his laptop, leaving her the sole winner. His version starts with the typical "Ordinary World," straight out of Vogler: an ordinary husband out by the garbage can of the suburban home, preparing to go to work. The Inciting Incident? A neighbor calls; Nick returns home to discover a break-in. Suddenly Nick is on a thrilling journey to discover who did it, which escalates when he's accused of murdering his wife. "All of a sudden I'm on a 'Law & Order' episode," Nick says, in one of many bits of self-reflexive media-making reminiscent of Mankiewicz's cold, self-deprecating dialogue in *All About Eve* (USA, 1950).

Amy's "she said" spirals downwards from a happily-ever-after courtship backstory to a series of dramatized entries from a fabricated diary that she's written out of revenge for her husband having slept with a younger woman. "I began to think of a different story, a better story," writes Amy,

> that would destroy Nick for doing this to me ... It would make me the hero,
> flawless and adored.
> Because everyone loves the Dead Girl.[98]

By the time the public has turned against Nick, his "he-said" has evolved from typical American reticence to some soul-searching on his part:

> I'd tried all my life to be a decent guy, a man who loved and respected women, a guy without hang-ups. And here I was, thinking nasty thoughts about my twin, about my mother-in-law, about my mistress. I was imagining bashing in my wife's skull.[99]

The film can't keep quite as many of these interior monologue observations, but since Nick and Amy are both writers, they have a perfect excuse for their voice-overs. When Amy fakes her death in order to frame her husband, she writes/says, "I'm so much happier now that I'm dead." What we see in the film is an underwater shot of a woman's corpse in the river. Her voice-over continues:

> And when they find my body, they'll know ... Nick Dunne dumped his beloved like garbage, and she floated down past all the other abused, unwanted, inconvenient women.[100]

For the literati among movie-goers, the woman's decaying corpse with her seaweed-like hair is more than a riff on the woman-as-victim cliché: it also evokes the title sequence of the Australian film adaptation of *Wide Sargasso Sea* (Australia, 1993),[101] Caribbean novelist Jean Rhys's riff on Charlotte Brontë's English classic, *Jane Eyre*. (The fantasy shot of seaweed entangling Amy's dead body may also bring to mind the garbage dump in Rio de Janeiro where Orfeu finds Eurydice's corpse in the 1999 Brazilian adaptation of the Orphic legend.) The idea of one novelist riffing on another's work is also apparent in a book by Kamel Daoud, which retells Albert Camus's *The Stranger* from the perspective of the Arab murder victim's Algerian brother. Daoud's *Meursault, Counter-Investigation* has been adapted into a play and is currently in development as a film.[102]

Rhys, like Flynn today, was concerned stretching structure beyond the classic plot points. In adapting Brontë's novel to her own, Rhys wrote:

> About my book. It is done in the way that patchwork would be done if you had all the colors and all the pieces cut but not yet arranged to make a quilt.[103]

Time is the pieces of patchwork with which a screenwriter stitches together an adaptation. In Virginia Woolf's novel, *Orlando*, the protagonist, "a being who lived for 400 years, first as a man and then as woman,"[104] is portrayed as male until page 67:

> He stretched himself. He rose. He stood upright in complete nakedness before us, and while the trumpets pealed Truth! Truth! Truth! We have no choice left but confess – he was a woman.[105]

Screenwriter/director Sally Potter grappled with the best approach to adapting *Orlando* (UK/Russia/Italy/France/Netherlands, 1992), which was famous for its uniquely associative literary style and which dealt with gender issues with light humor.

> The longer I lived with Orlando and tried to write a character who was both male and female, the more ludicrous maleness and femaleness became, and the more the notion of the essential human being – that a man and woman both are – predominated.[106]

These changes included moving the ending from 1928 – ten years after women got the right to vote in the UK – to 1992, when Potter's film was completed,[107] "in order to keep faith with Virginia Woolf's use of real time in ending the novel (with the story finishing just as she puts down her pen to finish the book),"[108] and telling the six-chapter, four-century story in nine acts, keeping the concept of a character who lives an extraordinarily long life, rather than only showing part of it or turning it into a mini-series – a choice that many other adaptations make. The film's ending includes both the music of David Bowie and a girl with a video camera, homage to Potter's parallel life as a late twentieth-century experimental filmmaker, celebrating both sexes.

If the male-female protagonist of Potter's *Orlando* suggests one creative riff on the concept of the Double Goddess, another is suggested by *The Stone Angel* (Canada, 2007), written and directed by Kari Skogland: the protagonist as a Double Goddess achieved by mixing one character's present and her past. Based on Margaret Laurence's classic novel of the same title, *The Stone Angel* intercuts the life of Hagar, a 90-year-old Canadian woman forced to comply with her son's demands, and Hagar's defiance against her father as a young woman. (There's actually a compelling scene that takes place in her childhood, as well, making her a Triple Goddess in construction, technically speaking: a Canadian *Daughters of the Dust* in its intertwining of the generations – although Julie Dash's *Daughters of the Dust* was an original film, not an adaptation, followed by Dash's novelization after the success of the film.)

The sentimental music score and frequent flashbacks of the film version of *The Stone Angel* impinge on the realistic "now" of Hagar's perspective, bleeding together her past and present perspectives of small-town Canadian life, whereas Margaret Laurence's prose bristles in starkly delineating its plot points. For example, midway through the novel, Hagar has escaped from her son's plan to drag her to a nursing home by running away to the rotting old skeleton of a house where she had once lived a passionate life as the wife of a wild and reckless farmer. She sits among the cobwebs and observes in canny detail the decaying, old items that had surrounded her as a housewife. When her husband's alcoholism destroyed their marriage, Hagar was forced to take a job in town keeping house for an old man to make ends meet. But just before the reader learns how stultifying it will be to return to Manawaka in such reduced circumstances, the novelist makes us feel that this new house might just be Hagar's salvation:

> To move to a new place – that's the greatest excitement. For a while you believe you carry nothing with you – all is canceled from before, or cauterized, and you begin again and nothing will go wrong this time.[109]

Throughout the tragedies of Hagar's life, her mother's gravestone looks down on it all – an imposing statue of pure white marble, especially imported from Italy, which "must have been carved in that distant sun by stonemasons who were the cynical descendants of Bernini, gouging out her like by the score..."[110] If the stone angel is a Demeter locked in the frozen Hades of Canadian winters, she is unable to speak to her daughter, let alone see her for who she really is: "Whoever carved her had left the eyeballs blank," writes Laurence.[111] But Hagar, at age 90, has experienced the full range of the female experience, including maidenhood and motherhood. As screen goddess in *The Stone Angel*, Hagar's face fills the screen with rage, passion, and despair. She alternates from cinematic Double Goddess to a wreck of a crone whose house has already been signed over to her son.

As useful as it may be to turn to Demeter, Persephone, and other goddesses to enrich the women's stories we are adapting (particularly if they are lightweight in substance, although I bristle at the misuse of the term "Chick Lit"), it may be perilous to the "now" in which we write our screenplays to rely too heavily on the history of myth to provide us inspiration. Now that cinema is turning increasingly to independent filmmakers whose backgrounds are often closer to the arts than the industry-driven Hollywood, we may catch up creatively with the thinking of poets like Denise Levertov, who wrote:

> Examination of my own work for the presence of myth has confirmed me in my belief that myth arises from within the poet and poem rather than being deliberately sought. I think I may have shown that dreams may be a more frequent and – in an age when the Western intellectual, along with the rest of the people, is rarely in live touch with a folkloric tradition of myth and epic – a more authentic source of myth in poetry than a scholarly knowledge would be, unless that scholarly knowledge is deeply imbedded in the imaginative life of the writer.
>
> I am thinking here of the contrast between the many academic set-pieces on mythological themes – usually on Greek or Roman ones – which read like exercises in the gentle art of saying nothing elegantly or of evading the here-and-how (and seem like the last echoes of the long period when every gentleman could construe a page of Virgil or Ovid, yet feel in his pulses nothing of what they meant) – between these on the one hand and the poems of writers like [Robert] Duncan, [Charles] Olson, [Ezra] Pound, David Jones, in whom scholarship is an extension of intuitive knowledge.[112]

It would be interesting to see which poets and screenwriters Denise Levertov might have included in her list, had she not been compiling it fifty years ago.

Elsewhere, Levertov describes the poet as a woman in labor, painfully struggling to push out a poem; a father, watching "a remote consequence of a dream of his" being born; [113] or a thirty-year-old man:

> All the books he has read are in the poet's mind (having arrived there by way of his eyes and ears, his apperceptive brain-centers, his heartbeat, his arteries, his bones) as it grasps a pen with which to sign yes or no. Life or death? Peace or war?[114]

Gloria Anzaldúa has compared writing to "a cactus needle embedded in the flesh. The more one tries to remove it, the deeper it gets. The act of writing gives birth to the soul through the body: 'When I write it feels like I'm carving bone. It feels like I'm creating my own face, my own heat – a Nahuatl concept'." [115] Of course, in creating the underpinnings of our stories in the post-male and post-female gaze world, we also remember the poet John Donne, who stated in 1633 that "the body makes the mind."[116] That can extend not only to what makes us write, but even to the concept behind the characters being created, such as the transgender father in Jill Soloway's television series *Transparent* (USA, 2014).

If you experience pain in reading this chapter, I hope that it will transform you into someone who education goes deeper than a mere degree, who is in touch with herself or himself, and who will touch others through your writing.

Notes

1 Joseph Campbell, *The Hero with a Thousand Faces* (Princeton, NJ: Princeton University Press, 1949).
2 Antoine Faivre, *The Golden Fleece and Alchemy* (New York: State University of New York, 1993), 8.
3 Christopher Vogler, *The Writer's Journey: Mythic Structure for Storytellers & Screenwriters* (Los Angeles, CA: Michael Wiese, 1992) and Christopher Vogler, *The Writer's Journey: Mythic Structure for Storytellers & Screenwriters* (Studio City, CA: Michael Wiese, 1992. 3rd edn, 2007).
4 Vogler, *The Writer's Journey*, 3rd edition, 96. Also described in the 1992 edition, 19.
5 Vogler, *The Writer's Journey*, 1998, 123, also in 3rd edn, 104.
6 Vogler, *The Writer's Journey*, 1998, 133, also in 3rd edn, 112
7 Vogler, *The Writer's Journey*, 1998, 144, also in 3rd edn, 123.
8 Vogler, *The Writer's Journey*, 1998, 153–154, also in 3rd edn, 131.
9 Vogler, *The Writer's Journey*, 1998, 163, also in 3rd edn, 140–141.
10 Vogler, *The Writer's Journey*, 1998, 24, extensively discussed in 3rd edn, 145–152.
11 Vogler, *The Writer's Journey*, 1998, 25, also in 3rd edn, 172.
12 Vogler, *The Writer's Journey*, 1998, 27, also in 3rd edn, 183–184.
13 Vogler, *The Writer's Journey*, 1998, 224, also in 3rd edn, 193.
14 Vogler, *The Writer's Journey*, 1998, 243, also in 3rd edn, 211.

15 Vogler, *The Writer's Journey*, 1998, 29, also in 3rd edn, 226–227.
16 Salman Rushdie, *The Wizard of Oz* (London: BFI Film Classics, 1992), 14.
17 Rushdie, *The Wizard of Oz*, 10.
18 Rushdie, *The Wizard of Oz*, 57.
19 Michael Kaminski, *The Secret History of 'Star Wars': The Art of Storytelling and the Making of a Modern Epic* (Kingston, ON: Legacy Books, 2008), 48, accessed October 24, 2016, www.legacybookspress.com/Books/The%20Secret%20History%20of%20Star%20Wars%20-%20Free%20Sample.pdf. Referring to Donald Richie, *The Films of Akira Kurosawa* (Berkeley, CA: UC Berkeley Press, 1965).
20 Susan Doll, "The Hidden Fortress," *Turner Classic Movies*, n.d., accessed October 24, 2016, www.tcm.com/this-month/article/290047%7C0/The-Hidden-Fortress.html.
21 Vikas Swarup, *Q&A* (New York: Scribner, 2005).
22 Jeff Goldsmith, "Still Slumming...," *Creative Screenwriting,* 16(2) (March–April, 2009), 41.
23 Simon Beaufoy, quoted in Goldsmith, "Still Slumming ...," 41.
24 Chris Vogler, *The Writer's Journey: Mythic Structure for Storytellers and Screenwriters,* 3rd edn. (Los Angeles, CA: Michael Wiese, 2007), p. xx.
25 Manohla Dargis, quoted in Manohla Dargis and A.O. Scott, "Sugar, Spice and Guts: The Representation of Female Characters on the Screen is Improving. But It's only A Start," *New York Times*, September 3, 2014, accessed November 7, 2016, www.nytimes.com/2014/09/07/movies/fall-arts-preview-representation-of-female-characters-in-movies-is-improving.html.
26 Martha M. Lauzen, "The Celluloid Ceiling: Behind-the-Scenes Employment of Women on the Top 100, 250 and 500 Films of 2016," Center for the Study of Women in Television and Film (San Diego, CA: San Diego State University, 2017), accessed July 25, 2017, http://womenintvfilm.sdsu.edu/wp-content/uploads/2017/01/2016_Celluloid_Ceiling_Report.pdf.
27 Mia Galuppo, "Study: Percentage of Women Working Behind the Camera in Indie Films Is 'Stagnant,'" *Hollywood Reporter,* May 5, 2016, accessed October 28, 2016, www.hollywoodreporter.com/news/2015-16-study-women-working-890642.
28 Martha M. Lauzen, "Boxed In 2015–16: Women On Screen and Behind The Scenes in Television," Center for the Study of Women in Television and Film (San Diego, CA: San Diego State University), accessed October 28, 2016, 9, http://womenintvfilm.sdsu.edu/files/2015-16-Boxed-In-Report.pdf.
29 Lauzen, "Boxed in 2015–16," 12.
30 Unnamed "studio distribution executive" quoted in Joshua L. Weinstein's "Box Office: 'Immortals, 'Jack & Jill' Need a Lot of Young Men," *The Wrap*, November 11, 2011, www.yahoo.com/movies/box-office-immortals-jack-jill-lot-young-men-072127751.html, accessed June 3, 2017, referenced in Julie Janata, "A Boxoffice Opportunity," in *Professional AWD (Alliance of Women Directors) Digest Number 2719*, November 13, 2011, accessed February 2, 2012.
31 Julie Janata, "A Boxoffice Opportunity," in *Professional AWD (Alliance of Women Directors) Digest Number 2719*, February 8, 2012, www.yahoo.com/movies/box-office-immortals-jack-jill-lot-young-men-072127751.html, accessed February 2, 2012.
32 Whitney Elkof, "'Wonder Woman' Hits $228 Million Global Debut," *Heroic Hollywood*, June 5, 2017, accessed June 7, 2017, heroichollywood.com/wonder-woman-228-million-global-debut/
33 Maureen Murdock, *The Heroine's Journey* (Boston, MA: Shambhala, 1990), 2.
34 Murdock, *The Heroine's Journey*, 2.

35 Murdock, *The Heroine's Journey*, 2.
36 Jane Alexander Stewart, A talk on the "Heroine's Journey," focusing on *The Silence of the Lambs*, Los Angeles County Museum of Art, March 28, 1998. Program notes excerpted from Dr. Stewart's article, "The Feminine Hero of *The Silence of the Lambs*." In Mary Lynn Kittelson (ed.), *The Soul of Popular Culture* (Chicago, IL: Open Court, 1998).
37 Ted Tally, *The Silence of the Lambs,* directed by Jonathan Demme (Los Angeles, CA: Orion, 1991), based on the 1988 novel by Thomas Harris (New York: St. Martin's, 1988).
38 Alexis Krasilovsky, "Of Spinners and Screenplays: A Woman's Journey into Adaptation," *Creative Screenwriting*, 1(3) (Fall, 1994), 67–84. I also critique the "Hero's Journey" from a-feminist standpoint in my article, "Issues in Adaptation: A Screenwriter's Journey into Myths and Fairy Tales," *Creative Screenwriting,* 1(1) (Spring, 1994), 111–122.
39 Dara Marks and Deb Norton, "Engaging the Feminine Heroic: Beyond the Hero's Journey – The Other Side of the Story," Hedgebrook: Women Authoring Change, April 12, 2015, accessed June 3, 2017, www.wgfoundation.org/screenwriting-events/hedgebrook-presents-engaging-the-feminine-heroic/
40 Pamela Jaye Smith, "Seminars, Workshops, Online Classes," accessed November 8, 2016, www.pamelajayesmith.net/seminars-classes/.
41 Helen Jacey, *The Woman in the Story: Writing Memorable Female Characters,* 2nd edn. (Los Angeles, CA: Michael Wiese, 2017), 98, 106.
42 Kim Hudson, *The Virgin's Promise: Writing Stories of Feminine Creative, Spiritual and Sexual Awakening,* foreword by Christopher Vogler (Los Angeles, CA: Michael Wiese, 2009, 2010).
43 Marion Woodman, *The Pregnant Virgin: A Process of Psychological Transformation* (Toronto: Inner City Books, 1985), 27, quoted in Kim Hudson,*The Virgin's Promise: Writing Stories of Feminine Creative, Spiritual and Sexual Awakening,* foreword by Christopher Vogler (Los Angeles, CA: Michael Wiese, 2009, 2010), 60.
44 Hudson, *The Virgin's Promise*, various.
45 Esther Harding, "Woman's Mysteries: Ancient and Modern," in Tamara Agha-Jaffar, *Demeter and Persephone: Lessons from a Myth* (Jefferson, NC: McFarland, 2002), 51.
46 Patricia Reis, *Through the Goddess: A Woman's Way of Healing* (New York: Continuum: 1991/1995), 127
47 Amanda Brown, *Legally Blonde* (Bloomington, IN: Anchor House, 2001).
48 Kim Hudson, "Getting to Know the Virgin's Promise with 'Legally Blonde,'" accessed October 20, 2016, 13, http://saswg.com/wp-content/uploads/downloads/2011/10/The-Virgin%E2%80%99s-Journey.pdf.
49 Karen McCullah Lutz and Kirsten Smith, *10 Things I Hate About You*, directed by Gil Junger (Burbank, CA: Touchstone, 1999), based on William Shakespeare's *The Taming of the Shrew*.
50 Karen McCullah Lutz, quoted in "Session 4: Comedy and Romantic Comedy," *Writers on Genre* (panel, Writers Guild Foundation, July 29, 2009).
51 Kim Hudson, "Getting to Know the Virgin's Promise with 'Legally Blonde.'"
52 Yassi, quoted in Azar Nafisi, *Reading Lolita in Tehran: A Memoir in Books* (New York: Random House, 2004), 257.
53 Azin, quoted in Nafisi, *Reading Lolita in Tehran,* 258.
54 Rodolfo Hoyos, quoted in "Rodolfo Hoyos, productor de RT Colombia en Caracas, habla de 'La virgin de la calle' nueva novella," online video clip, *YouTube*, June 30, 2013, accessed October 28, 2015, www.youtube.com/watch?v=xCxgDUCTq2I. Translated from Spanish by Rosalinda Galdamez.
55 Dave Kehr, "Romance, Men and Labels," "At the Movies" column, *New York Times*, October 1, 2003, E3.

56 Rachel Fell McDermott, *Singing to the Goddess: Poems to Kali and Uma from Bengal* (Oxford: Oxford University Press, 2001), 4.
57 McDermott, *Singing to the Goddess: Poems to Kali and Uma from Bengal*, 3.
58 John Harris and Mark Todd, *My Monster Notebook* (Los Angeles, CA: J. Paul Getty Museum, 2011), 12.
59 Valerie Estelle Frankel, *From Girl to Goddess: The Heroine's Journey through Myth and Legend* (Jefferson, NC: McFarland, 2010), pp. viii–ix.
60 W.B. Yeats, *A Vision* (New York: Collier Books, 1966, first published 1926).
61 Jacey, *The Woman in the Story*, 104–129.
62 Lidia Curti, *Female Stories, Female Bodies: Narrative, Identity, and Representation* (New York: New York University Press, 1998), p. xi.
63 Curti, *Female Stories, Female Bodies*, p. xiii.
64 Arthur Rimbaud, letter to Paul Demeny (Douai) from Charleville, France, May 15, 1871, "By Way of a Preface," *Illuminations and Other Prose Poems*, trans. by Louise Varèse (New York: New Directions, 1946, 1957), p. xxxiii.
65 Reis, *Through the Goddess*, 86–87.
66 Diane Purkiss, "Women's Rewriting of Myth." In Carolyne Larrington (ed.), *The Feminist Companion to Mythology* (London: Pandora, 1992), 441.
67 Reis, *Through the Goddess*, 59.
68 Reis, *Through the Goddess*, 59.
69 Reis, *Through the Goddess*, 58.
70 Reis, *Through the Goddess*, 59.
71 Betty De Shong Meador, *Uncursing the Dark: Treasures from the Underworld* (Asheville, NC: Chiron Publications, 1992); Judy Grahn and Betty De Shong Meador, *Inanna, Lady of Largest Heart: Poems of the Sumerian High Priestess* (Austin, TX: University of Texas Press, 2001); Samuel Noah Kramer and Diane Wolkstein, *Inanna, Queen of Heaven and Earth: Her Stories and Hymns from Sumer* (New York: Harper Perennial, 1983); as well as other Inanna scholars.
72 Meador, *Uncursing the Dark*, 69.
73 Maureen Murdock, *The Heroine's Journey* (Boston, MA: Shambhala, 1990), 109.
74 Murdock, *The Heroine's Journey*, 95.
75 Murdock, *The Heroine's Journey*, 97.
76 Clarissa Pinkola Estés, *Women Who Run with the Wolves: Myths and Stories of the Wild Woman Archetype* (New York: Ballantine Books, 1992/1996), 336.
77 Agha-Jaffar, *Demeter and Persephone*, 50.
78 Erich Neumann, "The Woman's Experience of Herself and the Eleusinian Mysteries." n *The Long Journey Home: Re-visioning the Myth of Demeter and Persephone in Our Time,* Christine Downing (ed.) (Boston, MA: Shambhala, 1994), 72.
79 Neumann, "The Woman's Experience of Herself and the Eleusinian Mysteries," 73.
80 Reis, *Through the Goddess*, 88.
81 Agha-Jaffar, Chapter 1 in *Demeter and Persephone*.
82 Robert Taylor, "Hero's/Heroine's Journey" (assignment, California State University, Northridge, Northridge, Spring, 2012). Unpublished work as part of CTVA 425 "Advanced Screenwriting" course.
83 Amit Taneja, "From Oppressor to Activist: Reflections of a Feminist Journey," in Shira Tarrant, *Men Speak Out: Views on Gender, Sex, and Power.* 2nd edn. (New York: Routledge, 2013), 243.
84 Amit Taneja, "From Oppressor to Activist: Reflections of a Feminist Journey," 243.
85 Arturo Ripstein, *El Lugar Sin Límites* (*The Place without Limits*) (Mexico: Conacite Dos).

86 Suzanne Jill Levine, *Manuel Puig and the Spider Woman: His Life and Fictions* (New York: Farrar, Straus & Giroux, 2000), 287. Quoted in Sergio de la Mora, "*El Lugar Sin Límite*: Ripstein in Review," August 21, 2014, accessed October 23, 2016, https://eatdrinkfilms.com/2014/08/21/el-lugar-sin-limites-ripstein-in-review/. Manuel Puig, *El beso de la mujer araño (Kiss of the Spider Woman)* (New York: Vintage Books, 1991; first published in Spain, 1976).
87 Alfredo Mirandé, "Hombres y Machos," in *Men Speak Out: Views on Gender, Sex, and Power,* Shira Tarrant (ed.) (New York: Routledge, 2nd edn, 2013), 63.
88 Mary M. Dalton, "Conquer or Connect: Power, Patterns, and the Gendered Narrative," *Journal of Film and Video*, 65(1–2) (Spring–Summer, 2013), 23–29.
89 Dalton: "Conquer of Connect," 23.
90 Carol P. Christ, "Learning from My Mother Dying," in *The Long Journey Home: Re-visioning the Myth of Demeter and Persephone in Our Time,* Christine Downing (ed.) (Boston, MA: Shambhala, 1994), 126.
91 Vladimir Nabokov, quoted in Alfred Appel's introduction, *The Annotated Lolita* (New York, NY: Vintage, 1991), p. xxi.
92 Paul Chitlik, *Rewrite*, 2nd edn. (Los Angeles, CA: Michael Wiese, 2013), 43.
93 Eric J. Leed, quoted in Manohla Dargis and A.O. Scott, "Sugar, Spice and Guts," 2. See also Eric J. Leed, *The Mind of the Traveler: From Gilgamesh to Global Tourism* (New York: Basic Books, 1991).
94 Gillian Flynn, *Gone Girl,* directed by David Fincher (Los Angeles, CA: Twentieth Century Fox, 2014); based on Gillian Flynn, *Gone Girl* (New York: Crown, 2012).
95 Vivian Gornick, *The End of the Novel of Love* (Boston, MA: Beacon Press, 1997), 3.
96 Gretchen Carlson, "Gretchen Carlson: My Fight Against Sexual Harassment," Opinion, *New York Times,* November 12, 2016, accessed November 13, 2016, 2, http://nyti.ms/2eO8VzX.
97 Flynn, *Gone Girl*, 406.
98 Flynn, *Gone Girl*, 234.
99 Flynn, *Gone Girl*, 358.
100 Amy's voice-over from *Gone Girl.*
101 Jean Rhys, *Wide Sargasso Sea*, Judith L. Raiskin (ed.) (New York: W. W. Norton, 1998); John Duigan, *Wide Sargasso Sea* (Los Angeles, CA: New Line, 1993).
102 Suzanne Ruta, "Naming the Arab: Kamel Daoud's /'Meursault, contre-enquête'/," *WWB Daily (Words without Borders)*, June 18, 2014, accessed November 26, 2016, www.wordswithoutborders.org/dispatches/article/naming-the-arab-kamel-daouds-mersault2.
103 Jean Rhys, letter of 1959, quoted in Vivian Gornick, "Jean Rhys," in *The End of the Novel of Love* (Boston, MA: Beacon Press, 1997), 59.
104 Sally Potter, *Orlando: A Biography: Film Screenplay* (London: Faber and Faber, 1994), p. xv.
105 Virginia Woolf, *Orlando* (Boston, MA: Houghton Mifflin, 1928, 1956), 67.
106 Potter, *Orlando,* p. xiv.
107 Sally Potter, *Orlando* (London: Adventure Productions, 1992).
108 Potter, *Orlando*, p. xiii.
109 Margaret Laurence, *The Stone Angel* (Toronto: McClelland and Stewart, 2004), 168.
110 Laurence, *The Stone Angel*, 1.
111 Laurence, *The Stone Angel*, 1.
112 Denise Levertov, *The Poet in the World* (New York: New Directions, 1960), 82.

113 Levertov, *The Poet in the World*, 107.
114 Levertov, *The Poet in the World*, 109.
115 Gloria Anzaldúa, quoted in Curti, *Female Stories, Female Bodies*, 116.
116 John Donne, quoted in Stanley Burnshaw, *The Seamless Web* (New York: George Braziller, 1970); originally in *Ivvenilia: or certaine Paradoxes, and Problemes* (London: E.P. for Henry Seyle, 1633).

Part III

A Survival Guide to Adaptation

NINE

The Process

The great director Akira Kurosawa was famous for his many adaptations. How did he start the process of making such an extraordinary film as *Rashōmon* (Japan, 1950), that would be acclaimed worldwide. How did he start the process of making such an extraordinary film?

The production came about when Daiei Studios asked Kurosawa to direct another film for them. (*Rashōmon* was not his first feature.) Kurosawa recalls:

> As I cast about for what to film, I suddenly remembered a script based on the short story "Yabu no naka" ("In a Grove") by Ryūnosuke Akutagawa. It had been written by Hashimoto Shinobu ... It was a very well-written piece, but not long enough to make into a feature film ... [Later] the memory of it jumped out of one of those creases in my brain and told me to give it a chance. At the same time I recalled that "In a Grove" is made up of three stories, and realized that if I added one more, the whole would be just the right length for a feature film. Then I remembered the Akutagawa story "Rashōmon." Like "In a Grove," it was set in the Heian period (794–1184). The film *Rashōmon* took shape in my mind.[1]

Adaptations may start with ideas, research, and extensive reading. But what you are reading is often based on ideas, research, and extensive reading, too. It's a never-ending process – one with which it's exciting to be involved. As Stephanie Harrison points out in *Adaptations: From Short Story to Big Screen*, in the case of *Rashōmon,* the 1922 Akutagawa story "In a Grove" hearkens back to "the *Konjaku Monogatari* (medieval Japanese tales, circa 1120), but the narrative form is similar to Robert Browning's *The Ring and the Book.*"[2]

> Robert Browning's poem, which also contains multiple conflicting testimonies, is based on a Roman murder (circa 1698) that Browning

> read about in what is referred to as the *Old Yellow Book*, a volume he bought from a market stall for one lira.[3]

Kurosawa loved reading novels, dramas, and short stories, and put his erudition to work as a filmmaker. "In order to write scripts," he advised,

> you must first study the great novels and dramas of the world. You must consider why they are great. Where does the emotion come from that you feel as you read them? What degree of passion did the author have to have, what level of meticulousness did he have to command in order to portray the characters and events as he did? You must read thoroughly, to the point where you can grasp all these things. You must also see the great films. You must read the great screenplays and study the film theories of the great directors. If your goal is to become a film director, you must master screenwriting.[4]

Whether your goal is to write, direct, become a hyphenate writer-director, or simply to study what makes a write or director great, this is the first step of the process. But in the words of Charlie Kaufman, who lies in bed in the film *Adaptation* (USA, 2002), fantasizing about how to adapt Susan Orlean's book *The Orchid Thief,* "There are too many ideas and things and people ... too many directions to go."[5] Better start now!

When Robert Nelson Jacobs was reading Joanne Harris' bestselling novel, *Chocolat*, in order to adapt it to the screen, he jotted down some questions (along with doodles in the margin that often helps the thinking process): "Does she play therapist to the locals? Does she have some unresolved issues? – guilt over death of the mother? Is this a period piece?..."[6]

The novel is about a freewheeling single mother who moves to a repressive French village, where she opens a chocolaterie. But further research is often required beyond reading the novel to be adapted. Inscribed along the inside cover of the book *The True History of Chocolate*[7] are more handwritten character development notes by Jacobs:

> maybe the V.O. starts: There ... Vianne Rochet, didn't talk about. She didn't talk about the fact that her great-grandmother was a descendent of Aztecs with whom her great-grandfather, a noted French adventurer in the late 19th century, "met and fell in love" – this would help integrate the Magical Realism element – the animism of ancient pre-Colombian religions – this exotic paganism takes the place of the more familiar, less intriguing witchcraft/paganism in the book – it's a similar idea, but more specific and offbeat.

Many screenwriters, unless they are working as part of a team, lead relatively solitary lives during much of the writing process. It's just you and the novel, short story, play, graphic novel, videogame, musical, manga, comic strip, song, or something else. But often that isn't enough.

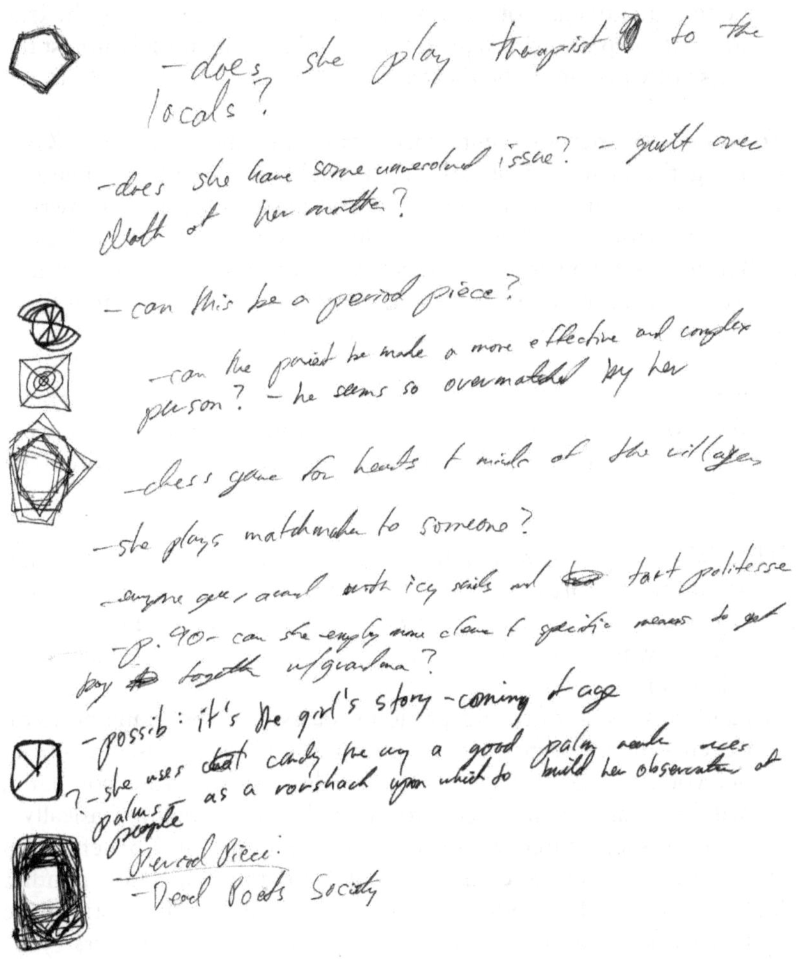

Figure 9.1 Robert Nelson Jacobs' notes on Joanne Harris' novel for the film *Chocolat* (UK/USA, 2000). Writers Guild Foundation Archive. Courtesy of Robert Nelson Jacobs and Miramax

For instance, the film *Mean Girls* (USA/Canada, 2004), was based on a 2002 self-help bestseller by Rosalind Wiseman, entitled *Queen Bees and Wannabees: Helping Your Daughter Survive Cliques, Gossip, Boyfriends & Other Realities of Adolescence*, it had no plot. *Mean Girls* screenwriter Tina Fey had to invent one, "borrowing elements from her own high school experience."[8]

For playwright Tom Stoppard, who co-wrote *Shakespeare in Love* (USA/UK, 1998), writing adaptations has always meant deferring to the creative ideas of the director:

> [A]lthough I've got my name on a handful of films, in every case they are films adapted from someone else's work, not original work, so one is a craftsman of a certain kind, one is there to serve the true author of the piece who is the director and that situation is almost the reverse of working in the theatre.[9]

For others, the development process can sometimes seem easy. While developing the character of Belle as a bright, well-read, independent character for the animated feature *Beauty and the Beast*, screenwriter Linda Woolverton said, "Nobody got in my way. I just conjured Belle up." But despite Woolverton's scripts having made $3 billion for Disney, there were no guarantees with the writing process when it came to writing *Alice Through the Looking Glass* (USA/UK, 2016):

> They came to me, I pitched it, and wrote it. Then they brought in a director who dismissed me and he rewrote it himself. There were 20 writers after me. ("Yet you kept the credit as sole writer?") I arbitrated.[10]

That Woolverton managed to keep sole credit as writer through arbitration underscores another important part of the Hollywood screenwriting process – belonging to the Writers Guild and having a good lawyer who will carefully craft your contract. (See Chapter 2: Career Issues.)

A standard version of the adaptation process involves taking notes on which events in the original source material will work best on screen. Whether you're keeping those notes on index cards or your computer, these will be invaluable in piecing together the plot, which is basically a series of events structured with cause and effect. You may benefit from using multicolored index cards: one color for the main plot, another color for Storyline B, another for Storyline C, and perhaps still more colors to track which events involve which principal characters: your protagonist[s], your opponent, your love interest, other allies, and/or family members, etc. That way you won't lose sight of someone we should care about who's introduced in Act I and may not reappear full throttle until somewhere in Act III (or another episode, if writing for TV).

As Dr. Ouelet says in *Ghost in the Shell* (USA, 2017), "What we do defines us," plot and character are two sides of the same coin. You'll need to research the events if your adaptation is based on a real life story, or, if justified in dramatizing the story, create fictional ones to mesh with the basic real life events.

Fabricated plot points abound in Oliver Stone's *Born on the Fourth of July* (USA, 1989), as analyzed by Jack Davis in *Oliver Stone's USA:*

> The academic historian typically does not, as Stone freely acknowledges doing, take "dramatic license" with historical facts. In *Born*, for instance, the peasant village Kovic's platoon destroys in the film bore

> no association with a real enemy firefight; Kovic actually broke his leg not while in the Bronx Veterans Hospital but after he returned from Mexico and was living alone in a New York apartment; he never went to Syracuse University with his girlfriend, who does not exist in the book, and – according to those who were there – the police were civil, not hostile, towards students protesting the Kent State incident.[11]

More recently, David Magee described the challenge of going through the novel, *Life of Pi*, in order to formulate a cohesive plot for the 2012 film:

> The book is so episodic. The sections are set in 100 chapters, some of them only half a page long. They don't have a narrative through-line to them. The opening is philosophical, about keeping animals in cages – it's not filmable. We had to create a through-line and shape it to Pi's growth (as a protagonist).[12]

If what you're adapting is a mammoth epic, scene cards can keep you focused on the essential events and characters: others can be combined or eliminated. On the other hand, if you're adapting a short story, it's likely that you'll have to fabricate additional characters and subplots to expand the story to feature-length, or to flesh out enough episodes for a series or mini-series, if writing for television. The adaptation process is like an accordion: compression and expansion allow it to come to life. But everyone has a different take on how to play it.

Eric Roth, who wrote the screenplay adaptation of F. Scott Fitzgerald's short story, "The Curious Case of Benjamin Button" (USA, 2008) and who won an Academy Award for Best Adapted Screenplay for *Forrest Gump* (USA, 1994), doesn't consider screenwriting an art form. "It's just a process," he says.[13] This is how he describes going about writing an adaptation:

> I always figure out what's going to be the first scene and the last scene. The middle is a big giant block. It's kinda fun if you let the characters take you where you're going. That's what I enjoy.[14]

While working on your scene cards and sorting through them to create a cause-and-effect order that will result in an outline and treatment, including character arcs, you will also need to work on your character backstories. A backstory is everything that happens to a character before the film or television episode begins, although it is sometimes revealed as the story unfolds – especially towards the end of Act II in a personal drama, as a result of great psychological pressure. Beyond the story as it's told in the novel or short story that you're adapting, how much do you really know or can imagine about the character whose life you have "adopted" for the purpose of adapting it to another medium?

Try to imagine yourself as a tailor, snip-snip-snipping the thread that signifies the beginning or end of a life. We Americans stash our elderly in nursing homes and talk of euthanasia. We've been uncomfortable showing the lives of the elderly onscreen. Is that changing with the booming audience of baby-boomers? We debate abortion; we study the embryo inside the womb. After many months, its life can be enriched if it heard Mozart or Beethoven while still unborn. It's more likely to grow up depressed if the mother was verbally or physically abused while pregnant. Can one's life be impacted even before conception? If you believe in reincarnation, your backstory may go back several centuries. With DNA studies, you can also go back to the many intertwined story threads that precede the person with the problem, age 18, whom we usually encounter for the first time in Act I, Scene i, of a movie. Regardless of where you choose to start and end, you'll want to zero in on some of the key events of your character's life, so that you'll be intimately familiar with his or her deepest secrets before you begin to write your screenplay. You may even find yourself becoming a medium, channeling your character's story!

Although research can be an essential part of mapping out the events of the story and character backstories, it's important not to overdo it, once you have the material you need in front of you. As Susannah Grant, the screenwriter of *Erin Brockovich* (USA, 2000) has said,

> I go after it without analyzing why, so that part of my brain won't shrivel up. ... I spent enough time with her [Brockovich] to feel the rhythms. The closer you can get to dreamtime, the better your work is going to be.[15]

Treatments/Outline

Mark L. Smith, who wrote the screenplay for *The Revenant* (Hong Kong/Taiwan/USA, 2015), sees an outline as the best antidote to writer's block: "I do an outline. It gets boring to me if I always know what will happen next. But if I write as I go, it's difficult."[16]

Outlines and treatment can vary in length and format, however the important thing is to keep them in present tense, emphasizing what happens. (If you're writing a television show, a Character Bible is a separate document from the event-driven outline or treatment.) You may find that adapting only half of a novel into a feature, as John Ford did with *How Green Was My Valley* (USA, 1941), is more effective than stretching it out over a lengthy television series; however, more writers make their living in TV than film these days, and you may have to choose between following your instincts for financial survival and following your heart as a creative writer in making hard decisions about timeline, framework, and format.

Once you have a treatment or outline in front of you, it should be easy to write the rough draft of your adaptation. Revise to shape the script into a page-turner that works as a film or television program, not a watered-down illustration of a novel. However, in today's film and television industries, several revisions have become the norm, using notes penned by the producer, director, and sometimes stars. For example, on Linda Woolverton's first draft film script of *Beauty and the Beast*, one of producer Jeffrey Katzenberg's handwritten notes reads:

> The storming of the castle and the objects defending it and Beast (who has decided not to fight) must be action-packed – not a lot of dialogue ... get on with it – not as written.[17]

But Linda Woolverton knows how to stand her ground as needed. "I make them justify the notes," she says. "You have to get along. I'm very cooperative. I listen. But they don't know what they want. They need us to tell them."[18]

Ultimately, the revised and polished screenplay is your responsibility, although you may get some help from unseen forces. As Denzel Washington said about the process of adapting August Wilson's play, *Fences* (USA/Canada, 2016) "Great writing will tell you what it wants."[19] It may just flow, or it may take months or even years of back and forth hard labor between you and various collaborators. What kept Mark L. Smith going on the revisions of *The Revenant* was, "Every scene had to be strong enough so people would keep turning the pages."

Second-rate Literature, First-rate Cinema; First-rate Literature, Second-rate Cinema

Adaptation is a double-edged sword: it's possible to make great art of near garbage, as Kurosawa did with a cheesy 1959 pulp fiction novel by Ed McBain entitled *The King's Ransom*, which sentimentalizes the kidnapping of a shoe company executive's son, and routinely seeks answers to the whodunit. In her pivotal essay, "Against Interpretation," Susan Sontag wrote: "Most American novelists and playwrights are really either journalists or gentlemen sociologists and psychologists. They are writing the literary equivalent of program music."[20] Yet Kurosawa was able to transform *The King's Ransom* into one of the best crime dramas ever made about a corporate executive and the drug addict out to bring him down: *High and Low* (*Tengoku to Jigoku*, Japan, 1963).

On the other hand, as Peruvian Nobel laureate Mario Vargas Llosa has written:

> Clearly, what works well in one form does not always work well in another. My novel *Pantaleón y las visitadoras* was made into a terrible film. I do not think you can establish a norm between good books and film. Some books have been made into marvelous films, and some have been destroyed by films. The great Spanish moviemaker Luis Buñuel once told me something about this relationship that I always remember. He said that only bad novels make good films. So I have never chosen a good novel to make a film; all the novels that I have adapted to film are bad novels.[21]

Notes on Two Manga

Katsuhiro Otomo's *Akira* (Japan, 1988) is an animated sci-fi film written by Katsuhiro Otomo and Izo Hashimoto about a teenage biker and his gang set in a future world of 2019, after Tokyo has been destroyed in an explosion in 1988.

The film is based mostly on the first part of Otomo's manga, in which "the army is working with the police to hunt down anti-government groups."[22] At the end of the film, Akira grows bigger than the Marshmallow Man of *Ghostbusters,* but is then reduced in power as containers of a strange chemical liquid in the Olympic Stadium shatter and spill on him, and the city destroys itself. It seems horrifyingly current.

Regarding the original manga, Otomo states: "I wanted the page count, the contents, the paintings, everything about the collected volumes to create a deep, full, American comic-style world."[23] Otomo discusses his choices of cover design, which were considered ground-breaking, in terms of nationalities and style:

> I didn't use the English and Chinese and whatever else on the cover because I was thinking about global distribution. I did it because I had this incredible enthusiasm to just try to make something new.[24]

Eventually, Otomo included Asian imagery in his illustration of tanks, teens, a warrior with a machine gun, and a city with Chinese signs in the background for Volume 3's cover:

> Volume 1 had an American image, and Volume 2 had a European image. I thought Volume 3 should project an Asian atmosphere, so I worked in the signs in the background and the color tones for the whole thing towards that end.[25]

Warner Brothers acquired the rights to *Akira* in 2002,[26] but development stalled after many attempts to reset the production from Tokyo to New York, and changing the race and age of the characters; Robert Brockway in cracked.com commented on the setting of the apocalyptic film in post-9/11 New York.[27] However, with the release of *Ghost in the Shell* (USA, 2017),[28] a live action American remake of *Akira* is again under consideration.

Ghost in the Shell, also based on a Japanese manga, is about a cyborg named Major (played by Scarlett Johansson), who finds out her life was stolen from her: Her real name is Motoko Kusangi. She is determined to stop whoever did this to her before it harms others (sort of like how authors sometimes feel when their work is ripped off by others, as their ideas may be the soul of their projects, but ideas per se aren't copyrightable).

"Maybe next time you'll design me better," says Major to Dr. Ouelet (Juliette Binoche), who is repairing her cyborg arm. Ditto the film – if there's a next time!

Notes

1 Akira Kurosawa, *Something Like an Autobiography* (New York: Knopf, 1982), 134, accessed April 12, 2017, https://lenguajecinematografico.files.wordpress.com/2013/07/kurosawa-akira-something_like_an_autobiography.pdf.
2 Stephanie Harrison, *Adaptations: From Short Story to Big Screen: 35 Great Stories that Have Inspired Great Films* (New York: Three Rivers Press, 2005), 527.
3 Harrison, *Adaptations*, footnote 527.
4 Akira Kurosawa, Appendix: "Some Random Notes on Filmmaking," 1975. In Kurosawa, *Something Like an Autobiography*, 143.
5 Charlie Kaufman, *Adaptation*, directed by Spike Jonze (2002; Culver City, CA: Columbia TriStar Home Entertainment, 2003).
6 Robert Nelson Jacobs, handwritten notes on the novel by Joanne Harris, *Chocolat*, for his adaptation, *Chocolat* (Santa Monica, CA and New York: Miramax and David Brown Publications, 2000), directed by Lasse Hallström. Writers Guild Foundation Archive.
7 Michael Coe and Sophie Coe, *The True History of Chocolate* (London: Thames & Hudson, 1996).
8 "*Mean Girls*," Wikipedia.org, accessed April 12, 2017, https://en.wikipedia.org/wiki/Mean_Girls.
9 Tom Stoppard, quoted in "Shakespeare on Film: *Shakespeare in Love,*" Study Guide, The Film Space, accessed April 6, 2017, 12, www.thefilmspace.org/shakespeare-on-film/resources/shakespeare-in-love/docs/shakespeare-in-love_studyguide.pdf.
10 Linda Woolverton, quoted from the Q&A moderated by Valerie Alexander following the screening of *Alice Through the Looking Glass* at the Writers Guild Theater, Beverly Hills, California, June 11, 2016.
11 Jack E. Davis, "New Left, Revisionist, In-Your-Face History: Oliver Stone's *Born on the Fourth of July* Experience." In Robet Brent Toplin (ed.), *Oliver Stone's USA: Film, History, and Controversy* (Lawrence, KS: University Press of Kansas, 2000), 144.
12 David Magee, quoted at a Q&A following the screening of *Life of Pi* at the Writers Guild Theater, Beverly Hills, California, January 11, 2013.
13 Eric Roth, quoted from "Eric Roth – Writers on Writing" event, Writers Guild Foundation, November 16, 2011.
14 Roth, "Eric Roth – Writers on Writing."
15 Susannah Grant, quoted from the panel, "Writers on Genre: Drama and True Stories," Writers Guild Foundation, July 2009.
16 Mark L. Smith, Q&A following the screening of *The Revenant,* Writers Guild Theater, Beverly Hills, California, December 13, 2015.
17 Jeffrey Katzenberg's note on Linda Woolverton's first draft film script for *Beauty and the Beast* (dated June 14, 1990), 90.
18 Woolverton, *Alice Through the Looking Glass* Screening and Q&A.
19 Denzel Washington, *Fences* Screening and Q&A moderated by Leonard Maltin, at the Writers Guild Theater, Beverly Hills, California, December 17, 2016.
20 Susan Sontag, "Against Interpretation," in *Against Interpretation and Other Essays* (New York: Farrar, Straus and Giroux, 1966), 11.
21 Mario Vargas Llosa, *A Writer's Reality,* Byron I. Lichtblau (ed.) (Syracuse, NY: Syracuse University Press, 1991), 92.
22 Dialogue from *Akira* (Japan, 1988) in English subtitles.
23 Katsuhiro Otomo, *Akira Club* (Milwaukee, WI: Dark Horse Comics, 2007; Dark House Manga, Mash-Room, 1995), 3.
24 Otomo, *Akira Club*, 4.
25 Otomo, *Akira Club*, 6.

26 Megan Peters, "Warner Bros. Reportedly Eyeing New Directors for Live Action Akira Film," *comicbook.com*, accessed April 13, 2017, http://comicbook.com/anime/2017/03/24/warner-bros-akira-live-action-film-update-director-anime/.
27 Robert Brockway, "5 Urgent Questions About the Live Action 'Akira' Remake," 2, *Cracked.com*, March 30, 2011, accessed August 19, 2011, www.cracked.com/blog/5-urgent-questions-about-live-action-akira-remake_p2/.
28 Ehren Kruger, Jamie Moss, and William Wheeler, *Ghost in the Shell* (Los Angeles, CA, Universal City, CA, Santa Monica, CA, Tokyo, Japan, Hong Kong: Paramount Pictures, Arad Productions, Steven Paul Production, Amblin Parners, Grosvenor Park Productions, Seaside Entertainment, Weying Galaxy Entertainment), directed by Rupert Sanders; based on the comic, Masamune Shirow, "The Ghost in the Shell."

Part IV

Renewing the Spirit in Myths and Fairy Tales

TEN

Fairy Tale Factors
From Spindle to Kindle

Writers for film and television have made use of free, public-domain myths and fairy tales in their work both as loose and faithful adaptations, as well as an endless source of influence for otherwise original storytelling. Although the sci-fi action adventure film *Aliens* (USA/UK, 1986)[1] credits twentieth-century writers James Cameron, David Giler, and Walter Hill for its story and Dan O'Bannon and Ronald Shusett for its characters, omitting the nineteenth-century Grimm Brothers and the seventeenth-century Charles Perrault and Giambattista Basile from its credit list, Walter Rankin points out numerous tie-ins of fairy tales to the film:

> As the film opens, the camera pans to the lone survivor of Ridley Scott's *Alien* (1979), Ripley (Sigourney Weaver), a sleeping beauty in a glass case who is awakened from hypersleep 57 years following her first encounter with the lethal alien being. With her dark hair, white skin, and red lips, she is later compared directly to Snow White ... And in the film's conclusion, Ripley leaves flares to find her way out of the unfamiliar darkness, much like Hansel and Gretel do in the forest with shiny pebbles and breadcrumbs. Yet the film's narrative structure and themes most closely parallel those of "Cinderella," in which a young girl loses her family and must struggle to survive on her own when a new mother arrives with her own threatening, self-serving family.[2]

As entertaining as these outer space versions of fairy tales such as "Sleeping Beauty" and "Hansel and Gretel" may be, when these classic European fairy tales were put into a U.S. setting for the first time, librarians were outraged at the travesty of someone modernizing them – although, as Michael Patrick Hearn points out, L. Frank Baum's *The Wonderful Wizard of Oz* shares more with *Robinson Crusoe* and *Gulliver's Travels* than fairy tales.[3] With its non-European setting, the book was banned by libraries for many years, even though it was the bestselling children's book of the year when it came out in 1900 to great reviews, was turned into the most successful Broadway play of its time in 1902, and was made into a silent film called *The Wizard of Oz* in 1910. The Oz series was so successful that Baum started a film company called Oz Film Manufacturing Company, producing several features. By 1934, one critic wrote, "Good heavens! The land of Oz is a fairyland run on Communistic lines, and is perhaps the only Communistic fairyland in all of children's literature."[4] Even when the MGM musical film came out in 1939 and took the nation by storm, the book was still being banned: librarians hated Hollywood as much as they hated so-called Communists.[5] But the books continued to sell:[6] the publisher hired other writers to continue writing the Oz books beyond Baum's death in 1919,[7] all the way up until the 40th book of the series came out in 1963.[8]

In the novel *Push*, when Precious mentions "The Wizard of Oz," she's thinking of the 1978 version with Diana Ross and Michael Jackson, called *The Wiz* (USA, 1978) – the adaptation of an African-American Broadway musical[9] based on *The Wonderful Wizard of Oz*. Going into that fantasy world helps Precious survive while her father is committing incest with her against her will as a young girl.

Novelist Salman Rushdie credits the 1939 version of Frank Baum's novel as "my very first literary influence."[10] While in hiding after a fatwa had been issued against him for writing his controversial book, *The Satanic Verses*, Rushdie wrote a book on *The Wizard of Oz* (USA, 1939),[11] with which he especially identified, as Oz provided a fantasy location where he could escape the ugliness of a trouble-ridden world and the dangers he might face were he to return home to Mumbai. Examining the differences between Baum's novel and the 1939 film, Rushdie writes that "*The Wizard of Oz* is one of the rare instances of a film improving on a good book," in part because of "the expansion of the Kansas section, which in the novel takes up precisely two pages at the beginning before the tornado arrives, and just nine lines at the end."[12]

Writing about Dorothy (played by Judy Garland) singing "Over the Rainbow," Rushdie writes:

> What she expresses here, what she embodies with the purity of an archetype, is the human drama of *leaving*, a dream at least as powerful as its countervailing dream of roots ... "Over the Rainbow" is, or ought to be, the anthem of all the world's migrants, all those who go in search of the place where "the dreams that you dare to dream really do come true." It is a celebration of Escape, a grand paean to the Uprooted Self, a hymn – *the* hymn – to Elsewhere.[13]

Rushdie glorifies the dreams of a girl who is stuck on a farm in Kansas where nobody understands her, until the *deus ex machina* of a tornado sweeps her away to the fantasy land of Oz. Traditionally, the storytellers themselves have been far less isolated than either Dorothy or Rushdie himself – although Dorothy does have the Scarecrow, the Lion, the Tin

Man, and her dog Toto for allies on her journey along the Yellow Brick Road. Frank Baum, whose *The Wonderful Wizard of Oz* was soon followed by *Patchwork Girl of Oz* (1913), must have been aware of the patchwork quilt parties that were also opportunities for women to come together and tell each other what was happening in their lives, although few male writers create female allies for their female protagonists. Earlier, in Europe, Karen Rowe explains, women came together to spin yarn and "spin yarns":

> In German the verb *spinnen* means also to fantasize, an apt talent for the one who spins not only cloth but tales as well. And as in the French *veillées,* so too German folk tales ... were assumed to have originated in ... the *Spinnstube*, for it was there that women gathered in the evening and told tales to keep themselves and their company awake as they spun. And it was from informants privy to the oral tradition that Wilhelm and Jacob Grimm gathered many of their folk tales.[14]

This idea of combining storytelling with spinning is something that we see in the parallel storytelling tradition of female West African griots, who braid hair and tell stories. Storytelling (or fortune-telling) while spinning is also recounted by Ovid in his epic Latin poem of AD 8, *Metamorphoses,* based on ancient Greek mythology.

For example, Ovid writes:

> She turned her thoughts to vengeance for these despicable murders.
> Her son! She cursed the day of his birth, which she now remembered,
> And how, when she'd lain in childbirth, the three mysterious sisters,
> Spinning between their fingers and thumbs the threads of life,
> Had decreed as a kind of whimsy that the length of the newborn baby's
> Life should be the same as ... that log over there, in the hearth[15]

The ashes of the hearth also give rise to the character of "*Cinder*"-ella (or Jacob and Wilhelm Grimm's "*Aschen*puttel"), a girl of such low self-esteem while in mourning for her mother, that her only place is to sleep is in the ashes of the fireplace. Not until a fairy godmother grants the girl magical powers does she land herself a prince and economic security in a castle. There are roughly 2,000 versions of "Cinderella" worldwide, from the ancient Chinese fairy tale "Yeh-hsien"[16] and Charles Perrault's seventeenth-century French "Cendrillon" or "Cinderella" in English (which led to the classic Disney version of 1950),[17] to a male Cinderella story set in Ireland, called "Billy Beg and the Bull,"[18] and contemporary film adaptations such as *Ever After: A Cinderella Story* (USA, 1998), in which Cinderella not only saves her prince, but in which we are given insights into what made her stepmother so evil.[19] Independent filmmakers and artists have also been reappropriating fairy tales, such as José Rodolfo Loaiza Ontiveros, whose Los Angeles art show "DisHollywood" includes a painting of Cinderella marveling at her new, punk-style shoe.[20]

Figure 10.1 Each culture wants to make Cinderella its own; some of us want a fairy godmother to make a career woman out of Cinderella, who can magically charm her own way to gender equity, with or without a Prince Charming. Courtesy of Warren Miller/The New Yorker Collection/The Cartoon Bank

Fairy tales are in the public domain, so when the economy is bad or producers simply want to avoid spending six or seven figure sums on best-selling novels, movie studios love to adapt them. We have Disney's classic *Snow White* (USA, 1937); the recent *Snow White and the Huntsman* (USA, 2012); *The Little Mermaid* (USA, 1987), with another in postproduction (USA, 2017); two *Beauty and the Beast*s (USA, 1991, 2017); *Frozen* (USA, 2013), based on Hans Christian Andersen's "The Snow Queen"; and that braying menagerie of musical fairy tales, *Into the Woods* (USA/UK/Canada, 2015), among others. Some of the TV shows based on adaptations include "Fractured Fairytales" from the *Rocky and Bullwinkle Show* (1959); the "Bedtime Stories" episode of *Supernatural* (2007) in which investigating the murder of two brothers with attributes like two of "The Three Little Pigs" also involves saving victims who resemble Little Red Riding Hood and other fairy tale characters;[21] *Once Upon a Time* (2012); the musical fairy tale series *Galavant* (2015–2016); and *Grimm* (2011–2017), a cop show which has been so successful in incorporating characters and events of various Grimms' fairy tales while solving its crimes that the show has led to "a *Grimm*-based merchandising bonanza in playing cards, pins, lunchboxes, and paperbacks," as well as Young Adult *Grimm* novels.[22]

Although we in the West are not always aware of the fairy tales, myths, and legends of other cultures, Brenna Kouf, the daughter of *Grimm*'s co-creator Jim Kouf, put together a database of such material "organized by continent and geographical regions, [which] is kept in the writers' room and sits on desks for the writers to draw from when researching ideas."[23]

But there's more to adapting fairy tales around the world than whatever the West can cull from them. For example, Kim Jee-Woon's stunning horror-thriller fairy tale, *A Tale of Two Sisters* (*Rose Flower Red Lotus*, Korea, 2003) is not an adaptation of the German fairy tale, "Snow-White and Rose-Red" by the Brothers Grimm. Instead, it's a modern-day retelling of a folktale from Korea's Josean dynasty (1392–1897), "Janghwa Hongryeon jeon" or literally "The Story of Janghwa [Rose Flower] and Hongryeon [Red Lotus]," a gruesome tale populated by ghosts, a dead mother, dead sisters, dead mayors, dead rats, and a faked miscarriage. Kim Jee-Woon's film aches with erotic subtext and sibling rivalry, and plunges the audience deeper and deeper into the surreal world of a murderous stepmother of two sisters who become so terrified, it's impossible to tell the difference between nightmare and waking horror. Kim Jee-Woon's is the sixth Korean adaptation of this story, which was later remade in the US as the critically unsuccessful *The Uninvited* (USA/Canada/Germany, 2009).

The Spanish film *Mama* (Canada/Spain, 2013), directed and co-written by Argentinian Andrés Muschietti based on his short film, *Mamá* (Argentina, 2008), contains similar elements of horror to those of *A Tale of Two Sisters*: two little girls dragged off to a terrifying locale, a crazed father intent on murdering them, a dead mother, and in this case, an allusion to the Latin American folktale of La Llorona – a ghost who laments the death of her children after she has drowned them in a river. Starring Jessica Chastain, *Mama* was successful at the box office, although at a panel held in 2014 at the Writers Guild of America, West entitled "The State of Modern Horror and the Latino Writer,"[24] panelists cautioned that by over-using well-known Latino folktales like La Llorona, writers run the risk of redundancy.

Italian novelist Goliarda Sapienza criticizes fairy tales through dialogue spoken by Beatrice's socialist lover Carlo in her epic novel, *The Art of Joy*:[25]

> Indeed, as our comrade Montessori says ... almost all fairy tales are evil: they are a tool to terrorize children and teach them to fear law and authority. We spoke about this at length, or rather, she talked to me about it, urging me to write a new kind of fairy tale ... Certainly her stance against the tales of Andersen, Grimm and many others is a valid one. But to expect all comrades – doctors, engineers or firemen – to force themselves to come up with different plots and adventures for the revolution every evening instead of sleeping...[26]

A modern-day adaptation of a fairy tale that proffers revolutionary twists for adult audiences is *Sleeping Beauty* (Australia, 2011) by Australian writer/director Julia Leigh, who is also a novelist. Leigh's disturbing yet fascinating film about a college girl working in a brothel explores women's work choices, male sexual fantasies, and questions of ethics (if you're old enough to watch the sex scenes). For younger audiences, there's another loose adaptation of "Sleeping Beauty," *Maleficent* (USA, 2014), this time taking the point of view of a now-adult fairy whose wings were cut off by the man she loved in her youth. At the end, Maleficent's love for her stepdaughter outweighs her quest for revenge, but most of the film was too dark and adult-centric to be as successful as some of screenwriter Linda Woolverton's other adaptations.

Catherine Breillat, the controversial novelist and filmmaker as well as Professor of Auteur Cinema at the European Graduate School, has also undertaken a "Sleeping Beauty" adaptation. *The Sleeping Beauty* (France, 2010) has a young girl as a protagonist who is condemned to sleep – but has many active adventures in her dream life, some of which are hybrid dreams with elements of Hans Christian Andersen's "The Snow Queen." Breillat's earlier fairy tale film, *Bluebeard* (France, 2009) isn't half as powerful as her earlier, original films *Fat Girl* (France/Italy, 2001) and the provocative *Romance* (France, 1999), which includes full frontal male and female nudity and explicit sex. She has also adapted four of her own books to the screen.

Breillat is not the first auteur or autrice to take on the "Bluebeard" fairy tale from a feminist perspective: That was the writer Angela Carter, whose 1979 story "The Bloody Chamber" was adapted into an erotic, feminist film, *The Company of Wolves* (UK, 1984) by Angela Carter as co-screenwriter with director and co-screenwriter Neil Jordan.

Writer/director Jane Campion focuses on the "Bluebeard" story in her fairy tale-like film, *The Piano* (New Zealand/Australia/France, 1993), which takes place in Aotearoa/New Zealand. Campion's film mimics yet another Grimm Brothers fairy tale, "The Handless Maiden," when the female protagonist is assaulted by her jealous husband with an axe. The film includes a play within the film, much like Shakespeare's play within a play idea, only this time, the Maoris in the audience are so shocked by the wife-murdering story on stage that they descend upon the stage, intent to put an end to Bluebeard.

Although it's a powerful film from a feminist perspective, it may have been even more fruitful to expand the roles of the Maoris to include their own mythology, instead of focusing solely on Western fairy tales and the Scottish ballad, "Barbara Allen." In Australia, "indigenous peoples embrace all phenomena and life as part of a vast and complex system-network of relationships which can be traced directly back to the ancestral Totemic Spirit Beings of The Dreaming."[27] If films are like dreams, how can this enrich our vision?

Margaret Bowater writes:

> The indigenous people of NZ, the Maori, have their own approach to dream interpretation, based on their own spirituality, mythology and oral tradition ... Being strongly connected with Maori spiritual

> beliefs, it is considered not appropriate for non-Maori people to seek to "colonise" this knowledge, before Maori themselves are ready to share it.[28]

Madonna Kobenschlag, in her book *Kiss Sleeping Beauty Good-Bye: Breaking the Spell of Feminine Myths and Models*, refers to Bluebeard as part of the "forbidden chamber" genre. In her 1979 analysis, she states:

> [In this tale] the woman's invasion into the man's hidden chamber is a breach of patriarchal etiquette: "The female must not inquire into the secrets of the male.[29]

In terms of dramaturgy, these are secrets that Campion's white characters reveal to the Maori, seeking intercultural peace. But Campion has been accused by Maori film critics such as Leonie Pihama of colonial gaze, in which the stereotype that Maori men are irrational and "unable to control their 'native warlike instincts'" is unchallenged by the screenwriter-director.[30] We had to wait for the next New Zealand film to get released in the U.S., Niki Caro's *Whale Rider* (New Zealand/Germany, 2002) based on the novel *The Whale Rider* by Witi Ihimaera, to explore the Maoris' own myths, legends, and religious beliefs.

Clarissa Pinkola Estés, author of *Women Who Run with the Wolves*, states that for a woman to know herself and her own individual nature, she must go into the dark chamber and confront "that captor, the dark man who inhabits all women's psyches, the innate predator"[31] who "… forbids the young woman to use the one key that would bring her to consciousness."[32] Estés explains:

> For women, the key always symbolizes entrée to a mystery or into knowledge. In fairy tales, the key is often represented by words such as "Open Sesame," which Ali Baba shouts to a ragged mountain, causing the entire mountain to rumble and crack open so he could pass through … And the words women need most in situations similar to the one described in Bluebeard are: What stands behind? What is not as it appears? What do I know deep in my ovaries that I wish I did not know? What of me has been killed, or lays dying?[33]

And as a filmmaker who does not recognize myself in the mirror of the screen in the dark film auditoriums, I venture to add: Which films go deep enough to present a true image of our creative souls?

Notes

1 James Cameron, *Aliens,* directed by James Cameron (Los Angeles, CA: Twentieth Century Fox, 1986).

2 Walter Rankin, *Grimm Pictures: Fairy Tale Archetypes in Eight Horror and Suspense Films* (Jefferson, NC: McFarland, 2007), 104.

3 Michael Patrick Hearn, "L. Frank Baum and the 'Modernized' Fairy Tale." In Michael Patrick Hearn (ed.), *The Wizard of Oz* (New York: Schocken Books, 1983), 271.
4 Stewart Robb, "The Red Wizard of Oz," *New Masses*, October 4, 1934, 8. In Suzanne Rahn, "Introduction: Analyzing Oz: The First Hundred Years," in L. Frank Baum's World of Oz: A Classic Series at 100 (Lanham, MD: ChLA-Scarecrow, 2003), p. xiv.
5 Hearn, *The Wizard of Oz*, "Preface," p. xii.
6 Hearn, *The Wizard of Oz*, "Preface," p. x.
7 Martin Gardner, "Why Librarians Dislike Oz," in Hearn,*The Wizard of Oz*, 190.
8 "L. Frank Baum: Royal Historian of Oz," *myantiquemall*, accessed April 4, 2017, www.myantiquemall.com/AQstories/baumbooks/BaumBooks.html.
9 Joel Schumacher, *The Wiz*, directed by Sidney Lumet (Los Angeles, CA: Universal Studios and Motown Productions, 1978), based on the 1974 Broadway musical libretto by William F. Brown and L. Frank Baum's *The Wonderful Wizard of Oz*.
10 Salman Rushdie, *The Wizard of Oz* (London: BFI Film Classics, 1992), 74.
11 Noel Langley, Florence Ryerson and Edgar Allan Woolf, *The Wizard of Oz*, directed by Victor Fleming (Culver City, CA: Metro-Goldwyn Mayer Studios, 1939).
12 Rushdie, *The Wizard of Oz*, 14.
13 Rushdie, *The Wizard of Oz*, 23.
14 Karen E. Rowe, "To Spin a Yarn: The Female Voice in Folklore and Fairy Tale," in Ruth B. Bottigheimer (ed)., *Fairy Tales and Society* (Philadelphia, PA: University of Pennsylvania Press, 1986), 65, quoted in Alexis Krasilovsky, "Of Spinners and Screenplays," *Creative Screenwriting,* 1(3) (Fall, 1994), 69.
15 Ovid, translated by David R. Slavitt, *The Metamorphoses of Ovid*, VIII (Baltimore, MD: Johns Hopkins University Press, 1994), 161.
16 "Yeh-hsien," in Judy Sierra, *Cinderella* (Phoenix, AZ: Oryx Press, 1992), 6–8.
17 "Cinderella, or the Little Glass Slipper (France)," in Sierra, *Cinderella*, 9–15.
18 "Billy Beg and the Bull," in J. Sierra, *Cinderella*, 44–52.
19 LaVeria Alexander and Alexis Krasilovsky, "*Cinderella* & *Ever After*: Retrieving the Heroine's Journey," *Creative Screenwriting*, 6(3) (May–June, 1999), 55–57.
20 José Rodolfo Loaiza Ontiveros, "DisHollywood," La Luz de Jesus Gallery, Los Angeles, August 2–September 1, 2013.
21 Cathryn Humphris and Eric Kripke, "Bedtime Stories," directed by Mike Rohl, *Supernatural*, Season 3 Episode 5, aired November 1, 2007. Special thanks to Luis Cuevas for his research on "Bedtime Stories" for CTVA 309, "Film As Literature," Department of Cinema and Television Arts, California State University, Northridge, September 25, 2013.
22 Louise Farr, "Partners in Crime: Jim Kouf & David Greenwalt Brew Police Procedural with Fantasy-Horror to Concoct *Grimm*," *Written By,* 19(4) (Summer, 2015), 26.
23 Louise Farr, "Name the Thing" (sidebar), in Farr, "Partners in Crime," 31.
24 Special thanks to Hugo Valencia, CTVA 425, "Advanced Screenwrting," Department of Cinema and Television Arts,' for his research notes on this panel. WGA/w panel, "The State of Modern Horror and the Latino Writer," Writers Guild, October 28, 2014 featuring Latino WGA screenwriters Daniel Dominguez and Trina Calderon (moderators) and panelists Fede Alvarez, Daniel Kenneth, Alvaro Rodriguez, and Al Septien.
25 Goliarda Sapienza, *The Art of Joy* (New York: Farrar, Straus & Giroux, 2013).
26 Sapienza, *The Art of Joy*, 209–210.

27 "Dreamtime," Wikipedia.org, accessed August 11, 2013, https://en.wikipedia.org/wiki/Dreamtime.
28 Margaret Bowater, "Dreamwork in New Zealand," accessed August 22, 2013, http://dreamtalk.hypermart.net/international/new_zealand_english.htm.
29 Madonna Kobenschlag, *Kiss Sleeping Beauty Good-Bye: Breaking the Spell of Feminine Myths and Models* (New York: Doubleday, 1979), 162.
30 Leonie Pihama, "Ebony and Invory: Constructions of Maori in *The Piano*." In Harriet Margolis (ed.), *Jane Campion's The Piano* (Cambridge: Cambridge University Press, 2000), 130.
31 Clarisssa Pinkola Estés, *Women Who Run with the Wolves: Myths and Stories of the Wild Woman Archetype* (New York: Ballantine, 1992), 44.
32 Estés, *Women Who Run with the Wolves*, 51.
33 Estés, *Women Who Run with the Wolves*, 56.

ELEVEN

The Beasts

From Cocteau to Cable

The earliest known version of "Beauty and the Beast," entitled "Cupid and Psyche," "appeared in the second century AD in *The Transformations of Lucian, Otherwise Known as the Golden Ass*, written in Latin by Apuleius of Madaura," who was born in what is now Algeria;[1] however, the best known version of this classic fairy tale was written in French in 1756 by Madame Jeanne-Marie Leprince de Beaumont as "La Belle et la bête," translated into English three years later as "Beauty and the Beast,"[2] and nearly 200 years later faithfully adapted to the screen by writer/director Jean Cocteau (France, 1946). One might say it is a primer for young ladies of the court who wish for high status and economic stability on how to put up with a man's ugliness and beastly manners if a castle comes as part of the package of falling in love with him.

Towards the end of the Cocteau's *La Belle et la bête* (*Beauty and the Beast)* one sees a statue of a woman with a bow and arrow – an allusion to the cult of Diana, the ancient Greek goddess of the hunt, protectress of animals, and a virgin in the sense of both sexual chastity and wholeness unto herself.

In 2001, I travelled to Lake Nemi, a day's trip from Rome and once part of the Grand Tour of writers like Stendhal, Longfellow, Goethe, Hans Christian Andersen, and Gogol: on its shores, in Roman times, the Sanctuary of Diana "attracted pilgrims from all over the Roman Empire."[3] The lake was known to the Romans as the Mirror of Diana:[4] this perfectly oval, volcanic lake, protected by steep forest-covered hills on all sides, is as pure as the magical mirror in Cocteau's *Beauty and the Beast*, which reflects one's true self, and as reflective as the mirror that's rippled like alchemical mercury in Cocteau's next film, *Orphée* (France, 1950), to transport the poet to the Underworld.

The town of Nemi is still fixated on the goddess Diana: the restaurants even serve wild boar from the surrounding forests, whose oak groves date back to the Bronze and Iron Ages. This is where the King of the Woods lives – the twice-born male consort of the fertility goddess, "afraid to rest or sleep in case he should be caught off his guard" and a challenger would "reach the sacred wood and break off the mysterious golden branch from a particular tree which grew somewhere in the forest."[5] This King of the Woods, described in James George Frazer's *The Golden Bough*, was so important that "in the 1st century CE ... the Emperor Caligula sent an assassin to dispose of him" because his reign had lasted too long.[6] The bloodthirsty succession of kings, one after another, reminded me of the endless cycle of writers, calling out their greatness, one generation after another, breaking the golden bough of tradition that grew before them, but leaving the roots of the great tree of literature. Being in those woods in person, I could feel the proximity of Diana to the nature goddesses before her, which had been assimilated into the cult of Diana along with the Egyptian cult of Isis, goddess of love and fertility. The cult of Diana itself became assimilated into Christianity, with the great annual Festival of the Goddess on the Ides of August being converted in "the Middle Ages ... into the Holy Feast of the Assumption of the Virgin – one of the most important dates in the Roman Catholic calendar."[7]

I have also been to Ephesus, on the west coast of Turkey, where the Temple of Diana was one of the greatest wonders of the ancient world, only a few miles from where the Virgin Mary is said to have been born. Imagining Paul of Tarsus (St. Paul, 5–67 CE) who preached in the Temple of Diana "during his evangelizing tour of the Mediterranean"[8] leading to riots and the eventual decline of the temple, I could envision the transformation of religious stories from one culture to another over the millennia and throughout the world.

In Cocteau's *Beauty and the Beast*, Diana guards the building where the Beast's fortune is kept: when thieves break in, she shoots them with her arrows. Diana is the triple goddess: goddess of nature and wildlife, goddess of the moon, and goddess of the magic arts. What role does nature play in the story? What role does moonlight play, or at least the idea of reflected light on a screen, which is one aspect of cinema? Where do the magic arts come in? Cocteau, who has such a hard time depicting women like Belle as real characters, is a genius of paying homage to the goddess. There may be other occult references in this film, and much of its strength lies in hidden truths. The mask of the Beast was actually designed from the death mask of Cocteau's lover at a time when homosexuality was still illegal. In some ways, the subtext of the Beast's story, full of anguish for an inability to express his love due to the necessity of remaining in hiding, is the story of many artists like Cocteau, sublimating their life energies into great films like *Beauty and the Beast*.

The idea of inanimate objects coming to life, which the magician-filmmaker Jean Cocteau had introduced in his film, *The Blood of a Poet* (France, 1930), is brought to a heightened level of aesthetic fulfillment in his 1946 *Beauty and the Beast*. Made when World War II had decimated the French film industry, there was no big studio budget available: it was Cocteau's creative thinking that gave this film its great artistry. Disney's animated *Beauty and the Beast* (USA, 1991) borrowed Cocteau's hauntingly human candlesticks and mantelpieces – along with the *mise-en-scène* of Busby Berkeley's great musical movie, *Gold Diggers of 1935* (USA, 1935) – putting forks, plates, candlesticks, and food to work in the magnificent filmic choreography that was state of the art for the early 1990s.

In the twentieth century, when women's status was not necessarily defined by the economic class of the man she marries, an updating seemed called for. Belle is an unusual girl for a rural French town in the 1991

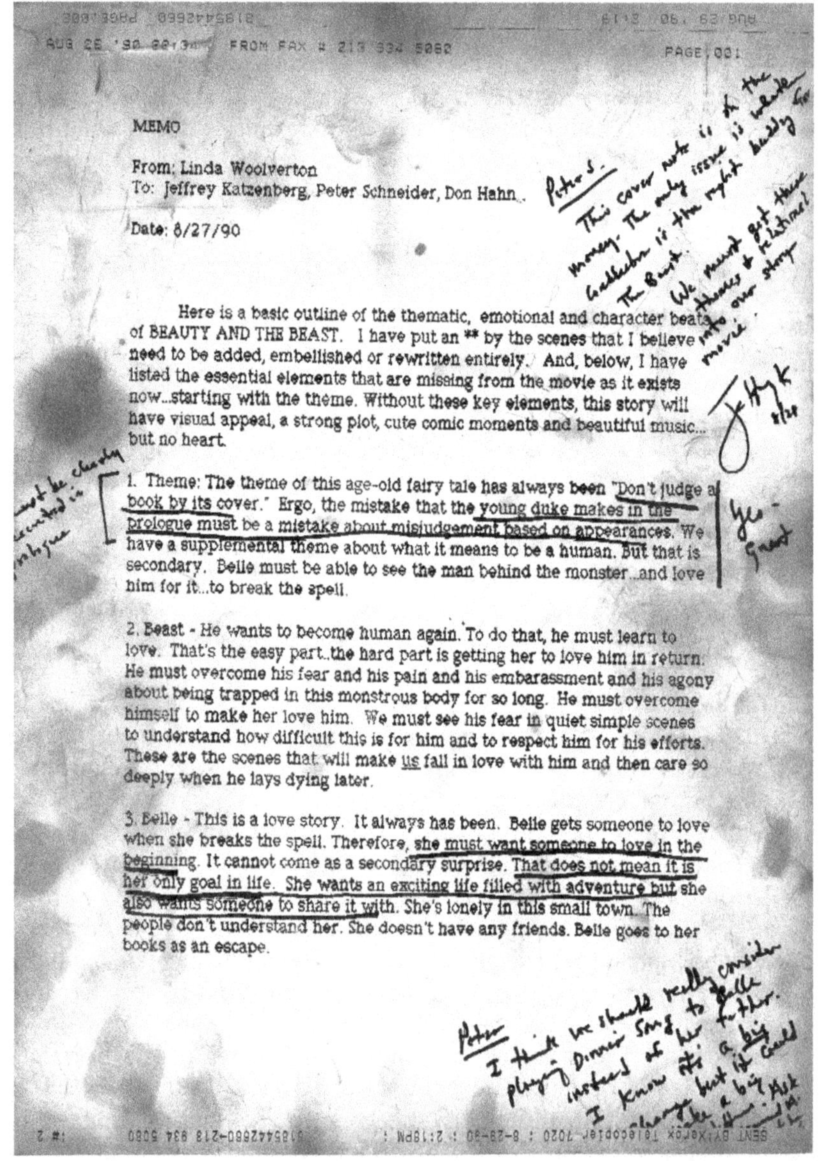

MEMO

From: Linda Woolverton
To: Jeffrey Katzenberg, Peter Schneider, Don Hahn

Date: 8/27/90

Here is a basic outline of the thematic, emotional and character beats of BEAUTY AND THE BEAST. I have put an ** by the scenes that I believe need to be added, embellished or rewritten entirely. And, below, I have listed the essential elements that are missing from the movie as it exists now...starting with the theme. Without these key elements, this story will have visual appeal, a strong plot, cute comic moments and beautiful music... but no heart.

1. Theme: The theme of this age-old fairy tale has always been "Don't judge a book by its cover." Ergo, the mistake that the young duke makes in the prologue must be a mistake about misjudgement based on appearances. We have a supplemental theme about what it means to be a human. But that is secondary. Belle must be able to see the man behind the monster...and love him for it...to break the spell.

2. Beast - He wants to become human again. To do that, he must learn to love. That's the easy part...the hard part is getting her to love him in return. He must overcome his fear and his pain and his embarassment and his agony about being trapped in this monstrous body for so long. He must overcome himself to make her love him. We must see his fear in quiet simple scenes to understand how difficult this is for him and to respect him for his efforts. These are the scenes that will make us fall in love with him and then care so deeply when he lays dying later.

3. Belle - This is a love story. It always has been. Belle gets someone to love when she breaks the spell. Therefore, she must want someone to love in the beginning. It cannot come as a secondary surprise. That does not mean it is her only goal in life. She wants an exciting life filled with adventure but she also wants someone to share it with. She's lonely in this small town. The people don't understand her. She doesn't have any friends. Belle goes to her books as an escape.

Figure 11.1 Memo from Linda Woolverton to Jeffrey Katzenberg, Peter Schneider, Don Hahn, dated August 27, 1990, outlining "the thematic, emotional and character beats of BEAUTY AND THE BEAST." Writers Guild Foundation Archive. Courtesy Linda Woolverton and Walt Disney Studios

Disney version,[9] also set in France of yesteryear, but with feminist values at its core: screenwriter Linda Woolverton's Belle loves to read, thinks for herself, and takes an active role in achieving her goals.

On screenwriter Linda Woolverton's memo to producers Jeffrey Katzenberg and Peter Schneider and lyricist Don Hahn, outlining "the thematic, emotional and character beats of BEAUTY AND THE BEAST," Jeffrey Katzenberg comments in handwriting, "This cover note is on the money. The only issue is whether Candleabra is the right buddy for the Beast." He has underlined that Belle "wants an exciting life filled with adventure but she also wants someone to share it with," with no response other than "Peter, I think we should really consider playing Dinner Song to Belle instead of her father."

In another lengthy memo written in response to notes from producer Michael Eisner, dated November 12, 1990,[10] Woolverton provides a detailed beat sheet of Beast's character arc, beginning with the "PROLOGUE":

> A spoiled, overindulged boy in the Prologue, the Prince is transformed into a Beast because of his own selfish, unkind, unloving behavior.[11]

Comprised of all the scenes in which Beast appears, this memo specifies "how his character develops in each scene and the adjustments that will be necessary to accomplish this,"[12] including notes on Beast's behavior in twenty scenes such as "BEAST AT BELLE'S DOOR," "THE WOLF FIGHT," "BEAST GIVES BELLE THE LIBRARY," in which:

> As he stands on the balcony, gazing down at Belle playing [in] the snow, the Beast articulates his feelings for the first time. Now we know that he's fallen for her. His behavior from this point on is that of an awkward adolescent in a monstrous body who's trying to get the girl.[13]

But the executives left the screenwriter largely to her own devices in developing Belle, giving Woolverton the freedom to develop Belle as a much more liberated character than prior Disney films.

Linda Woolverton has stated that her main quest in writing *Beauty and the Beast* was to make a proactive heroine, a character who saves the beast through her actions as well as her love.[14] She's well-read, although at first the producers simply wanted her to be good at baking a cake, and she doesn't want or need to be an object conquered by Gaston, the handsome but not-too-smart town bully. She chooses to save her father's life by submitting herself to the will of the Beast, and is not a passive victim. In some ways, Belle's journey and sojourn in the Beast's castle is a prototypical "Heroine's Journey." In the ancient Greek version, Persephone goes down to Hades as a result of kidnapping and rape, but becomes the Queen of the Underworld, gaining wisdom and power in the process. In "Beauty and the Beast," Beauty sacrifices herself to a Beast, allowing herself to be locked up in the Beast's castle. But in the process she learns to love him, which leads to a powerful position at his side. Ultimately, Beauty becomes the Queen of the Beast's castle, ruling all the furniture and utensils. Her favorite perk?: The castle comes with a library. It takes two complex character arcs for Belle to fall in love with the Beast, but it's love at first sight for his books.

Ellen Snortland's book *Beauty Bites Beast: Awakening the Warrior Within Women and Girls*, offers a way for proactive female protagonists and their female allies to defend themselves, taking Belle way beyond the confines of her small-minded town or high-walled castle, with a chapter entitled "A Woman's Home is Her Castle, the World Her Playground – When She Defends Them."[15] Furthermore, the feminist art group which calls itself the Guerrilla Girls eschews "Beauty and its beasts" in their book *Bitches, Bimbos and Ballbreakers: The Guerrilla Girls' Illustrated Guide to Female Stereotypes*:

> In the days when few could afford the amount of food needed to get there, fat used to be considered the epitome of female beauty. Now, the higher her social class, the more likely a woman is to starve herself to thinness ... [I]f women could only cut in half the time we spend making ourselves look good (and chastising ourselves for not looking good enough) we could take over the world. Then, we could pass a law: no more impossible notions of beauty.[16]

The Geena Davis Institute on Gender in Media's study, "Gender Disparity On Screen and Behind the Camera in Family Films" noted a small waist size in 22.9 percent of female characters vs. 4.5 percent of male characters in family films, where women "often serve as eye candy."[17]

Despite its active, attractive heroine, Disney's 1991 *Beauty and the Beast* probably fits the "Hero's Journey" better than the "Virgin's Promise" that was discussed in Chapter 8. As Linda Woolverton's memos underscore, the character who experiences the greatest transformative journey is the Beast; although Belle travels bravely from a provincial town to an imposing castle through a forest full of wolves, we don't see Belle getting a PhD or becoming a scientist like her dad, despite all those books in the Beast's library. Instead she gets a handsome husband, with the leisure time to read for personal edification or fun. It would be interesting to imagine a sequel: How violent can they make an action-packed divorce between Beauty and the Beast?

In the meantime, we can luxuriate in watching Disney's $300 million remake of the 1991 version through our 3-D glasses – a hybrid of live action and digitally rendered characters as state-of-the-art for 2017 as the now-obsolete techniques which created monsters for Douglas Fairbanks to slay in the romantic fantasy-adventure film *The Thief of Bagdad* (USA, 1924). The 2017 *Beauty and the Beast* is a beauty of a film, exhibiting far better aesthetic taste than most American studio productions of the past, especially in its glittering atlas whose magic is used to transport us to Paris, and animated decorations that lovingly coalesce on the skirt of Belle's gown as if they were sweet swirls of icing landing on a French gâteau. But this twenty-first-century version of an eighteenth-century Belle is much too feisty to settle for being a fashion plate: She ties some of her beautiful gowns into a rope in an attempt to escape from her Rapunzel-like tower. Other elements that the screenwriters Stephen Chbosky and Evan Spiliotopoulos add to the new *Beauty and the Beast* (which gives an on-screen "Based on ..." credit to Linda Woolverton's earlier script) is a backstory explanation to why the Prince was turned into a Beast in a long-winded voice-over which nevertheless counts on our empathy, and a backstory to Belle's mother's death, set in a garret that looks like it's next door to Baz Luhrmann's Moulin Rouge. The screenplay also updates the characters: Brooks Barnes describes Chip, Mrs. Potts' chipped teacup of a son, as "more of a skate dude,"[18] and Mr. Gad's manservant is a gay character with a happy ending: although he pines and sighs after the unattainable Gaston, LeFou ultimately finds a transvestite to dance with at the ball.

Yet Cocteau's *La Belle et la bête* can be interpreted as a gay version of the story itself at a time when it was illegal to be gay: there's a tragedy in the portrayal of a Beast who can't come out from behind his mask, as well as in the unnatural relationship between Belle and the Beast trying to fit a heteronormative pattern that's only a fairy tale for them.

Two TV series also feature the love relationship between a "normal" woman and a not-so-human male: *Beauty and the Beast* (USA, 1987–1990), in which a district attorney has fallen in love with a man who looks like a lion, and *Beauty and the Beast* (Canada, 2012–2016), in which Belle is a detective in love with a man-beast who has been genetically engineered by the government.

In contrast, Angela Carter's short story, "The Tiger's Bride," features a Beauty who is "erotically transformed into an exquisite animal herself."[19] Salman Rushdie writes, "It is Carter's genius, in this collection, to make the fable of Beauty and the Beast a metaphor for all the myriad yearnings and dangers of sexual relations."[20]

While there is beauty, greatness, and eroticism in more than one adaptation of *Beauty and the Beast* already, it remains to be seen where genius can take us next in adapting the dark side of fairy tales to film and television, with or without their happy endings.

Notes

1 Maria Tatar, introduction to Jeanne-Marie Leprince de Beaumont, "Beauty and the Beast," in Maria Tatar, *The Annotated Classic Fairy Tales* (New York: W. W. Norton, 2002), 58–59.
2 Tatar, *The Annotated Classic Fairy Tales*, 59.
3 Margaret Stenhouse, *The Goddess of the Lake: Legends and Mysteries of Nemi* (Rome: Press Time, 1997), 49.
4 Stenhouse, *The Goddess of the Lake*, 124.
5 Stenhouse, *The Goddess of the Lake*, 127.

6 James George Frazer, paraphrased in Stenhouse, *The Goddess of the Lake*, 128.
7 Stenhouse, *The Goddess of the Lake*, 47.
8 Stenhouse, *The Goddess of the Lake*, 116.
9 Linda Woolverton, *The Beauty and the Beast*, directed by Gary Trousdale and Kirk Wise (Burbank, CA: Buena Vista Pictures, 1991).
10 Linda Woolverton, Memo, "Re: The Character Arc of the Beast," "To All Concerned" (November 12, 1990), 1.
11 Woolverton, Memo, "Re: The Character Arc of the Beast," 1.
12 Woolverton, Memo, "Re: The Character Arc of the Beast," 1.
13 Woolverton, Memo, "Re: The Character Arc of the Beast," 4.
14 Comments by Linda Woolverton, panelist, "Global Storytelling: Portrayals of Women and Girls," panel moderated by Cathy Schulman, President, Mandalay Pictures, Geena Davis Institute on Gender in Media, "2nd Global Symposium on Gender in Media" (symposium, Los Angeles, October 6, 2014).
15 Ellen Snortland, "A Woman's Home is Her Castle, the World Her Playground – When She Defends Them," in *Beauty Bites Beast: Awakening the Warrior Within Women and Girls* (Columbia, SC: B3 Books, 2001), 101.
16 Guerrilla Girls, *Bitches, Bimbos and Ballbreakers: The Guerrilla Girls' Illustrated Guide to Female Stereotypes* (New York: Penguin, 2003), 3.
17 Marc Choueiti and Stacy L. Smith, "Gender Disparity On Screen and Behind the Camera in Family Films: An Executive Summary," The Geena Davis Institute on Gender in Media, 15.
18 Brooks Barnes, "*Beauty and the Beast*: Disney's $300 Million Gamble," *New York Times*, March 8, 2017, accessed March 18, 2017, 2–3, https:/nyti.ms/2mFy47U.
19 Salman Rushie, "Introduction," in Angela Carter, *Burning Your Boats* (New York: Henry Holt, 1995), p. xii.
20 Rushie, "Introduction," p. xii.

Part V

Global Storytelling Revisited

It's no longer enough to focus on Hollywood with a few art films and Academy Award-winners for Best Foreign Film thrown into the mix. Bollywood in India and Nollywood in Nigeria make far more films each year than Hollywood, and many other countries, especially Australia, Brazil, Canada, China, France, Germany, Iran, Japan, Korea, Mexico, Senegal, and the UK, also make films and television programs of international renown. Several factors can contribute towards making an adaptation international:

- its literary sources, whether a Peruvian-based novel by the Nobel Prize-winner Mario Vargas Llosa, reset in New Orleans, or a novel by Naguib Mafouz, set in Cairo, Egypt, that's reset in Mexico City as a film;
- the sources of financing, especially today when it is almost impossible for an American production company to make a big-budget film without the participation of Germany, Taiwan, the UK, Australia, or other countries (and sometimes vice versa);
- the background of above-the-line talent, such as Menno Meyjes, the Dutch-born screenwriter of Steven Spielberg's *The Color Purple*;
- the international make-up of the cast and crew, exchanging directions through interpreters from French, Spanish, or English to Hindi, Polish, or Korean and back;
- and the role of international film festivals that welcome filmmakers from around the world, some of whom have been exiled from their own countries, such as Iran.

TWELVE

Stories without Borders

Ugetsu

Kenji Mizoguchi's *Ugetsu* (Japan, 1953)[1] is a classic film that takes its inspiration not only from Japanese theater and history, but from a French short story by Guy de Maupassant and classic Japanese ghost stories which were in turn influenced by ancient Chinese fiction. Although Akira Kurosawa is the Japanese filmmaker most American film lovers know well today, Kurosawa himself felt that Kenji Mizoguchi was Japan's greatest filmmaker. Unlike Kurosawa, who repeatedly adapted world literature for a world audience, Mizoguchi made his films for Japanese audiences. It is largely due to the greatness of Mizoguchi's artistry that they resonate with audiences throughout the world.

In the 1950s, Mizoguchi adapted three stories from Japanese literature in quick succession, winning major awards at the Venice Film Festival three years in a row. *The Life of Oharu* (Japan, 1952) was based on Saikaku Ibara's seventeenth-century novel, *Life of an Amorous Woman*, an erotic masterpiece considered obscene in 1950s America, although the film adaptation of it, which appeared on Andrew Sarris and other critics' top ten lists, is one of the most devastating feminist portrayals of a woman's fall from society ever made. *Ugetsu* (Japan, 1953), was based on two ghost stories written in the eighteenth century by Akinari Ueda. "The House Amid the Thickets," set in the fifteenth century, is about a man who after leaving his wife, returns unaware that she has become a ghost. "The Lust of the White Serpent," set during the eleventh century Heian period, is about a man who falls in love with a beautiful woman who turns out to be a snake demon. Mizoguchi's third award-winning adaptation of the 1950s, *Sansho the Bailiff* (Japan, 1954), also set in the Heian period, in which the children of a noble family are sent to a slave camp when their father is exiled, was based on a short story by Mori Ōgai, one of the founders of modern Japanese literature.[2]

Ugetsu takes place during the same period of civil war in which Kurosawa sets *Rashōmon* (Japan, 1950): sixteenth-century Japan (although the wars began with the Onin War of fifteenth-century Japan – 1467–1477, and the story "The House Amid the Thickets" is set shortly before this, in 1455). Mizoguchi's screenwriter, Yoshikata Yoda, states that originally, Mizoguchi had no intention of making an anti-war film, and wanted "the horrors of war ... [to] be filtered through an atmosphere of beauty, refinement and ghostliness,"[3] focusing on "the purity and translucence of Ueda's story."[4] But later, in his notes to the screenwriter, Mizoguchi wrote:

> The feeling of wartime must be apparent in the attitude of every character. The violence of war unleashed by those in power on a pretext of the national good must overwhelm the common people with suffering – moral and physical. Yet the commoners, even under these conditions, must continue to live and eat. This theme is what I especially want to emphasize here. How should I do it?[5]

In the early 1950s, Japan was still recovering from the devastating impact of World War II. It was much easier to address the people's suffering in historical dramas rather than risk the American-led Allied Occupation censors' disapproval of a contemporary Japanese film about war. However, the Allied Occupation ended in 1952, a year before *Ugetsu* was released, which might explain Mizoguchi's change of heart about expressing the hardships of a war on Japanese soil.

Although they were dealing with adaptations of various storylines, Mizoguchi admonished his screenwriter not to be

> old-fashioned. For one thing, in order to make characters that are not artificial, it is essential for the author to observe people outside the framework of both his and the director's own experience or predetermined ideas. Don't follow the trite paths others have traveled before. I think it is important to discover something new that others have not yet become aware of.[6]

Mizoguchi's passion for the arts, including his own filmmaking, is apparent in every detail of his main character, Genjuro, a potter who is willing to risk being killed by soldiers in order to fire his pots to perfection and bring them to market. Mizoguchi was also able to infuse the suffering of prostitutes he knew personally in the tragic portrayal of Ohama, a farmer's wife who is raped by soldiers and forced into prostitution after her husband Tobei abandons her in his foolish quest to become a samurai. Satirizing a man's obsession for success in something for which he is unqualified is reinforced by Guy de Maupassant's "How He Got the Legion of Honor," first published in France as "Décoré" in 1883.

Even in the minor details of *Ugetsu,* however, Japanese history comes to life: When the ghost of Lady Wakasa mentions that her family had met their demise at the hands of someone named Nobunaga, the screenwriters are paying homage to the powerful feudal leader Oda Nobunaga (1534–

1582), who, "[i]n his attempt to unify Japan as one country ... was killed by one of his own generals when unification was easily in sight."[7]

Mizoguchi, who "spoke of his film as a representative of Japan's aesthetic tradition" when screening *Ugetsu* at the Venice Film Festival in 1953,[8] wanted his films "to be like picture scrolls."[9] According to Asian Studies scholar Arlene Stone, Heian narrative scroll paintings called *emakimono* were "a purely Japanese art form..."[10]

> made from pasted single sheets that formed a long roll and could be viewed from right to left ... As the scroll was unrolled, the narrative proceeded in what some would now call cinematic fashion, except that scroll images do not move continuously like film, but consecutively like the viewing of slides ... Painters arranged text with their paintings so that when the scroll was unrolled ... a continuous sequence could be followed. In this way secular stories (*setsuwa*) came into being.[11]

The richness of *Ugetsu*'s shots, with their *mise-en-scène* and long takes usually shot from a moving crane, serve an important storytelling function. A screenwriter usually thinks of creating a "page-turner"; one might also think of the Director of Photography Kazuo Miyagawa's storytelling contribution as his moving camera constantly moves us forward, the 35mm film (in the days before digital projection) winding its way from one section of Mizoguchi's cinematic scroll to the next.

Although the richness of its visual storytelling is part of what makes Mizoguchi's work a masterpiece – the boat slowly making its way through the thick fog, the lovers cavorting in the sun-dappled garden – perhaps the strongest influence on *Ugetsu* is the grave, mysterious style of fifteenth-century Noh theater, which frequently features ghosts as well as a travelling priest who questions the main character – both of which are central to *Ugetsu*'s plot. Even in its details, Noh's influence predominates. As Tadao Sato points out,

> Lady Wakasa ... is wearing a Noh costume [which] Mizoguchi borrowed ... especially from a Noh performer [and] ... her makeup and facial expression were reminiscent of various Noh masks and the way she walked imitated a Noh performance ... [and the view from the garden in the Kutsuki mansion] where she appears looks just like a Noh stage.[12]

Therefore, it should come as no surprise that one of Noh's most influential figures, the actor, playwright, and theoretician of Noh theater Komparu Zenchiku (1405–1470?), wrote a Noh drama entitled *Ugetsu* (*Rain and Moon*), in which a travelling priest named Saigyo stops at the house of an old couple. In return for finishing a poem, he is allowed to spend the rainy night with them. In the morning, the couple disappears, transformed into deities. Another diety has become a shrine priest who has materialized in order to thank Saigyo for the greatness of his poetry. At the end of the play, the priest "dances in praise of the virtue of poetry."[13] How can an ambitious filmmaker like Mizoguchi not have been inspired by a play like *Ugetsu*, with its reactions of ghosts and humans alike to the greatness of one's art?

Bride and Prejudice

In the US, there are probably as many anglophiles who revere English literature as there were Japanese scholars in the Heian era reciting Chinese texts. There have been lots of Jane Austen films made in the last two decades in particular. Part of the reason is that these films are adaptations of novels written in the early 1800s, and therefore in public domain. The question is, when it's considered a great classic like the work of Jane Austen, just how free are you, as a producer, screenwriter, or director, to change the story? The answer varies considerably not only from culture to culture, but from filmmaker to filmmaker.

English director Gurinder Chadha's Bollywood-style romantic musical *Bride and Prejudice* (UK/USA/India, 2004)[14] changes the character of Elizabeth Bennet, who was played by Keira Knightley in the faithful adaptation of *Pride and Prejudice* (France/UK/USA, 2005), to Lalita Bakshi, played by Bollywood star Aishwarya Rai. Instead of Austen's focus on the practical wisdom of marrying in an England where women rarely supported themselves and achieved economic security and status through marriage, resetting the film in Amritsar lets screenwriters Berges and Chadha explore Indian love values such as arranged marriages, the issue of lifelong marriage vs. divorce, and historical English dowries vs. contemporary Indian dowries or their equivalent.

Midaq Alley

Although English, American, and Indian adaptations of Jane Austen's novels abound, they may not have been adapted in Iran or Arabic countries as yet; but those regions have their own great literatures, including the novels of Egyptian Nobel laureate Naguib Mahfouz, who introduced himself to the Swedish Academy as a product of the 1,400 year old Islamic civilization and the 7,000 year old Pharaonic civilization of Egypt.[15]

In a book review of Mahfouz's novel *Midaq Alley (Zuqâq al-Midaq)*,[16] reviewer Louis Proyect writes:

> A decisive factor in the ongoing war against Arab Peoples is the general lack of knowledge about and sympathy for their culture. To destroy a people, it is much easier to do so under a cloak of ignorance and misrepresentation.[17]

Yet the characters of *Midaq Alley* also suffer from ignorance. As Proyect states,

> [T]here is no final understanding among the novel's characters about why they suffer, least of all a political one. Their choices appear limited between a kind of blind acceptance of "god's will" and the meager outlets afforded by factory jobs or army bases of the occupying power of the moment.

Such characters are so universal, though they are the specific fictional inhabitants of one impoverished neighborhood in Cairo, that I could easily imagine them languishing in the forgotten alleyways of today's American South or the Midwest; in adapting the novel to the screen, Jorge Fons reset Midaq Alley in Mexico City, and populated it with the criminals, prostitutes, homosexuals, and lovelorn characters that Mahfouz had created with such compassion.

Proyect also states:

> Mahfouz was not only committed to social justice, he was also highly critical of religious fundamentalism ... Refusing to focus on anti-Zionism, like Nasser's government of Egypt in 1952, Mahfouz defined the real enemy as: "poverty, ignorance, disease and dictatorship." He calls these the "genuine and historic enemies," and makes them central to the themes of "Midaq Alley" and many of his other novels.[18]

Midaq Alley (*El Callejón de los Milagros*, Mexico, 1995) doesn't put the politics of Naguib's novel center stage any more than *The Grapes of Wrath* (USA, 1940) did when it overlooked much of the left-wing politics of John Steinbeck's novel in favor of focusing on one farm family's bitter journey out of the Dust Bowl during the Great Depression. However, with the phenomenal success of *Midaq Alley*, "the most awarded film in Mexican history,"[19] Jorge Fons opened the door for new generations of young filmmakers to work in the film and television production center of Mexico City, the fourth largest of its kind in North America.[20]

Devdas

In India, many adaptations have been made from the classic novel, *Devdas,* written in Bengali in 1917 by Saratchandra Chatterjee, who is widely acclaimed as a *katha sahityik*, or master storyteller.[21] Pramathesh Chandra Barua directed three versions of *Devdas* between 1935 and 1937, in Bengali, Hindi, and Assamese;[22] other versions have been made in Tamil and Malayalam.[23] In P.C. Barua's 1936 version, Devdas is being sent to Calcutta to get an education, not as punishment for misbehavior, but the result is the same: the lovers are wrenched apart.

Bimal Roy's faithful, classic *Devdas* (India, 1955) begins with Devdas and Paro sharing an idyllic childhood out in nature, which plays a similar role to Catherine and Heathcliff's childhood romance in Emily Brontë's *Wuthering Heights*: Devdas's bird is not that different from the one whose feather Catherine guards as a special treasure in Andrea Arnold's adaptation of *Wuthering Heights* (UK, 2011), except that Devdas and Paro sing traditional Hindi songs to it instead of local English ones. In Roy's version, Devdas is sent off to Calcutta to study as a consequence of his many pranks and general misbehavior. Devdas's loss takes on a spiritual quality as another song begs Krishna to show his face again. "Radha is roaming alone, looking lost," the singers sing to Krishna, in return for the rupees that Devdas left his childhood friend Paro before he was dragged off. When a much older Paro – now a beautiful maiden of marriageable age – hears that Devdas is back in town, she pauses to notice the bird in the tree, symbolizing that Radha has waited for Krishna's return. At the end of the tragic story, when Devdas coughs up blood, dying of alcoholism, Paro faints: Bimay Roy's cutting between them filmically demonstrates their powerful bond.

The Bollywood adaptation of *Devdas* (India, 2002)[24] starring Aishwarya Rai Bachchan as Paro and "King of Bollywood" Shahrukh Khan as Devdas – pays homage to Chattopadhyay, Barua, and Roy in one of its opening title cards. The film proceeds to open its story with Devdas's return from London after a ten-year absence: an exciting use of *in media res*. Devdas's home looks like the world's biggest, most sumptuous mansion, full of family members, neighbors, servants, and dancing girls, all out to celebrate in Bollywood musical fashion. When Paro hears word of Devdas's return, it's a pay-off for having kept her love-light lit for a decade of loneliness and longing: the lamp with which she dances is a metaphor for her passion, her love, and Devdas himself.

As Sreejata Guha points out, the Devdas of the novel "is certainly not the conventional romantic hero, admirable and desirable, a Krishna archetype."[25] He's too stubborn to remain a prodigal son of wealthy parents, too proud to admit his love for the girl next door whose mother was once a lowly dancer; he even hits Paro, before his irredeemable descent

Figure 12.1 The Bollywood adaptation of *Devdas* (India, 2002) focuses on the never-ending passion between Paro (Aishwarya Rai Bachchan) and Devdas (Shahrukh Khan), and the tragic, alcoholic demise of its flawed hero. Image courtesy of Eros International. Produced by Red Chillies Entertainment and Mega Bollywood

into alcoholism. Instead, as Anjali Gera Roy points out in her study of Hindu Sanskritic and Perso-Arabic sources of Hindi films, Devdas "is a Hindu avatar of Qais, who is driven mad by unrequited love and becomes *majnun* or possessed, in whom countless poets saw the symbol of their own state."[26] Bollywood star Shahrukh Khan, in explaining his portrayal of Devdas, says, "I played him as a metaphor, not as a character."[27] Guha points out that in the novel, too,

> it is as a metaphor that Devdas succeeds. The specific events in his life are incidental; it is as a metaphor for unfulfilled love that he captures the readers' imagination.[28]

Life of Pi

In trying to write a script that would appeal to a global audience and do justice to Yann Martel's best-selling novel about an Indian boy who survives 227 days at sea with a Bengal tiger in his lifeboat, director Ang Lee claimed with some hyperbole that the screenplay of *Life of Pi* (USA/Taiwan/UK/Canada/France/India, 2012) went through four hundred drafts as he and screenwriter David Magee "wrote our hearts and brains out."[29] The more modest Magee states:

> I didn't write 160 drafts, but there were about 160 times I sat down and we wrote new scenes to try. Sometimes, the changes would be a few lines, and sometimes it would be a third of an act that we rewrote.[30]

Life of Pi's visual storytelling was so strong that the film would have been better served if structured as a story without bookends – the white writer in Montreal who served as a filter and sounding board for Pi's first version of his seafaring story, or the Japanese insurance investigators who listen to Pi's second version at the end. I can understand Magee's hesitancy, when confronted with "the section at sea [which] is a hundred chapters – some of them only half a page long: they don't have a narrative through-line to them," as well as his enthusiasm for "this sense of humor that the older Pi would have about his life and his journeys while telling it to a Westerner."[31] Yet I felt that clutching to a narrative device of in-your-face listeners – which worked so well in novels written for girls in the nineteenth century to lend a moral perspective to otherwise delightful romps – weighed down the sky's-the-limit fantasy appeal of the adaptation. We could have broken out of the Pondicherry zoo and into the limitless expanse of the sea with its sailor's yarns without the presence of those on-screen listeners sitting in their chairs, with whom I'd rather not feel obliged to identify as a passive member of the audience, when there's such a unique and an adventurous young fellow in a storm-tossed boat on-screen whose journey I'm eager to follow instead, no holds barred. *Life of Pi* contains a magnificent story, but since the story *is* so magnificent, it's redundant to make it a film about storytelling, even if the novel itself was partly about storytelling.

And yet, I can understand the difficulties of making these decisions. As David Magee describes it:

> The novel jumps around a lot. I thought of starting with the Japanese investigators. Ang said no, we need the storyteller in India first, as it's a film about storytelling.[32]

But the opening wasn't their only problem in terms of narration. As Ang Lee describes it:

> We'd still be playing with the ending, but we had to release the film. Getting the right balance, interpretation and structure, when do you bring back the narrator? For a while we tried to do it without the Japanese investigators.[33]

From beginning to end, the film is woven through with storytelling concerns: It even tells the story twice. Magee insists:

> This is about how different people choose different narratives to comprehend the world. Without getting all philosophical, it's like the Plato and the Cave thing: We're all looking at the same shadows, but we're picturing different things behind us ... So the stories come out different. But what we're trying to express is the same.[34]

As a screenwriting professor who has investigated storytelling and the complexities of narrative perspectives in adaptations for decades, I'd like to agree with Magee – especially given how much I love the sequences which he wrote that were set on the open seas, including montage scenes which Ang Lee further developed using state-of-the-art visual effects. They did their utmost to honor author Yann Martel, who has described the subtext of his novel, *Life of Pi,* as "Life is a story. You can choose your story. A story with God is the better story."[35]

But when it really comes down to it, I feel that many adaptations would be better served if you just told the story, period – with or without God. Do you really need some French-Canadian writer or some Japanese insurance investigators to hold our hands while we watch the film, when the story itself is so powerful? When the French critic Alexandre Astruc explained the greatness of *Ugetsu* by stating that "The obsession of the artist is artistic creation,"[36] he was referring to Mizoguchi's *mise-en-scène*, not his screenwriter Yoshikata Yoda's story construction. While characters who tell the same story from different perspectives is a thrilling component of both Akira Kurosawa's *Rashōmon* and David Fincher's *Gone Girl* (USA, 2014) thanks to their screenwriters – as we're constantly in suspense as to whether or not they are telling the truth – this narrative device simply kills time in *Life of Pi*. It detracts from Ang Lee's true genius as an auteur, which is centered in his *mise-en-scène*.

Notes

1 Matsutarō Kawaguchi (adaptation) and Yoshikata Yoda (scriptwriter), *Ugetsu*, directed by Kenji Mizoguchi (Tokyo: Daiei Studios, 1953).
2 "Mori Ōgai," Britannica.com, accessed April 3, 2017, www.britannica.com/biography/Mori-Ogai.
3 Mark Le Fanu, *Mizoguchi and Japan* (London: BFI, 2005), 59.
4 Yoshikata Yoda, interviewed by Kaneto Shindo, "Kenji Mizoguchi: The Life of a Film Director," DVD, Criterion, 1975, Ch. 19 01:39:09.
5 Kenji Mizoguchi, quoted in Philip Lopate, "From the Other Shore," in *Ugetsu* (accompanying pamphlet to DVD) Criterion, 4.
6 Kenji Mizoguchi, letter to his scriptwriter Yoshikata Yoda, quoted in Keiko I. McDonald (ed). *Ugetsu: Kenji Mizoguchi, Director* (New Brunswick, NJ: Rutgers University Press, 1993), 107.
7 Bret Freemyer, "Nobunaga Reference in *Ugetsu*," research for CTVA 309, "Film As Literature," Department of Cinema and Television Arts, California State University, Northridge, April 19, 2005, 1.
8 Donald Kirihara, *Patterns of Time: Mizoguchi and the 1930s* (Madison, WI: University of Wisconsin Press, 1992), 5.
9 Kenji Mizoguchi quote, recalled in an interview with Mizoguchi's Director of Photography, Kazuo Miyagawa, in the documentary, *Kenji Mizoguchi: The Life of a Film Director*, by Kaneto Shindo (New York: Criterion, 1975), Ch. 19.
10 Itsuji, referenced in Arlene Stone, *"Cloistered" Women*, Part Three, Chapter Six (unpublished manuscript).
11 Stone unpublished research, *"Cloistered" Women*.
12 Tadao Sato, "The Subject and Form of Traditional Theater Made into a Film – *Ugetsu*," in McDonald, *Ugetsu*, 163.
13 Richard Emmert, synopsis, "Ugetsu (Rain and Moon)," Kotay.net, accessed October 18, 2012, www.kotay.net/keith/WorldTour97/noh.html.
14 Paul Mayeda Berges and Gurinder Chadha, *Bride and Prejudice*, directed by Gurinder Chadha (London: Pathé Pictures International, 2004); based on the novel *Pride and Prejudice* by Jane Austen.
15 Naguib Mahfouz, "Nobel Lecture," 1988, accessed April 2, 2017, www.nobelprize.org/nobel_prizes/literature/laureates/1988/mahfouz-lecture.html.
16 Naguib Mahfouz, *Midaq Alley: A New Translation*, trans. by Humphrey Davies (New York: American University in Cairo Press, 2011).
17 Louis Proyect, "Naguid Mahfouz: *Midaq Alley*," book review, *Swans Commentary*, April 14, 2003.
18 Proyect, "Naguid Mahfouz: *Midaq Alley*."
19 *Midaq Alley*, imdb.com, accessed April 2, 2017, www.imdb.com/title/tt0112619/combined.
20 "Cinema of Mexico," Wikipedia.org, accessed April 2, 2017, https://en.wikipedia.org/wiki/Cinema_of_Mexico.
21 Sreejata Guha, "Introduction," *Saratchandra Chattopadhyay's Devdas*, trans. by Sreejata Guha (New Delhi: Penguin, 2002), p. vii.
22 P.C. Barua, *Devdas* (1936), written and directed by P.C. Barua, Vintage DVD, back cover notes.
23 Sreejata Guha,"Introduction," p. xii.
24 Prakash Kapedia and Sanjay Leela Bhansali, *Devdas*, directed by Sanjay Leela Bhansali (Mumbai: Mega Bollywood, 2002).

25 Sreejata Guha, "Introduction," p. ix.
26 Anjali Gera Roy, "*Qissa* and Popular Hindi Cinema." In Lina Khatib (ed.), *Storytelling in World Cinemas, Vol. 2, Contexts* (New York: Wallflower/Columbia University Press, 2013), 187.
27 Sharukh Khan, quoted in Guha, "Introduction," p. xi.
28 Guha, "Introduction," p. xii.
29 Ang Lee, at a Q&A with screenwriter David Magee following the screening of *Life of Pi* (2012), based on the novel by Yann Martel, Writers Guild Theater, Beverly Hills, California, January 11, 2013.
30 David Magee, quoted in Richard Stayton, "Taming the Tiger," *WGAW Written By,* 16(6) (November–December, 2012), 25
31 Stayton, "Taming the Tiger," 25.
32 David Magee, Q&A, Writers Guild Theater.
33 Ang Lee, Q&A, Writers Guild Theater.
34 Stayton, "Taming the Tiger," 29.
35 Yann Martel, quoted in Jennie Renton, "Yanna Martel Interview," *Textualities,* 2005, accessed April 1, 2017, http://textualities.net/jennie-renton/yann-martel-interview.
36 Alexandre Astruc, "What is *mise-en-scène*?," *Cahiers du Cinema* 100 (October, 1959), 268.

THIRTEEN

Regional vs. International Perspectives

Universalizing Regional Stories

China and Japan

Lu Wei, co-screenwriter of *Farewell, My Concubine* (China/Hong Kong, 1993) and *To Live* (China/Hong Kong, 1994) – both huge successes at the Cannes Film Festival – read Robert McKee's *Story*[1] in the early 1980s. Critic Wang Tianbing's long-time friend Lu Wei was amazed that McKee's book didn't focus on the miserable fates suffered by literary geniuses, like so many Chinese books about writing; instead it taught practical writing skills: "Such a thing could only come from American culture, he thought."[2]

Lu Wei went on to write "possibly the only writing guidebook that has many practical functions written by a Chinese writer," developed from Wang Tianbing and Lu Wei's "writing conversation" entitled "When Will the Chinese Movie Industry Grow Up?" that had been published in *Tianya* magazine in 2006 as part of the Chinese movie industry's 100th anniversary celebration.[3] According to Wang Tianbing, under Lu Wei's "normal Chinese appearance, there's a deeply Westernized brain."[4] But this approach enabled Lu Wei to bring Chinese cultural treasures such as the *Kunqu* and Beijing Operas, shadow puppetry, and the *laoqiang* singing style to life in films that Western audiences could understand and value.[5] Wang Tianbing recollects:

> [I]t still shocks me tremendously that he's put so much time into studying so many foreign literary classics and movie masterpieces. You can see in his films the compassion of Anton Chekhov, the power of Akira Kurosawa and the structure of Bernardo Bertolucci. His acute sense of cultural conflict is just like David Lean's. His awareness of local culture can be compared to Francis Ford Coppola's. His passion for historical restoration in the backgrounds salutes the films of Andrei Tarkovsky. You can see many clues of these features in *Farewell My Concubine* and *To Live*.[6]

Lu Wei studied Western films, as well as films from Eastern cultures that incorporated a dual East/West sensibility such as Akira Kurosawa's, in order to expand the viewership of films with themes of particular significance to Chinese history and culture. Kurosawa's *Ran* (Japan, 1985), is based not only on Shakespeare's *King Lear* (1606), but on the history of Mōri Motonari (1497–1571), a sixteenth-century Japanese feudal lord (*daimyō*) with three sons.[7] *Ran*'s story of the three arrows – unbreakable in their unity, but easily snapped one by one – comes from a lesson Motonari imparted to his three sons in order to keep them from fighting each other. It addresses Kurosawa's fears that the three superpowers – the US, the Soviet Union, and China – would destroy the world without unifying behind the idea of nuclear disarmament. Kurosawa created a powerful hybrid by mixing the samurai genre with a mainstream Western approach to Shakespearian adaptation.

India

Filmmakers in India have turned to Western culture as a source for regional entertainment that sometimes also resonates beyond borders, and which also includes their own regional cultural references. For example, Rajiv Menon's *Kandukondain, Kandukondain* (*I Have Found It*, India, 2000) is a loose adaptation of Jane Austen's *Sense and Sensibility* that also pays homage to Tamil poet/writer Subramania Bharati by including the song "Suttum Vizhi," based on his poem. The sisters speak together: "The one, born for me will come in search of me. Holding his hand I will go round the world," and when the music begins, one of them identifies what she hears as "Bharathiyar poetry."

Set in South India, as well as in Scottish castles and at the pyramids of Egypt, *Kandukondain, Kandukondain* was mostly made in Kollywood. That's right: Kollywood, India's second largest film industry in Chennai, formerly known as Madras, on the east coast of India. Chennai's Kodambakkam district is its region's version of Hollywood, hence the "K" in "Kollywood."

This Kollywood adaptation of *Sense and Sensibility* stars Aishwarya Rai, former Miss World and Bollywood's top female star. "Meenu" (or "Meenakshi") is as passionate about Tamil dancing and poetry as Marianne Dashwood was for Shakespeare's sonnets, Edmund Spenser's "The Faerie Queene," and English country dancing. The song she sings also references an "ocean of milk" – part of one of the best known episodes of traditional Hindu mythology, the *Samudra Manthan* or "Churning of the Ocean," found in the Sanskrit classics – the *Bhagavata Purana*, the *Mahabhrata* and the *Vishnu Purana* – which are part of a Sanskrit culture that is over three thousand years old.[8]

Adaptations from other regions of India include the award-winning *Adajya* (Assam, 1993), written and directed by Santwana Baoloi, based on the Assamese novel *Dontal Hatir Une Khonda Howdah* by Mamoni Raisom Goswami; and *Zulfiqar* (West Bengal, 2016), written and directed by Srijit Mukherji, a Bengali adaptation of Shakespeare's *Julius Caesar* and *Antony and Cleopatra* set in Kolkata.

Israel and Mexico; Iran and France

Ligiah Villalobos, who has also worked as a studio executive for the Walt Disney Company, describes her work as screenwriter on the adaptation of *Bonjour Monsieur Shlomi* (Israel, 2003) for Salma Hayek's company:[9]

> I was brought in to make an Israeli film, a Latino film. So one of the things I had to do before I even took on the project, was to make sure that I could actually do that. That I felt that an Israeli family could be adapted into my own culture and a Latino family experience. And the thing that I discovered while watching Shlomi[10] is how similar Mexican families are to Israeli families. Both passionate, both a little nutty, both involved in every aspect of each family member's lives, etc. So even though I did have to change some things and make it authentic to my own culture's experience, the core of the family was very similar ... That process was fun.[11]

Marjane Satrapi and Vincent Paronnaud's *Persepolis* (France/USA, 2007), a French/Iranian film which takes place in Tehran, Iran, and Vienna, Austria, is based on an autobiographical graphic novel by Marjane Satrapi. Co-writer/co-director Satrapi states:

> We tried not to put the finger all the time on this stupid notion of East and West, and Muslim and Christian. I have always said: if there is a real separation in the world, it's between the stupid fanatics and everyone else.[12]

This quote is from a woman in a country where 64 percent of the students in 2008 were women, but women had half the rights of men. Satrapi, writer and director said, "These women have to prove themselves. The only way to get emancipated is through education..."[13] In my opinion, this makes your responsibility to become well-educated and to impart what you know to the world through your screenwriting even more imperative.

Africa

Looking back at an historic meeting of African writers in Uganda in 1962, whose commonality was writing in the English language, Kenyan novelist and playwright Ngũgĩ wa Thiong'o lamented in the mid-1980s:

> We never asked ourselves: how can we enrich our languages? How can we "prey" on the rich humanist and democratic heritage in the struggles of other peoples in other times and other places to enrich

Figure 13.1 Persepolis, written and directed by Vincent Paronnaud and Marjane Satrapi (France/USA, 2007), based on the graphic novel by Marjane Satrapi. Image courtesy of Sony Pictures Classics. Produced by 2.4.7. Films

> our own? Why not have Balzac, Tolstoy, Sholokov, Brecht, Lu Hsun, Pablo Neruda, H.C. Anderson, Kim Chi Ha, Marx, Lenin, Albert Einstein, Galileo, Aeschylus, Aristotle and Plato in African Languages? And why not create literary monuments in our own languages?[14]

While some of the African books of recent years that have received the greatest accolades in the West continue to be written in English or French, such as Ben Okri's visually rich *The Famished Road*, which won the 1991 Booker Prize in the UK but has yet to be adapted, and MacArthur Genius Grant recipient Chimamanda Ngozi Adichie's *Half of a Yellow Sun*, which was adapted into a Nigerian film in 2013, Ngũgĩ's own highly acclaimed 2006 novel, *Wizard of the Crow*, was written in Kikuyu.[15] For those of us who are tired of formula movies with thin plots and little meaning – whether in Hollywood or Nollywood – there is a wealth of material available for adaptation in a variety of African cultures today.

International Perspectives in a Global World

Adaptation not only allows us to bring great classic stories to life in new forms that new generations can appreciate, but it helps to preserve classic art forms such as the English social dancing seen in Ang Lee's traditional adaptation of *Sense and Sensibility* (USA/UK, 1995), the Indian poetry referenced in *Kandukondain, Kandukondain* (*I Have Found It*, India, 2000), the Korean *p'ansori* of *Chunhyang* (South Korea, 2000), the Peking Opera of *Farewell, My Concubine* (China/Hong Kong, 1993), and the Chinese shadow puppetry of *To Live* (China/Hong Kong, 1994).

Zhang Yimou, in discussing the power of visual effects to "dissolve boundaries,"[16] also cautions us, however, that there is a dangerous side to the transmission of images worldwide:

> It might be a transitional historical development; however, I think the mass duplication of American popular culture, Hollywood films, popular songs from Taiwan or Hong Kong, or the mass idolization of pop stars by youngsters can strangle the very personality of our urban culture.[17]

Furthermore, Zhang Yimou claims:

> [L]ocal trends will be assimilated into global trends when images cross national or geographical boundaries. And it is only logical to predict such global assimilation through mass media will go on at a breakneck speed. My view towards globalization is that individuality should always conquer conformity. As a filmmaker is a creator, a creator must have originality, be it fashionable or unfashionable. And to be original is to be unique, to be different.[18]

Zhang Yimou and his screenwriters have mostly worked on adaptations, not from original screenplays. Yet even when adapting someone else's unique vision, you still have the opportunity to play a unique duet with the original author's voice, by channeling him or her as your double or by adding a further dimension of your own experiences and insights.

Notes

1 Robert McKee, *Story: Style, Structure, Substance, and the Principles of Screenwriting* (New York: HarperCollins, 1997).
2 Wang Tianbing and Lu Wei, "When Will the Chinese Movie Industry Grow Up?" Tianya, Haikou City, Hainan Province, China: 2006, referred to in Wang Tianbing, "Preface: To get to know Lu Wei and understand the secret of movie-making," in Lu Wei and Wang Tianbing, *The Secret of Screenwriting* (Shanghai: Shanghai Jiao Tong University Press, 2013), trans. by May Wu, 5.
3 Wang, "Preface," 5.
4 Wang, "Preface," 3.
5 Wang, "Preface," 3.
6 Wang, "Preface," 3.
7 "Mōri Motonari," Wikipedia.org, accessed April 13, 2017, https://en.wikipedia.org/wiki/M%C5%8Dri_Motonari.
8 Juan Mascaró, "Introduction," *The Baghavad Ghita* (New York: Penguin Classics, 1962), 9–10.
9 Shemi Zarhin, *Bonjour Monsieur Shlomi (Hakochavin Shel Shlomi*, Israel: United King Films, 2003), directed by Shemi Zarhin. The Latino adaptation was written by Ligiah Villalobos for Salma Hayek's company, but in the aftermath of the writers' strike, with the director Rodrigo Garcia busy on another film, it remained unproduced.
10 Ramat Hasharon, *Bonjour Monsieur Shlomi* (Israel: United King Films, 2003).
11 Ligiah Villalobos, interviewed by author via email, September 9, 2016.
12 Marjane Satrapi, quoted in Laurie Koh, "The Voice of Dissent: Marjane Satrapi Draws a Revolution in Persepolis," *Film Arts: The Magazine of the Independent Filmmaker* (March–April, 2008), 16.
13 Strapi in Koh, "The Voice of Dissent," 16.

14 Ngũgĩ Wa Thiong'o, *Decolonising the Mind: The Politics of Language in African Literature* (Rochester, NY: James Currey, 1986), 8.
15 Ben Okri, *The Famished Road* (New York: Nan A. Talese, 1991); Chimamanda Ngozi Adichie, *Half of a Yellow Sun* (New York: Knopf/Anchor, 2006); Ngũgĩ wa Thiong'o, *Wizard of the Crow* (London: Harvill Secker, 2006).
16 Zhang Yimou, quoted in Kwok-Kan Tam, "Cinema and Zhang Yimou," 1996, in Frances Gateward, *Zhang Yimou: Interviews* (Jackson, MS: University of Mississippi Press, 2001), 110.
17 Zhang in Tam, "Cinema and Zhang Yimou," 108.
18 Zhang in Tam, "Cinema and Zhang Yimou," 110.

Part VI

Modern Perspectives on Romance

FOURTEEN

Love and Romance Adaptations

Hollywood and the Harlequin Plot

Why deal with romance? One reason might be its total annual sales value of $1.08 billion,[1] with this genre representing 34 percent of the fiction market in the US alone.[2] "More than 44 million print and 28 million electronic romance books were sold in 2015,"[3] presenting a vast array of work in this genre, some of which may be worth adapting. Romance also prevails in the music industry, which grossed $42.93 billion globally in 2016, a higher figure than the global box office revenue of films in all genres.[4] Remembering Godard's words, "Money is the language of film," we can cash in on romance, and we can revolutionize it.

Before 1960, the main plot of 85 percent of all Hollywood films was romance.[5] Today, romance maintains a second class status as subplot – unless *La La Land* (USA, 2016) represents a breakthrough and not just a moment of nostalgic glory. Teenage boys determine the film market with their love of action adventure, even though lower budgeted films in which romance often plays a vital role sometimes give a greater return in relation to their production costs than action films. What may be secondary, at best, to the men who green-light mainstream films – and they are almost always men – is still central to the lives of most women. Yet love and romance also affect – willingly or otherwise – the lives of most men.

Film, television, cable and internet producers, writers, and directors have an obligation to become master alchemists of love. Most romance films are stuck in the heady first stage of love, when phenylethylamine (PEA) allows us to make love for hours on end – a stage which lasts only "six months or two years, if you're lucky."[6] We ignore the stories implicit in the rest of the time line, although the problems of love and the end of love are rife with dramatic potential. As student Chelsea Matthews has stated, "Staying together through the hard times is what makes the audience hopeful for a happy romantic relationship."[7]

Independent and experimental cinema, cable television, and webisodes – to which women, minority, and LGBT filmmakers have greater access – have dealt with these issues for years, while mainstream cinema lags behind. By taking heed of cultural critics such as bell hooks, who states: "Profound changes in the way we think and act must take place if we are to create a loving culture,"[8] a lucrative new market can finally be realized.

Love in China

Mo Yan's novel, *Red Sorghum,* asks, "What is love?" Through the tempestuous love affairs of the film adaptation, the question is answered visually and dramatically, with great eroticism in the acting. But the novel goes further in its definitions:

> The first ingredient of love – fanaticism – is composed of heart-piercing suffering: the blood flows through the intestines and bowels, and out the body as feces the consistency of pitch. The second ingredient – cruelty – is composed of merciless criticism: each partner in the love affair wants to skin the other alive, physically and psychologically. They both want to rip out each other's blood vessels, muscles, and every writhing internal organ, including the heart. The third ingredient – frigidity – is composed of a protracted heavy silence. Icy emotions frost the faces of people in love. Their teeth chatter so violently they can't talk, no matter how badly they want to.[9]

Love in Japan

The Tale of Genji by Murasaki Shikibu, completed in 1021 CE in Japan, is the world's first novel still considered to be a classic. Like Dante Alighieri's *The Divine Comedy*, it was written in the vernacular of its culture: In Dante's case, Italian instead of Latin; in Shikibu's, Japanese instead of the Chinese preferred by many writers and scholars of the Heian Era. However, instead of being a religious journey through Hell, Purgatory, and Heaven, *The Tale of Genji* recounts the many love affairs of a handsome and noble prince. It seems to lack any structure: as described in the novel *Sex and the Cyborg Goddess*, Shikibu's novel remains

> without any real suspense until the last chapter, well after the main protagonist had already died – not that Murasaki Shikibu had indicated how or when he died. And the ending was so abrupt, leaving it up in the air whether or not the girl who'd tried to drown herself would be dragged back to the general, or be left a nun, hidden away from the floating world.[10]

Yet the exploits of Prince Genji, "who seem[s] to have hidden beautiful courtesans in every corner of each of his palaces, each one of them drenching the corners of her kimono with more and more tears,"[11] is highly addictive in its beauty and nuances of tone.

Film, television, and the internet are the "vernacular" media of our time: college students spend more time at their computers and television sets than reading books, which may help explain why *The Tale of Genji* has lived on in so many adaptations including movies, anime, and "twenty-odd manga versions."[12] In one adaptation of *The Tale of Genji*, Horikawa Tonko's film, *Love of a Thousand Years: The Tale of Genji* (*Se'nen no koi: Hikaru Genji monogatari*, Japan, 2001), the famous writer Murasaki Shikibu teaches Empress Shoshi – "in other words, incorporating the author into the film as a kind of story within a story."[13]

Gay and Lesbian Love Story Adaptations

When Amy writes at the end of *Gone Girl*, "We are on the eve of becoming the world's best, brightest nuclear family,"[14] we take her words as false and ironic. The novel has thoroughly deconstructed this possibility at the same time as manifesting its veneer. Flynn has taken her characters to the nearest decimal point before what McKee calls "the end of the line": they've done everything they possible could other than turn gay.[15]

Passionate and problematic love stories with gay and lesbian characters abound in contemporary literature and film adaptations such as *Aimee and Jaguar* (Germany, 1999), *Brokeback Mountain* (USA/Canada, 2005), *Moonlight* (USA, 2016), and *The Handmaiden* (South Korea, 2016).

In *Moonlight*, the charged silence that Barry Jenkins uses conveys even more passion and longing than stated words of dialogue. A screenwriter must be careful not to be seduced by the power of language. When his characters don't talk, it opens up a greater opportunity for the audience to identify with the longing his characters feel for each other, regardless of our individual sexual preferences.

Jenkins describes bringing one such scene to the screen in directing his screenplay of *Moonlight*, based on an unproduced play by Tarell Alvin McCraney that was already more visual than talky:

> So Trevante Rhodes hangs up the phone, sits on the bed, puts the phone against his head, he's rubbing the phone against his forehead, he lays back, looks at the screen, and the phone drops to his chest. That's how, through concrete imagery, you're revealing the interior of the character to the actor, and the actor can perform and externalize it onscreen without resorting to voiceover – which I'm a fan of but I try not to lean on.[16]

What *Moonlight* offers the gay community, the black community, and because of its powerful universality, everyone who is searching for love – sometimes after a lifetime of being misunderstood – is hope.

While gay and lesbian literature of the mid-twentieth century often ended in broken hearts and suicide, to the dismay of the LGBT community, more recent novels have ended happily, including a more positive depiction of same-sex eroticism. The doctoral dissertation of Sarah Waters focused on lesbian and gay fiction from 1870 to the present.[17] Waters built on her dissertation as a bestselling British author of lesbian literature. Her novel *Fingersmith*,[18] set in mid-nineteenth-century England, is about a young thief named Sue, who goes along with a con man's scheme that she pretend to be a maid and convince Maud Lilly to marry him, so they can lock the gentlewoman in a madhouse and share her fortune. In the process, however, Maud and Sue fall for each other, although they can't admit it to the world at large.

Part Two of the novel delineates at great length the torturous deception that Maud encounters after marrying Gentleman, before his ultimate demise. Dragged to Mrs. Sucksby's den of iniquity in the most depraved part of London, where Gentleman and Mrs. Sucksby intended to pass her off as the thieving Sue in order for them to benefit from Maud's stolen inheritance, she is finally made to see the truth of her upbringing.

> "Go on, Mrs Sucksby ... Tell the rest. As for you, Maud: listen hard, and know at last what your life was lived for."
>
> "My life was not lived," I say in a whisper. "You have told me, it was a fiction."
>
> "Well" – he finds a match, and strikes it – "fictions must end. Hear now how yours is too."[19]

Similarly, in Part Three, when the illiterate maid Sue is sent to the madhouse in a spine-chilling reversal (as the reader has assumed that Maud, the recently married Mrs. Rivers, will end up there instead, making Sue rich), the doctor believes that Sue is really Mrs. Rivers, and will punish her cruelly for her fantastical alibis and for not being able to read.

> "Terrible plots? Laughing villains? Stolen fortunes and girls made out to be mad? The stuff of lurid fiction! We have a name for your disease. We call it a hyper-aesthetic one. You have been encouraged to over-indulge yourself in literature; and have inflamed your organs of fancy."[20]

Chan-Wook Park's *The Handmaiden* resets *Fingersmith* in 1930s Korea during Japanese colonial rule.[21] In the screenplay by Chung Seo-Kyung and Chan-Wook Park, Miss Hideko (Maud) tries to hang herself, but is saved by Sookee (her maid), who admits she wanted to trick Miss Hideko – and is told that *she*, the maid, is being tricked to go to the madhouse. The surprise element of the novel is missing along with the stench and overall realism of the madhouse, truncating at least two hundred pages of Maud and Sue's parallel miseries. But the film is far more intense, due to the splendor of its visual eroticism, landscapes and architecture augmented by extraordinary cinematography. It also reworks the class issues that Sarah Waters raised in her British-based novel by contrasting

Figure 14.1 The Handmaiden, directed by Chan-wook Park, written by Seo-Kyung Chung and Chan-wook Park (South Korea, 2016), based on the novel *Fingersmith* by Sarah Waters. Image courtesy of Amazon Studios. Produced by Moho Film and Yong Film

its decadent, colonializing Japanese antagonists to desperate Koreans who will try any scheme to help them survive.

The Handmaiden's plot provides extra layers of fantasy that weren't in the novel: Miss Hideko brings Sookee to her uncle's library and shows her maid his rare collection of pornographic books, which the maid tears up, kicking them into one of the reflecting pools. Then the two women run off together. (In the novel, Sue knows nothing about the perverse collection until the very end.) Elsewhere in the film, Uncle Kouzuki says, "A story is all about the journey," wanting to hear about Count Fujiwara's wedding night.

Instead of the triple she-said construction (Maud's, Sue's, and Mrs. Sucksby's accounts), *The Handmaiden* gives the novel's primary antagonist Gentleman more of a backstory in Count Fujiwara's own perverse perspective, making it a she-said, she-said, he-said story. Mrs. Sucksby is a forgettable part of the general depravity of the handmaiden's poor background, never revived in the end. Instead, the film shows Count Fujiwara committing suicide and killing Uncle Kouzuki with mercury-laced cigarettes, whose smoke fills the library after Kouzuki has chopped off Fujiwara's fingers. (Fujiwara says, as he expires, that at least he is dying "with his cock intact.") In the novel, he is murdered, presumably by a vengeful Maud, but Mrs. Sucksby takes the rap and hangs for it.

Ultimately, the exquisite cinematography by Chung-hoon Chung provides another important narrative perspective – the ultimate, ironic "male gaze" layer of visual commentary when the lovers reunite. Miss Hideko and Sookee take their cue for their final lovemaking scene from the lesbian pornography that Miss Hideko's uncle had forced her to read out loud to entertain the men in his library, and it's also shot from a voyeuristic male perspective, not each other's. This is especially ironic as earlier lesbian scenes were much more intimate, with the camera eye in sync with this multi-layered story's suspension of disbelief. The novel ends with Maud, now co-inheritor of the estate, showing Sue the pornography that she herself is now writing professionally. The film's ending serves as a reminder that audiences watching an erotic thriller can sometimes be swindled by the screenwriter, director, and cinematographer just as the characters of the novel and adaptation make it their business to swindle one another. What's exciting – even tantalizing – is how they do it.

Notes

1 "Romance Statistics" Romance Writers of America, figure for 2013, accessed March 8, 2017, www.rwa.org/p/cm/ld/fid=580.
2 "Romance Statistics" Romance Writers of America figure for 2015, accessed August 23, 2017, www.rwa.org/p/cm/ld/fid=580.
3 "A Profitable Affair: Opportunities for Publishers in the Romance Book Market," Nielsen.com, July 5, 2016, accessed March 8, 2017, www.nielsen.com/us/en/insights/news/2016/a-profitable-affair-opportunities-for-publishers-in-the-romance-book-market.html.
4 "Statistics and Facts about Music Industry in the U.S.," Statista.com, accessed March 8, 2017, www.statista.com/topics/1639/music and "Statistics and Facts about the Film Industry," Statista.com, accessed March 8, 2017, www.statista.com/topics/964/film.
5 Virginia Wright Wexman, *Creating the Couple: Love, Marriage, and Hollywood Performance* (Princeton, NJ: Princeton University Press, 1993), 3. Wexman cites the study *The Classical Hollywood Cinema* by David Bordwell, Janet Staiger, and Kristin Thompson for this data.
6 Pat Love, "What Is This Thing Called Love?" *Family Therapy Networkers: Psychotherapy and Modern Life*, 23(2) (March/April, 1999), 37.
7 Chelsea Matthews, mini-theme assignment: "Manifesto to Hollywood," CTVA 309, "Film As Literature," California State University, Northridge, December 8, 2014, 2.
8 bell hooks, *All About Love: New Visions* (New York: William Morrow, 2000), p. xxiv.
9 Mo Yan, *Red Sorghum* (New York: Viking Press, 1993), 272–273.
10 Alexis Rafael, *Sex and the Cyborg Goddess* (Los Angeles, CA: Amazon, 2017), 32.
11 Rafael, *Sex and the Cyborg Goddess*, 31.
12 Lynne K. Miyake, "Graphically Speaking: Manga Versions of 'The Tale of Genji,' in "Monumenta Nipponica, 63(2) (Autumn, 2008), 359, accessed June 5, 2017, http://muse.jhu.edu/article/256376.
13 Lynne K. Miyake, email to Alexis Krasilovsky, July 4, 2013.
14 Gillian Flynn, *Gone Girl* (New York: Crown Publishers, 2012), 415.
15 Robert McKee, *Story: Style, Structure, Substance, and the Principles of Screenwriting* (New York: HarperCollins, 1997), 319–320.
16 Barry Jenkins, quoted in Ernest Hardy, "Dancing in Serious Moonlight," *Written By*, 21(2) (February–March, 2017), 36.
17 Sarah Waters, "Wolfskins and Togas: Lesbian and Gay Historical Fictions, 1870 to the Present" (doctoral dissertation, Queen Mary, University of London, London, 1995).
18 Sarah Waters, *Fingersmith* (New York: Riverhead Books, 2002).
19 Waters, *Fingersmith*, 357.
20 Waters, *Fingersmith*, 447.
21 Park Chan-Wook and Chung Seo-Kyung, *The Handmaiden,* directed by Park Chan-Wook (Wook, Seoul: Moho Film, 2016); inspired by the novel *Fingersmith* by Sarah Waters.

Part VII

Bringing Up the Classics

FIFTEEN

From Ancient Greece to Hollywood and Nollywood

Some Ancient Greeks in Modern Times

It's possible to criss-cross back and forth between literature and cinema when it comes to how Homer's eighth-century BCE epic poem the *Odyssey* is retold in the novels of James Joyce, Thomas Wolfe, and Alberto Moravia, and a variety of films and television programs, such as the Japanese-French anime, *Ulysses 31* (1981), a television series which "updates the ancient setting into a 31st-century space opera."[1]

The Coen Brothers' *O Brother, Where Art Thou?* (USA, 2000), set in the Deep South of 1930s America, plays with sections of the *Odyssey* in which "Odysseus warns his men against killing the sacred oxen that belong to the sun god Helios, but his men slaughter the cow anyway and Odysseus' ship is struck by lightning, killing all but him."[2] The Coen Brothers' characters make reference to the cow motif as the film progresses. As Gabriel Walter observes:

> George "Baby Face" Nelson, the notorious bank robber ... starts shooting at the cops and then at a herd of cattle. Delmar remarks, "Oh, George, not the livestock." At the end of the film, George is sent to the electric chair, and during the parade to the execution, someone leading a cow behind the mob yells, "Cow killer!"[3]

However, as A.O. Scott has pointed out, *O Brother, Where Art Thou?* is less a retelling of the founding epic of Western civilization than a portable anthology of Americana, a tinker's van festooned with scraps of *Moby-Dick*, *The Wizard of Oz* and Preston Sturges's *Sullivan's Travels*, the source of the film's title."[4]

An Italian novel in which a screenwriter and a director fight it out about how best to adapt the *Odyssey* is Alberto Moravia's *Il Disprezzo* (also known as *A Ghost at Noon*),[5] written almost fifty years before the Coen Brothers took such liberties with Homer's epic poem. *Il Disprezzo* was in turn adapted by Jean-Luc Godard as the film *Contempt* (France, 1963), a contemptible exploitation of Moravia's novel about movie exploitation, starring Brigitte Bardot.

Eleazar Meletinsky, in his book *The Poetics of Myth*, describes the set-up to Moravia's rambunctious screenwriter-producer-director team as follows:

> The protagonist, Molteni, a screenwriter, is asked by a producer named Battista to write a screen treatment of Homer's Odyssey. Battista intends to transform the Odyssey into a Hollywood-type spectacular, but the German director Rheingold wants a psychoanalytic approach to the theme.[6]

Molteni says to Rheingold, the German director:

> "No, Homer's Odyssey is not yours, Rheingold. And I'll say more, since you force me to it: I find Homer's Odyssey altogether enchanting and yours altogether repulsive!"
>
> "Molteni." This time Rheingold appeared really indignant.
>
> "Yes, to me it's repulsive," I went on, becoming heated now, "this desire of yours to reduce, to debase the Homeric hero just because we're incapable of making him as Homer created him, this operation of systematic degradation is repulsive to me, and I'm not going to take part in it at any price."

Moleni proceeds to ask the director if he's even read *Ulysses*, James Joyce's masterpiece of English literature written in 1940. It's a particularly insulting question for the 1940s–1950s, when there were at least forty books published that were based on the classics.

> "I've read everything that concerns the Odyssey," replied Rheingold in a deeply offended tone, "but you..."
>
> "Well," I continued passionately, "Joyce ... made Ulysses a cuckold, an onanist, an idler, a capricious, incompetent creature ... [and] Penelope a retired whore ... Circe a visit to a brothel, and the return to Ithaca the return home at dead of night through the streets of Dublin, with a stop or two on the way to piss in a dark corner. But at least Joyce had the discernment not to bring in the Mediterranean ... He placed the whole story in the muddy streets of a northern city, in taverns and brothels, in bedrooms and lavatories ... everything modern, in other words debased, degraded, reduced to our own miserable stature. But you – you lack Joyce's discretion."[7]

Of course, Godard's adaptation of Moravia's novel about the *Odyssey* takes place precisely on the Mediterranean, the better to observe Brigitte Bardot's body sunning on a yacht.

Similarly to James Joyce's *Ulysses*, *The Bacchae of Euripides* by Africa's first Nobel laureate, Wole Soyinka, reset an ancient Greek story into a modern locale – in Soyinka's case, Nigeria during a period of civil unrest. Commissioned by the National Theatre in London in 1973, *The Bacchae of Euripides* was written and performed in English,[8] unlike Bruno Coppola's faithful film adaptation, *The Bacchae* (Greece, 2010), which was produced for the National Theatre of Northern Greece. Soyinka also adapted one of his own plays into the screenplay for a film: *Kongi's Harvest* (Nigeria, 1970), starring Soyinka as an African dictator. Directed by American Ossie Davis, it was also in English.

However, in 1984, Kenyan novelist and critic Ngũgĩ wa Thiong'o called for African writers to explore their own cultural traditions, and bemoaned the impoverishment of being trapped by their exposure to the European novel specifically, and having to write in English, French or Portuguese, instead of in their own languages:

> The brilliant minds of a Chinua Achebe, a Wole Soyinka or a Kofi Awoonor want not to revitalize the African novel but to create a new tradition, that of the Afro-European novel.[9]

In fact, in addition to his novels and plays, Wole Soyinka had directed a Nigerian narrative film in 1983 about politics, entitled *Blues for a Prodigal*, that was partly in the Yoruba language, but it was seized at its premiere in Lagos because of its critical stance against the government.[10] Dapo Adeluga of the University of Ibadan praised Soyinka's *Blues for a Prodigal* partly for using a variety of languages:

> The use of Yoruba and its dialects and of a few other Nigerian languages, of English (including Pidgin) in its varieties carries further Soyinka's attempt to use language in a manner that would more readily reach the majority of his audience than the "difficult" intellectual dramas of which many critics have complained, albeit unjustly, in the past. This film establishes Wole Soyinka as a multi-talented artist with a strong fascination with the medium of the cinema and a vibrant awareness of current trends in film-making.[11]

More recently, Nollywood director Tunde Kelani directed a Yoruba-language adaptation of Femi Osofisan's novella *Maami*,[12] a story about a poverty-stricken single mother and her young son. Kelani has stated that a central concern of his in the making of *Maami* (Nigeria, 2011) and other films, is "[celebrating] writers and their work" and exposing books "to what he sees as a public that reads less and less."[13]

Ancient Greek mythology is also at work in Barry Jenkins' Oscar-winning film *Moonlight* (USA, 2016): its protagonist is named Chiron after a centaur mentioned in Homer's *Iliad* and known for self-healing. But in *Moonlight*'s Act One, as a little boy, Chiron is mostly referred to as "Little" (with overtones of Malcolm Little, before Islam transformed him into Malcolm X), and later, as a grown man, struggling with self-identity issues behind his drug dealer mask, as "Black." Tarell Alvin

McCraney, author of the original source material on which *Moonlight* was based, explains:

> The notion of a wounded healer was really important to me, the story of how Chiron takes Zeus's unwanted children and raises them in this other place ... I just wanted to remind myself that this goes back into antiquity. The name itself had a great weight to it.[14]

McCraney points out that myths and legends are used "in everyday life to tell our origin stories and to tell who we are," whether they're the mythological characters used by Shakespeare "in order to explode them," or characters based on the Yoruba gods of Western Africa:[15]

> To me, it's the same thing – it's about finding out why our ancestors used these origin stories and these myths to talk about their everyday life; it's probably because they were dealing with the same thing.[16]

Shakespeare Then and Now: The Many Romeos and Juliets

Even before the talkies were invented, permitting movie audiences to hear Shakespeare's dialogue, several theatrical-looking adaptations of Shakespeare's *Romeo and Juliet* were produced, among many of his other plays. These silent productions included the Gaumont Company's *Romeo and Juliet* (UK, 1908), the Vitagraph Company's *Romeo and Juliet* (USA, 1908), Film d'Arte Italiana's *Romeo and Juliet* (Italy, 1911), and Vitagraph's *Indian Romeo and Juliet* (USA, 1912), in which, according to Judith Buchanan, a "Native American landscape becomes the backdrop for the story which focuses on the forbidden romance, secret marriage and tragic ending of a Mohican princess and a young Huron brave."[17] Buchanan also describes two American *Romeo and Juliet* productions – one by Fox and the other by Metro – made for the tercentenary of Shakespeare's death in 1916.[18]

The Moving Picture World of August 19, 1911, reviewed the two-reel (half-hour) American adaptation of *Romeo and Juliet* produced by the Thanhouser Corporation in 1911, comparing it to Vitagraph's one-reel production of 1908:

> This is the first attempt of an Independent manufacturer to produce a two-reel attraction ... The Vitagraph story was excellently well told, the acting was superb, the settings magnificent, the adaptation clever. The two-reel production, however, makes the story plainer to a person who has never read the classic tragedy ... The Thanhouser adaptation ... makes the story very plain to every grade of intelligence, a merit which cannot be estimated too highly.[19]

A rave review for an adaptation of a play without spoken dialogue is all the more astounding when one considers the tediousness of George

Cukor's *Romeo and Juliet* (USA, 1936), where the characters actually talk. While screenwriter Talbot Jennings only used around 45 percent of Shakespeare's dialogue,[20] the characters seem to drone on forever, partly due to the miscasting of its stars. For what should be a love story between two young lovers – Juliet is about to turn fourteen in the play, and Romeo is only somewhat older – Norma Shearer was thirty-four when she played Juliet, Leslie Howard was a forty-three-year-old Romeo, and John Barrymore was in his mid-fifties, playing a teenage (or possibly 20-something) Mercutio.

In 1961, an adaptation of a successful 1957 Broadway musical, *West Side Story*, that was based on Shakespeare's *Romeo and Juliet*, won ten Oscars – the most that a film in the musical genre had ever won. Originally, the writers intended one of the gangs to be Jewish, in order to deal with the anti-Semitism of 1950s America; the other was meant to be Polish-American. This was changed to a Puerto Rican gang and a white gang, although the lead Puerto Rican character was played by a non-Puerto Rican, Natalie Wood.

Franco Zeffirelli successfully directed and co-wrote a more faithful adaptation of Shakespeare's story of the star-crossed lovers by casting much younger actors for his *Romeo and Juliet* (UK/Italy, 1968) and filming most of the story in beautiful, romantic Italian locations with only a few street scenes shot on a studio set.

Among other adaptations of *Romeo and Juliet* is Mira Nair's *Mississippi Masala* (UK/USA, 1991), written by Sooni Taraporevala. Set in Mississippi, this loose adaptation shows a love affair between an African-American man (played by Denzel Washington), and an Indian immigrant from Uganda, Africa, whose family was exiled along with other non-Africans by Idi Amin, making this a transnational Montague vs. Capulet story.

Baz Luhrmann's *Romeo + Juliet* (USA, 1996), co-written with Craig Pearce, updates the story to a modern-day Verona Beach, where two rival Mafia gangs equipped with guns, cars, and motorcycles spell doom for the star-crossed lovers played by Claire Danes and Leonardo DiCaprio. While the scenery and costumes are updated, the dialogue is not. However, in an interview with *Creative Screenwriting* after the film's release, Baz Luhrmann admitted to cutting the language of *Romeo and Juliet* by a third to one-half – perhaps less of a "crime" than Franco Zeffirelli, who, Luhrmann claimed, "rewrote extra dialogue."[21]

On being asked by interviewer Erik Bauer, "If Shakespeare was a contemporary filmmaker, what kind of movies do you think he'd be making?" Luhrmann replied:

> You can't answer that with any degree of certainty. ... What you can scientifically look at is the world in which he wrote these plays, and the fact that he was an actor in a company that was basically going broke. So he had to pack the house, a sort of 3,000-foot theater, with everybody from the street sweeper to the Queen of England, in the middle of the day, every day. You know, he just stole stories

> lock-stock-and-barrel. Whatever was popular. He stole "Romeo and Juliet" – it was the popular Italian novella at the time. He just stole it – adapted it virtually in a few days.[22]

Luhrmann is referring here to Matteo Bandello's "Romeo and Juliet," written in 1554,[23] the main elements of which, according to further research by Francisco Menendez, "are in existence in both *Il Novelino* (1476) and *Istoria novellamente ritovata* [sic] *di due Nobili Amanti* (c. 1530)." "Citing *Shakespeare's Sources* by Kenneth Muir,[24] which includes the poet Arthur Brooke," Menendez states that "there is no evidence that William Shakespeare knew of Arthur Brooke's sources," but rather, that Shakespeare would certainly have been familiar with Brooke's "long narrative English poem" of 1562, *The Tragical Historye of Romeus and Juliet* based on these earlier Italian works.[25] Furthermore,

> Shakespeare definitely improved the dramatic circumstances of Brooke's "Romeo and Juliet." Shakespeare made Juliet fourteen years old, much younger than the character in Brooke's poem, heightening the innocence and tragic loss of the tale. He also compressed the action of the play from the three months in Brooke's poem to four urgent days in which the action must take place. This strengthens the dramatic irony and the seemingly inevitable outcome of the story.[26]

E. Talbot Donaldson, an award-winning interpreter of medieval texts, also considers Brooke's poem "[t]he chief immediate source for Shakespeare's play."[27] For additional sources, it's hard to imagine that Shakespeare wouldn't have been familiar with Ovid's *Metamorphoses* (8 AD), in which two ill-fated love stories pertain: that of Orpheus and Euridice, and that of Pyramus and Thisbe, which a woman tells her sister, while spinning wool:

> There once was a handsome youth named Pyramus, and next
> Door lived the loveliest girl in the East, whose parents had called her
> Thisbe. These two became acquaintances, friends, and, in time,
> There was love that ought to have led to marriage, but the parents
> Of both, displeased, wanted something better or richer...[28]

In *Troilus and Criseyde* by Geoffrey Chaucer (c. 1342–1400), we have a story of ancient love that, as literary scholar Robert Adams has noted, implicitly predates Chaucer:

> [A]nd "as I rede" plainly characterizes the narrator as here not a dreamer or a pilgrim but a reader, retelling for the benefit of modern lovers as much of this story of ancient love as he can discover in his "olde books." Yet this most avowedly bookish of all Chaucer's works is also his most immediately vivid and absorbing – so much so that it has been described as "the first modern novel."[29]

Chaucer's own source was Boccaccio's *Il Filostrato* (1338), whose source in turn was Guido delle Colonne's Latin version of a twelfth-century Trojan legend as told in French by Benoît de Sainte-Maure. While Shakespeare would have been directly influenced by at least some of these sources in writing his much darker play of lovers stymied in a world of political strife, *Troilus and Cressida* (1602), they may have indirectly influenced his earlier play, *Romeo and Juliet* (1591–1595) as well.

A writer as obsessed with love as with his writing becomes the theme of John Madden's romantic comedy, *Shakespeare in Love* (USA/UK, 1998), written by Marc Norman and playwright Tom Stoppard. Through a series of imaginary events that may have inspired a hot-blooded young Shakespeare to write his masterpiece, the film simultaneously parodies and celebrates the writing process, rehearsals, and first performance of *Romeo and Juliet*.

Of writing *Shakespeare in Love*, Stoppard says:

> As with all fiction involving historical characters the story is taking place in a parallel world. One is making a fairy tale out of the life of a genius who lived. It's rather helpful to the people who are telling the story that so little is known about William Shakespeare because it means that you can use quite a lot without contradicting other things that might have been known about him. So this fiction which exists in the parallel world of the filmmaker's imagination coalesces with the historical Shakespeare without contradicting him.[30]

Crime and Punishment Redux

Dostoevsky's *Crime and Punishment* starts with a student who owes his landlady rent, a predicament with which some of the readers of this book may identify:

> [F]or some time past, he had been in an overstrained, irritable condition, verging on hypochondria. He had become so completely absorbed in himself, and isolated from his fellows that he dreaded meeting, not only his landlady, but any one at all. He was crushed by poverty, but the anxieties of his position had of late ceased to weigh upon him. He had given up attending to matters of practical importance; he had lost all desire to do so.[31]

If you think that you don't have a chance in hell of ever writing an adaptation that will cover not only your rent, but a spread in Malibu and a decade's worth of spec scriptwriting time, then you are exempt from reading the rest of this chapter. Otherwise, you may wish to take this opportunity to study one of adaptation's best examples. Writer/Director Woody Allen's *Match Point* (UK/Ireland/Luxembourg, 2005) begins with socially ambitious tennis instructor Chris Wilton (played by Jonathan Rhys Meyers) reading *Crime and Punishment*, the psychologically penetrating novel that soon segues from Raskolnikov's financial predicament to the idea of getting away with murder. The close-up of the book in Chris' hands, emblazoned with the title *Crime and Punishment*, clues us in immediately to its serving as a major reference for Woody Allen; however, it was not the only creative work that influenced *Match Point*.

For a more faithful adaptation of Dostoevsky's 1866 novel, Pierre Chenal's *Crime and Punishment* (France, 1935) follows the storyline of the novel, though it resets it in Paris. It was highly applauded for the psychological realism of its actors' performances, with Harry Baur as the inspector and Pierre Blanchard as Raskolnikov, the dropout law student. Josef von Sternberg's Hollywood version starring Peter Lorre and Edward Arnold also appeared in 1935. Other adaptations include *Crime and Punishment* (USSR, 1970), *Crime and Punishment* (Finland, 1983), and *Crime and Punishment* (Australia, 2015).

Alfred Hitchcock's psychological thriller, *Strangers on a Train* (USA, 1951), also deals with the idea of murder. In this film, written by Raymond Chandler and Czenzi Ormond, a professional tennis player meets a criminal on a train, who tells him of a plan for a perfect murder: each man will kill the other's victim without leaving any clues behind. The tennis player agrees, and the criminal murders the tennis player's wife. Woody Allen uses elements of this story in his own plot, where a former tennis pro meets a friend's sister and begins to date her, ultimately murdering another woman in a choice of lust for social position over love. Can he get away with it? His guilt goes right back to *Crime and Punishment*.

Woody Allen loves culture just as much as the critic-turned-filmmaker François Truffaut loved books. In addition to novels, plays, and films, Allen includes references to Donizetti's opera, *L'Elisir d'amore* or *The Elixir of Love* (1832) – about a poor man in love with a wealthy woman – and Verdi's opera *La Traviata* (1853), which is based on *La Dame aux camélias* (1852), a play that was in turn an adaptation of Alexandre Dumas, fils' novel (1848) with the same title. Why *La Traviata*? Maybe because the opera (which also influenced Baz Luhrmann's *Moulin Rouge*) deals with the idea of true love versus a realistic appraisal of the role love can play in surviving financially. Another reason for using opera in *Match Point* is that it's a costly art form appreciated by the wealthy, demonstrating Chris' desire to move up the social ladder. Aesthetically, the operas don't always match the action: Verdi's *Othello* (1887) is included in the soundtrack, but as Charalampos Goyios points out, the lyrics have no correlation to what's happening on screen – although there is that lingering feeling that Othello, who kills his beloved wife, is one more layer of Chris, who loves Nola, the pregnant lover whom he kills in order to marry a richer woman.[32] There's also a musical in the soundtrack while he murders the old woman who lives downstairs from Nola: It's *The Woman in White* by Andrew Lloyd Webber. The musical is based on a novel by Wilkie Collins (1859) that deals with murder and intrigue, which itself led to many film, television, and computer game adaptations as well

Figure 15.1 Woody Allen's *Match Point* (UK/Ireland/Luxembourg, 2005): Chris Wilton (Jonathan Rhys Meyers) wants to do away with Nola Rice (Scarlett Johansson), if he can get away with murder. Image courtesy of Icon Film Distribution. Produced by BBC Films, Thema Production, Jada Productions, and Kudu Films

as inspiring the plot of Sarah Waters' novel *Fingersmith*[33] – which was recently adapted as *The Handmaiden* (South Korea, 2006).

We can go dizzy listening to these medleys of referentiality! In the book *Referentiality and the Films of Woody Allen*, film scholar and director D.E. Wynter points out that the lyrics of the musical *The Woman in White,* ending in "I had to drown your bastard. / I had no other choice. / Before the child was due, / I'd had enough of you,"[34] form "essentially the climax of *Match Point*."[35]

Later in *Match Point*, we see Chris' fiancée Chloe asking him, "Have you seen my Strindberg book?" – a book which we find Chris reading while Nola storms out in the rain. Wynter has discovered that

> Allen derives the infrastructure for the relationship between the two main characters in *Match Point* from August Strindberg's *Miss Julie* (1888) and constructs his thematic examination of the unpunished criminal upon the narrative groundwork laid by Strindberg in his plays *There Are Crimes and Crimes* (1899) and *Pariah*, a one-act play (1889).[36]

As Wynter points out, both *Miss Julie* and *Match Point* take place in "a lavish country estate,"[37] both of their male leads mimic the upper class in order to fit in and advance themselves in the world,[38] and both female protagonists manifest their "internal oppression" by acting inappropriately, with tragic consequences.[39] Peeling away the layers of referentiality still further, Wynter notes that "Allen and Strindberg both allude heavily to *The Tragedy of Macbeth* in the final acts of *Match Point* and *There Are Crimes and Crimes*, respectively."[40]

That Woody Allen loves to borrow from culture is not always seen as a positive. In "Game Set," Elbert Ventura comments:

> Ever the insecure arriviste, Allen has always been anxious to show his autodidactic erudition. A shot of Chris reading *Crime and Punishment* sees nothing more than a typical Allen name-check; a line like "We had an interesting conversation about Dostoevsky" can be dismissed as lazy shorthand signifying intellectual seriousness. But the references to Dostoevsky actually prove to be trenchant, serving as they do the film's thematic touchstone.[41]

Other notable works inspired by *Crime and Punishment* include Theodore Dreiser's novel, *An American Tragedy* (1925),[42] and Robert Bresson's film, *Pickpocket* (France, 1959). Dreiser's *An American Tragedy* shares the psychological depth of *Crime and Punishment*, but its plot was based on the 1906 murder of Grace Brown by a young man who was intent on moving up in the world socially once he could dispose of his working class girlfriend. The newspaper stories of the era detailing the court case and electrocution of Chester Gillette carried the world by storm, much like the O.J. Simpson trials of a later era. Dreiser's 800-page novel, exploring every detail of the story with obsessive power, inspired the Soviet director Sergei Eisenstein to write a screenplay adaptation of *An American Tragedy* for Paramount Studios during his visit to Hollywood in 1930, but he was unsuccessful in convincing the studio to go ahead with it. Instead, the film project went to director Josef von Sternberg, whose *An American Tragedy* (USA, 1931), written by Samuel Hoffenstein, was intensely disliked by Dreiser. However, even worse is *A Place in the Sun*, the 1951 Hollywood adaptation of Dreiser's *An American Tragedy* and a 1926 play that was also based on the novel. Despite winning its screenwriters Michael Wilson and Harry Brown an Oscar for Best Screenplay, among its several other Oscars, *A Place in the Sun* only wins one award in my book: Most Kitschy Adaptation.

Quite the opposite is Robert Bresson's *Pickpocket* (France, 1959), a loose adaptation of Dostoevsky's novel. The plot of this film is similar to *Crime and Punishment*, except that instead of murdering his mean old landlady, the protagonist (Michel) feels justified in pickpocketing similarly unworthy people to whom he feels vastly superior morally and intellectually, in order to finance his worthier life. However, Paul Schrader (who co-wrote the adaptation of Martin Scorsese's *Raging Bull)* points out in his book, *Transcendental Style in Film: Ozu, Bresson, Dreyer,* that Bresson "has an antipathy toward plot: 'I try more and more in my films to suppress what people call plot. Plot is a novelist's trick.'"[43] While many critics give Robert Bresson an outstanding rank in the pantheon of film as literature for exploring the spiritual underpinnings of his characters, Bresson himself would not have agreed to validating literature in relationship to filmic style. In the documentary *Au hasard Bresson* (West Germany, 1967), Bresson states: "I think the muse of painting can be friends with cinema, but the muse of literature can't really."[44] Bresson also disparages the relationship of theater to film as an art form:

> I believe all the elements: image, sound – and "sound" includes sound effects, dialogue and music – should affect and transform each other. Without transformation, it isn't art. That's why I consider today's cinema a reproduction, not a true art, because it's just a copy of another art: theater. If we want cinema to be a true, independent art, there must be transformation.[45]

Notes

1 "*Odyssey,*" Wikipedia.org, accessed April 5, 2017, https://en.wikipedia.org/wiki/Odyssey.
2 Book XII, "The Singing Sirens, and the Terrors of Scylla and Charybdis" and Book IV, "Odysseus and the Swineherd," in Homer, *The Odyssey* (New York: Mentor Classics, 1937), 140, 164, summarized by Gabriel Walter, Midterm Presentation essay, CTVA 420, "Screenplay Adaptation," Department of Cinema and Television Arts, California State University, Northridge, Spring 2011, 5.
3 Walter, 5.
4 A.O. Scott, "Movie Review: Hail, Ulysses, Escaped Convict," *New York Times*, December 22, 2000, accessed April 4, 2017, www.nytimes.com/movie/review?res=9C03E1D91F39F931A15751C1A9669C8B63.
5 Alberto Moravia, *Il Disprezzo* (Milan: Bompiani, 1954). Published in English as *Contempt*, trans. by Angus Davidson (New York: NYRB Classica, 2004). Also known as *A Ghost at Noon*.
6 Eleazar M. Meletinsky, *The Poetics of Myth*, trans. by Guy Lanoue and Alexandre Sadetsky (New York: Garland, 1998), 332.
7 Dialogue from the protagonist Molteni in Alberto Moravia, *Il Disprezzo* or *A Ghost at Noon* (1954) quoted in Meletinsky, *The Poetics of Myth*, 333.
8 Special thanks to Strongman Osom for his research into Nigerian author and screenwriter Wole Soyinka for CTVA 309, "Film As Literature," Department of Cinema and Television Arts, California State University, Northridge, December 17, 2012.
9 Ngũgĩ Wa Thiong'o, *Decolonising the Mind: The Politics of Language in African Literature* (Rochester, NY: James Currey, 1986), 70.
10 Maya Jaggi, "Ousting Monsters," *Guardian*, November 2, 2002, accessed April 4, 2017, www.theguardian.com/books/2002/nov/02/theatre.artsfeatures.
11 Dapo Adelugba, "Wole Soyinka's 'Blues for a Prodigal': A Review," *Africa Media Review*, 3(2) (1989), 75, accessed April 4, 2017, http://pdfproc.lib.msu.edu/?file=/DMC/African%20Journals/pdfs/africa%20media%20review/vol3no2/jamr003002007.pdf.
12 Femi Osofisan, *Maami* (Lagos, Nigera: *The Guardian*, 1987).
13 Tunde Kelani, quoted from an interview with the blog "Africa is a Country," in morayooshodi, "Filmmaker Tunde Kelani Brings Nigerian Literature to Life," October 31, 2013, accessed April 4, 2016, www.zodml.org/blog/filmmaker-tunde-kelani-brings-nigerian-literature-life#.WOQQB461taY.
14 Tarell Alvin McCraney, quoted in E. Alex Jung, "*Moonlight*'s Tarell Alvin McCraney on Writing the Original Source Material, Take Inspiration From Myths, and Creating Heroes With Black Skin," *Vulture*, November 29, 2016, accessed February 18, 2017, www.vulture.com/2016/11/tarell-alvin-mccraney-on-writing-moonight.html.

15 McCraney, in Jung, "*Moonlight*'s Tarell Alvin McCraney on Writing the Original Source Material."
16 McCraney, in Jung, "*Moonlight*'s Tarell Alvin McCraney on Writing the Original Source Material."
17 Judith Buchanan, *Shakespeare on Film* (Harlow: Pearson Longman, 2005), 26, 37, 261, 262.
18 Buchanan, *Shakespeare on Film*, 34.
19 "Review: *Romeo and Juliet* – Thanhouser – two reels," *Moving Picture World*, in "Volume 2 – Filmography: 'Romeo and Juliet,' Part I," August 19, 2011, accessed April 5, 2017, www.thanhouser.org/tcocd/Filmography_files/cdpgwg.htm.
20 Tatspaugh, Patricia, "The Tragedy of Love on Film." In Russell Jackson *The Cambridge Companion to Shakespeare on Film* (Cambridge: Cambridge University Press, 2000), 137, cited in "*Romeo and Juliet* (1936 film)," Wikipedia.org, accessed June 6, 2017, https://en.wikipedia.org/wiki/Romeo_and_Juliet_(1936_film).
21 Erik Bauer, "Re-Revealing Shakespeare, An Interview with Baz Luhrmann, *Creative Screenwriting,* 5(2) (1998), 32; also available as "Re-Revealing Shakespeare: Baz Luhrmann on Romeo + Juliet," accessed April 5, 2017, https://creativescreenwriting.com/re-revealing-shakespeare-baz-lurhmann-on-romeo-juliet/.
22 Bauer, "Re-Revealing Shakespeare," 32.
23 Francisco Menendez, "Redefining Originality: Peace and Luhrmann's Conceptualization of 'Romeo and Juliet,'" *Creative Screenwriting,* 5(2) (Spring, 1998), 36.
24 Kenneth Muir, *Shakespeare's Sources* (London: Methuen, 1957), 21–30, cited in Menendez, "Redefining Originality," 36 footnote 41.
25 Menendez, "Redefining Originality," 36.
26 Menendez, "Redefining Originality," 36 fn. 41; further credits Olin H. Moor, *The Legend of Romeo and Juliet* (Columbus, OH: Ohio State University Press, 1950).
27 E. Talbot Donaldson, *The Swan at the Well: Shakespeare Reading Chaucer* (New Haven, CT: Yale University Press, 1985), 120.
28 Ovid, *The Metamorphoses of Ovid,* trans. by David R. Slavitt (Baltimore, MD: Johns Hopkins University Press, 1994), Book IV Lines 57–62, 65.
29 Robert Adams, *The Land and Literature of England* (New York: Norton, 198), 43.
30 Tom Stoppard, quoted in "Shakespeare on Film: *Shakespeare in Love,*" Study Guide, *The Film Space*, accessed April 6, 2017, www.thefilmspace.org/shakespeare-on-film/resources/shakespeare-in-love/docs/shakespeare-in-love_studyguide.pdf.
31 Fyodor Dostoevsky, *Crime and Punishment* (New York: Bantam Classics, 2003, originally published in 1866), 1.
32 Charalampos Goyios, "Living Life as an Opera Lover: On the Uses of Opera as Musical Accompaniment in Woody Allen's *Match Point*," *Senses of Cinema*, 40 (July, 2006), accessed April 6, 2017, http://sensesofcinema.com/2006/feature-articles/match-point/.
33 "*The Woman in White* (novel)," Wikipedia.org, accessed April 6, 2017, https://en.wikipedia.org/wiki/The_Woman_in_White_(novel).
34 Lyrics from Andrew Lloyd Webber, *The Woman in White* (musical), Act II Scene iv. In D.E. Wynter, "'Darling, Have You Seen my Strindberg Book?': Dialogism as Social Discourse in *Match Point,*" in Klara Stephanie Szlezák and D.E. Wynter (eds.), *Referentiality and the Films of Woody Allen* (New York: Palgrave Macmillan, 2015), 139.
35 Wynter, "'Darling, Have You Seen my Strindberg Book?'," 139.
36 Wynter, "'Darling, Have You Seen my Strindberg Book?'," 137.

37 Wynter, "'Darling, Have You Seen my Strindberg Book?'," 140.
38 Wynter, "'Darling, Have You Seen my Strindberg Book?'," 140.
39 Wynter, "'Darling, Have You Seen my Strindberg Book?'," 141.
40 Wynter, "'Darling, Have You Seen my Strindberg Book?'," 151.
41 Elbert Ventura, "Game, Set," Reverse Shot Online, accessed November 23, 2012, www.reverseshot.com/legacy/winter06/newreleases/matchpoint.html.
42 Theodore Dreiser, *An American Tragedy* (New York: Boni & Liveright, 1925).
43 Robert Bresson, quoted in Paul Schrader, *Transcendental Style in Film: Ozu, Bresson, Dreyer* (Berkeley, CA: University of California Press, 1972), 64.
44 Robert Bresson, interviewed in Theodor Kotulla, *Au hasard Bresson,* documentary (Munich, Germany: Iduna Film Produktiongesellchaft, 1967).
45 Bresson in Kotulla, *Au hasard Bresson.*

SIXTEEN

Chunhyang, Orpheus, and Other Myths

The Song of Chunhyang: A Korean Myth

The Song of Chunhyang is neither a novel nor a play, but a *p'ansori*: "an epic singing narrative native to Korea and perhaps the most minimal theatre form in the world ... that requires many hours to perform."[1] As such, it poses many challenges for film and television adaptation. But, simply put, *Chunhyang* is Korea's *Romeo and Juliet*. This passionate love story between Mong-nyong, the teenage son of a governor, and Chunhyang, the beautiful young daughter of a former courtesan – interwoven with passages of their servants' ribald comedy and tragedy as the lovers are torn apart – is universal in its appeal.

According to Kim Chong-Un and Richard Rutt, "the oldest datable version was written as a long poem in Chinese by Yu Chin-han in 1754,"[2] although according to Ah-Jeong Kim and R.B. Graves, it is conjectured that some of the "old folklore, shamanistic ritual, and legends [that] evolved into the existing *p'ansori* narrative ... trace as far back as the Three Kingdoms period (37BCE– 935CE)."[3] Although *The Song of Chunhyang* is revered throughout Korea by the well-educated and non-educated alike, "it is packed with Chinese literary allusions and poetic quotations which would be meaningless to real peasants,"[4] such as the verse "fitting partner for a lord" from the well-known marriage song of "the ancient *Shih ching* (*Book of Songs*), or poems written by T'ang poets such as Li Po."[5] As Richard Rutt and Kim Chong-Un point out, "References to Chinese stories are so numerous in *Ch'unhyang ka* that full annotation of them in a translation would only be pedantic."[6] However, at the time the story takes place, it was the custom for Korean students to complete their education by competing at a poetry contest to see who could write the best verse in Chinese, and Mong-nyong winning out over all the rest is central to what makes him such a desirable character in *Ch'unhyang*, even when his parents drag him off to the capital, forcing him to leave his newly married teenage bride.

Altogether, there have been at least a dozen film adaptations of *Chunhyang* in North and South Korea, as well as television series, a children's musical, and a manga. These include Han Sang-Hoon's "Korean traditional literary classic," *Sung Choon-Hyang* (South Korea, 1987), written by Kim Yong-Jin,[7] and Korea's "first digital animation," *The Love Story of Choon-Hyang* (South Korea, 1999), directed by Andy Kim.[8] The screenwriters of *The Love Story of Choon-Hyang*, Park Yang-Ho, Kim Yon-Ok, and Hong Jae-Ho, updated the story in a similar fashion as Baz Luhrmann's *Romeo + Juliet* so that "Choon-Hyang and Mong-Nyong listen to fast tempo music and even use cell phones and beeper."[9]

In *Chunhyang* (South Korea, 2000), director Im Kwon-Taek and screenwriter Myung-Kon create a fascinating mélange of the poetry and music of traditional Korean *p'ansori,* beautiful Korean landscapes, and a romantic storyline. But I found the montage sequences jarring: I'm used to the precise editing that weds landscape to lovers in films like Bimal Roy's classic *Devdas* (India, 1956) and Andrea Arnold's *Wuthering Heights* (UK, 2011). Perhaps the images sync up with the words in Korean, but they're disturbingly unconnected in English, marring the film's aesthetics and its ambitious attempt to convey Korean aesthetics to a Western audience.

However, Huh Moon-Young takes a more positive critical stance:

> Each and every gesture of the characters is saturated with the rhythm of pansori. From the very beginning, Chunhyang is an experiment that attempts to build cinema beyond the traditional cinematic grammar of western cinematic language with the aesthetic resources of the Korean performing arts.[10]

A recent television version, *Sassy Girl Chun Hyan*g (literally *Delightful Girl Chun Hyang,* South Korea, 2005) co-written by the Hong sisters, Hong Jung-eun and Hong Mi-ran, updates the story into a modern-day teenage romantic comedy "fusion-style" series, mixing *p'ansori* with rap. It aired in Korea, Taiwan, Japan, and Thailand and was later remade in Indonesia as *Cinta Remaja* (Jakarta, 2006–2007).[11]

Orpheus: Singing Our Lives with His Song

Myths have supplied plotlines and characters for centuries. For example, the myth of Narcissus was recently reset in the world of Los Angeles modeling: *The Neon Demon* (USA/Denmark/France, 2016) by Danish writer/director Nicolas Winding Refn. Among the myths that have had the most play, however, is the story of Orpheus, which has wound its way through literature from the eighth century BCE Greek poet Hesiod's *Works and Days* and Latin poet Virgil's *The Georgics* (36–26BCE), to Ovid's *Metamorphoses* (AD 8) and beyond.

In the nineteenth century, American education was something only the wealthy could afford; in those times, one would be considered uneducated if one did not read the AD 8 *Metamorphoses* in its original Latin and probably had memorized it, the way Korean scholars memorized classic Chinese poetry for their education in the eighteenth and nineteenth centuries, as reflected in the storyline of various versions of *Chunhyang*. Stilted translations have kept generations of English speakers from appreciating Ovid's writing, but David Slavitt's 1994 translation revitalizes it. For example, in the wedding scene:

> The guests were concerned, alarmed,
> and then, in a matter of moments, horrified, for the bride,
> on the grass among her attendant naiads, stepped on a viper,
> whose sharp and envenomed fangs killed her at once. The
> wedding abruptly turned to a wake. Orpheus, the bridegroom,
> all but out of his mind with grief, went into mourning,
> carrying his complaint to the ends of the earth and beyond.[12]

This time we can hear something of Orpheus' grief projected across the universe and into Hades, even before he pleads to the God of Hades to restore his beloved's life "in the name of love" in a song so passionate it might even revive the spirit of Jim Morrison or some reigning punk musician of the 1980s, bitten by the serpent of heroin overdose in a dirty needle. I refer to musicians because Orpheus was the rock star of his culture and generation, but others have also invoked his spirit. Even Ted Hughes, the husband of the suicidal poet Sylvia Plath, wrote an Orpheus and Eurydice story in his *Tales from Ovid*,[13] as if that could expiate his grief or perhaps guilt for the suicide of his wife. For Eurydice's perspective, we have to go back to an earlier version, Virgil's in 36–26BCE, where Eurydice cries out:

> What utter madness is this? See, once again
> The cruel Fates are calling me back and darkness
> Falls on my swimming eyes. Goodbye forever.[14]

Writers throughout the millennia have appropriated the Orpheus myth. For example, in 1321, we see Virgil reappear as Dante's guide through Hell in Dante Alighieri's *La Divina Commedia* (*The Divine Comedy*). But in the last hundred years, filmmakers, too, have seen themselves as Orpheus, using their filmic music, as it were, to express their grief about love, to get love back into their lives, or simply to play to the universe.

Jean Cocteau – poet, novelist, dramatist, and filmmaker – was considered one of the greatest cultural forces of the twentieth century. He was a leading member of the surrealist movement, which emphasized the unconscious in artistic creation. As a young man in 1923, Cocteau became addicted to opium after the death of his lover. He described his recovery in *Opium: The Diary of an Addict*;[15] during his recuperation he produced the play *Orphée*, about a modern, middle-class couple living in Thrace (where the original Orpheus died) – which Cocteau would later reset in Paris and the surrounding countryside in his film adaptation of *Orphée*.

Cocteau was so intrigued by the myth of Orpheus that he revisited it three times; once as a rebellious, revolutionary upstart as a young filmmaker in his 1930 film, *The Blood of a Poet* (in which a lifeless statue, formerly smashed to bits, holds a lyre), determined to break with the history of old, lifeless art by old, dead men, yet ironically putting himself into history in the process. Yet even as a young upstart with a manifesto-like film, this creator of *poésie cinématographique* couldn't help but be influenced by an earlier poet, Arthur Rimbaud, whose *A Season in Hell* (*Une Saison en Enfer*) of 1873 firmly establishes the journey through hell that the writer must take as an initiation.

In his prime, twenty years after *The Blood of a Poet*, Cocteau wrote and directed *Orphée* (France, 1950), set not in Ancient Greece, but on the Left Bank of Paris – the 1940s equivalent of San Francisco and New York and their 1990s Poetry Slams – where a famous poet is scorned by a new generation for having written a manifesto that involves technology as language, and becomes obsessed with death. Ten years later, when he was nearing the end of his life, he made *Le Testament d'Orphée* (France, 1960), which includes an interrogation of an eighteenth-century time-travelling poet played by Cocteau himself, who admits:

> I have often been tempted to scale that fourth wall on which men inscribe their dreams and their loves ... that creativity which is the highest form of humanity's spirit of contradiction.[16]

Echoes of *Orphée* appear in the Wachowski sisters' *The Matrix* (USA, 1999), from the character whose name is Morpheus, to the mirror transformation of computer hacker Neo, which harkens back to the mirror made of mercury (that alchemical substance, which a magician like Cocteau would have appreciated) into which Orphée dips his hands in order to time travel.

The danger is not to let the computer take over the function of storytelling to the point where it's replaced by formula. In Henry Miller's *The Time of the Assassins*, the Swiss poet, critic, and professor of moral philosophy, Henri-Frederic Amiel, conjectures:

> I imagine this kind of thing will be the literature of the future – a literature à l'américaine, as different as possible from Greek art, giving us algebra instead of life, the formula instead of the image, the exhalations of the crucible instead of the divine madness of Apollo.[17]

Apollo is the sun god, and it's to the sun that Orpheus is first seen singing, in order to make the dawn arrive over Rio de Janiero in the opening scene of *Black Orpheus* (Brazil/France/Italy, 1959).[18] This version of the Orpheus story, as well as the play *Orfeu da Conceição* which inspired it, uses as its hybrid source Afro-Brazilian culture, combining Afro-Brazilian initiation rites with the Orphean legend, and is set during the exotic springtime ritual of Rio's Carnaval that takes place each year just before Lent.

In the Dogon initiation ceremonies of West Africa as studied by Marcel Griaule, initiates learn by stages involving sacrifice of a "fourth dimension" to understand the structure of the universe. "Giri so" means "word at face value, including mythological meanings." "Beena so" means the word on the side, like subtext. "Bolo so" means the word from behind, as in a synthesis of meanings, including historical meanings, and "so dayi" is "the clear world edifice: knowledge in its ordered complexity."[19] Applied to the Greek myth, there is no rite of passage – coming into eloquence as a tragic poet – without sacrifice, in this case represented by the death of Eurydice.

African ritual is referenced most prominently in the scene in which Orpheus, grief-stricken for his loss of Eurydice, goes to a Macumba chapel where one of the observants falls into a trance and takes on the voice of the dead Eurydice. But the moment that Orpheus turns to look at her, wild in his desire to be with his beloved again, Eurydice's voice disappears forever, leaving only a haggard old woman, exhausted from her trance.

Black Orpheus incorporates Afro-Brazilian beliefs in a similar way that *The Matrix* includes biblical references to Nebuchadnezzar, Babylon, Zion, and the Trinity – inspirationally, but also to offer a Western audience a dose of exoticism. The religious characters of the slums of Rio look to the goddess Bahiana – "inspiration for hundreds of poets, fine artists and … musicians and composers" – for their salvation, "in spite of … suffering, poverty, and sometimes even persecution."[20]

Like the 1959 *Black Orpheus*, Carlos Diegues' 1999 *Orfeu* is also based on *Orfeu de Conceição*, but it updates the story by setting it against the drug wars of Rio's favelas during Carnaval.[21] This combo of good ideas and kitsch begins when Euridice's plane lands on the runway. Euridice is an Indian girl visiting her Aunt Carmen. We know Euridice is sweet and innocent because of the kitten she picks up, which sadly turns her into more of a cliché than a tragic figure; her rival Mira, on the other hand, lugs around an issue of *Playboy*, bragging to anyone who will listen that she's that month's cover girl. The first time Euridice makes love to Orfeu, he asks, "Where'd you learn to love like that?" Her answer: "In Acre, watching TV." But there's plenty of action in *Orfeu*: The police storm the favela, looking for drug dealers like the drug lord Lucinho, who used to be Orfeu's friend in childhood. (Ah, those kites they used to fly together!) As the tension mounts, Euridice's disappearance brings up contemporary issues like sex trafficking and rape – promising material, but not for long. When Orfeu sees her in the mirror, the glass cracks in a hokey homage to Cocteau's *Orphée*. He's advised to "Never look back," but the audience can't resist: We see a dismembered hand in the garbage along with an ever-symbolic snake, followed by a victim porn shot of Euridice whose dead body bleeds in the rain. "Sleep, Euridice. When the rain's over we'll go home," says Orfeu – scarcely a poetic eulogy, though maybe a cadence or two is lost in translation from the Portuguese. Like a crowd of zombies, the Bacchantes rush up to Orfeu, who is holding the corpse of Euridice in his arms. They're out to revenge the player who wounded them in love. These stick figures react with the same anonymity of the extras screaming out "Kali Ma!" in *Indiana Jones and the Temple of Doom.*

A more recent adaptation of the Orpheus myth is an update of Offenbach's 1858 operetta, *Orphée en enfers*, which had "lampoon[ed] the deadly seriousness of Gluck's *Orphée et Euridice* and a range of other easy targets."[22] As Fiona Maddocks describes the 2011 version, "translated and reinvented for Scottish Opera and Northern Ireland Opera" by Rory Bremner, Mount Olympus is "a sky-high champagne bar with views on the City of London. There's bunga bunga, gang bang and can-can; debagging and phone hacking and serial shagging…"[23] Aha! Perhaps a twenty-first-century parody of *Orfeu* is also in order, or can Sylvia Plath arise from her grave and give us an update on the tragic myth from Eurydice's perspective?

The Nine Lives of the Bible

The first film depicting the Passion of Christ was not Mel Gibson's *The Passion of the Christ* (USA, 2004) – controversial for its graphic violence and anti-Semitism – but Georges Hatot's and Louis Lumière's French production made in 1899. However, the first really big production based on the Bible was *La Passion ou La Vie de Notre Seigneur Jésus-Christ* (*The Passion or the Life of Our Lord Jesus Christ*), also made in France, in 1906. It was director Alice Guy's masterpiece and Gaumont Studios' blockbuster hit: According to film historian Alison McMahan, *La Passion's* cast included 300 extras, 25 sets, and was the longest (660 metres) and costliest production to date.[24] Another director, Zecca, directed two films on the Passion of Christ for Pathé Studios, one released in 1903 and the other in 1907, but Guy's is more important, using deep focus, diagonal compositions, a thematic relationship between exterior and interior spaces, and was more thoroughly researched.[25]

D.W. Griffith's *Intolerance* (USA, 1916) included a Passion Play of Christ's betrayal and crucifixion, setting the stage for two more American epic extravaganzas involving the Passion: Cecil B. DeMille's *The King of Kings* (USA, 1927) and George Stevens' *The Greatest Story Ever Told* (USA, 1964) which according to its critics at the time, was perhaps the most boring story ever told. Further embarrassment comes when the opulent, ever-escalating special effects become outdated, thus exposing the adaptation for its hype.

In Italy, poet, novelist, and filmmaker Pier Paolo Pasolini also adapted part of the Bible in 1964. As Millicent Marcus states in *Filmmaking by the Book*, when it comes to Pasolini's *Gospel According to St. Matthew*, "Adaptation study meets perhaps its most formidable challenge … where all the standard difficulties … are immeasurably complicated by the sanctity of the textual source."[26] Citing Matthew 10:19–20, "For it is not ye that speak, but the Spirit of your Father which speaketh in you," Marcus concludes that "A faithful adaptation of Scriptures … requires a cinematic equivalent to this narrative voice that presents itself as God's writing."[27] Pasolini's idea was:

> To follow the Gospel According to St. Matthew point by point, without making a script or adaptation of it. To translate it faithfully into images, following its story without omissions or additions. The dialogue too should be strictly that of St. Matthew, without even a single explanatory or connecting sentence, because no image or inserted word could ever attain the poetic heights of the text. It is this poetic elevation that so anxiously inspires me. And it is a work of poetry that I want to make.[28]

Although Pasolini followed the rules of adaptation religiously when it came to story and dialogue, he set his Gospel in Southern Italy a substitute for "the Hebrew World of 2,000 years ago," celebrating a similar "Third-World, rural, pre-industrial, subproletarian society."[29] A much looser adaptation of biblical material is Krzysztof Kieślowski's ten-part television drama series, *The Decalogue* (Poland, 1985), in which most of the Ten Commandments are enacted in a Warsaw housing project, unlike Cecil B. DeMille's blockbuster film, *The Ten Commandments* (USA, 1956), which was shot in Egypt, Mt. Sinai and the Sinai Peninsula. In 1993, 20th Century Fox was developing an American send-up of *The Ten Commandments* in which "ten different creative types – including Bill Murray, Mike Myers, and Rick Moranis – [would] contemporize one of the Ten Commandments, which [would] all be thematically linked."[30] The associate producer of the project explained that "When Moses came down with tablets and said, 'thou shalt remember the Sabbath,' there was no Super Bowl Sunday."[31] And while *Life of Brian* (UK, 1979, re-released 2004), takes place in Tunisia, re-using sets left over from Franco Zeffirelli's television mini-series, *Jesus of Nazareth* (Italy/UK, 1977) that convey a biblical setting,[32] the Monty Python troupe satirize biblical stories that simultaneously make fun of British politics.

Martin Scorsese's *The Last Temptation of Christ* (USA/Canada, 1988) is an adaptation of Greek Orthodox Nikos Kazantzakis' 1955 novel by the same name, which explores the human side of a Jesus Christ who comes down from the cross to marry Mary Magdalene, have sex with her, raise a family, and later, when he remarries, commits adultery. For a month before the film opened, "conservative Christians ... denounced the film as blasphemous, staged demonstrations, called for boycotts and shaped a national campaign to have the picture destroyed or withdrawn."[33] Fifteen years later, however, *Time* magazine labeled Mary Magdalene "[t]he year's surprise 'It' girl," as popular writers like Dan Brown, author of the bestselling *The Da Vinci Code* (which would get its own adaptation in 2006), along with feminist scholars, strove to reexamine the significance of her life and her relationship to Jesus Christ.[34]

Writer/director Denys Arcand's *Jesus of Montreal* (*Jésus de Montréal*, Canada,1989) is a film about five actors whose lives are changed as a result of updating a Passion Play at the behest of a priest who soon demands that they restore the play to its original, conservative version. But the actors have taken their roles seriously, with dire consequences. Arcand uses his Passion players to satirize Canadian culture, religious and medical institutions, and to raise issues of commercialism vs. spiritual values and religious hypocrisy.[35] In an interview, Denys Arcand discusses his main character, Daniel Coulombe, who collapses under the cross from which he is unable to get down when the authorities close down the production in which he plays the role of Jesus:

> My Jesus of Montreal also dies. But he tried to protest, to say something different and he nearly succeeded. That's why, at the end of the film, his eyes and his heart are donated for transplant. Things are always beginning again, life is a perpetual struggle and voices of protest must always be raised.[36]

Cheick Oumar Sissoko's *La Gènese* (France/Mali, 1999) is based on Chapters 24, 25, 34, 37, and 38 of Genesis, but filmed entirely in West Africa, using only African actors speaking in Bambara. California Newsreel describes the film as using "the story of Jacob and Esau to explore internecine wars from Liberia to Somalia and from Congo to Kosovo."[37] Sissoko observes:

> Because La Gènese associates universal themes with a profound anchorage in African reality, I believe it constitutes a new stage in our cinema.[38]

Many other films and television programs use the Bible to supply themes, characters, and story elements. *Ghostbusters* (USA, 1984) adds the theme of the Apocalypse in the form of a giant Marshmallow Man run amok in Manhattan to augment the climax of the film. Frank Darabont's *The Shawshank Redemption* (USA, 1994), based on Stephen King's novella, *Rita Hayworth and the Shawshank Redemption*, evokes Christ's Last Supper when Andy Dufresne and his twelve fellow prisoners take a break from tarring the prison roof to drink beer – all except Andy, who, like Jesus who will "'drink no more' (Mark 14:25) until he is in the kingdom of heaven,"[39] has given up drinking. The Bible is directly referenced in Frank Darabont's screenplay after the warden discovers that Andy has escaped from Shawshank Prison:

```
INT - NORTON'S OFFICE - DAY (1966)

Norton opens his safe and pulls out the "ledger" - it's
Andy's Bible. The title page is inscribed by hand: "Dear
Warden. You were right. Salvation lay within." Norton flips
to the center of the book - and finds the pages hollowed out
in the shape of a rock-hammer.[40]
```

Biblical themes are often used in the episode titles of Aaron Sorkin's television series, *The West Wing* (USA, 1999–2006), such as "In Excelsis Deo," "Shibboleth," "The Fall's Gonna Kills You," and "Isaac and Ishmael," as Alexandra Karova pointed out in her Teaching Assistant lecture in my "Screenplay Adaptation" class.[41] Karova has also discovered numerous analogies between Mark Zuckerberg's character as written by Aaron Sorkin in *The Social Network* (USA, 2010) and biblical characters such as David, who slays Goliath the way Zuckerberg "outshin[es] the Winklevoss twins with his intellectual gifts,"[42] and "between the antagonist Sean Parker and Bathsheba, who "seduces [King] David by bathing across from his palace, where she knows he can see her ... (Samuel 11:2),"[43] explaining that "Parker is introduced to the audience naked and post coital in a white bed sheet,"[44] and just happens to be across the street from Mark in Palo Alto, all too ready to have him move in. Although *The Social Network* is officially an adaptation of Ben Mezrich's *The Accidental Billionaires: The Founding of Facebook, A Tale of Sex, Money, Genius, and Betrayal,* Sorkin's extensive knowledge of biblical literature enriches the story and gives it depth just as much as his references to Shakespeare's *Othello* and *Macbeth.*

Notes

1 Ah-Jeong Kim and R.B. Graves, *The Song of Ch'unhyang: Musical Text,* compiled by Master Singer Kim Yon-su. Seoul: Literature Translation Institute of Korea, e-publication forthcoming, accessed September 4, 2015, 1.
2 Kim Chong-Un and Richard Rutt, trans. "Introduction" to "The Song of a Faithful Wife, Ch'un-hyang," in *Virtuous Women: Three Classic Korean Novels* (Korea: Royal Asiatic Society, K.N.C for Unesco, 1974), 237.
3 Kim and Graves *The Song of Ch'unhyang*, 4.
4 Kim and Rutt, "Introduction," 239.
5 Kim and Rutt, "Introduction," 245.
6 Kim and Rutt, "Introduction," 245.
7 Joo Jin-Sook and Kim Mee-Hyun, *Everlasting Scent of the Classic: Choon-Hyang Jeon* (brochure), 5th Pusan International Film Festival, 37.
8 Joo and Kim, *Everlasting Scent of the Classic*, 38.
9 Joo and Kim, *Everlasting Scent of the Classic*, 38.
10 Huh Moon-Young, "Excerpt from *Cine 21...*," 237 (January 26–February 1, 2000), quoted in Joo and Kim, *Everlasting Scent of the Classic*, 41.
11 "*Sassy Girl Chun Hyang,*" Wikipedia.org, accessed October 4, 2016, https://en.wikipedia.org/wiki/Sassy_Girl_Chun-hyang.
12 Ovid, *The Metamorphoses of Ovid*, VIII, trans. by David R. Slavitt (Baltimore, MD: Johns Hopkins University Press, 1994), 195.
13 Ted Hughes, *Tales from Ovid* (London: Faber & Faber, 1997).
14 Virgil, *The Georgics*, Book 4, lines 484–497.
15 Jean Cocteau, *Opium: The Diary of an Addict* (London: Longmans, Green & Co., 1932); originally published in French in 1930.
16 Jean Cocteau, *The Testament of Orpheus* (*Le Testament d'Orphée,* Paris: Cinédis).
17 Henri-Frederic Amiel, quoted in Henry Miller, *The Time of the Assassins: A Study of Rimbaud* (New York: New Directions, 1946), 127.

18 Marcel Camus and Jacques Viot, *Black Orpheus,* directed by Marcel Camus (Paris: Dispat Films, 1959); based on the play *Orfeu da Conceição* by Vinicius de Morales, first performed in 1956.
19 Marcel Griaule and Germaine Dietterle, *The Pale Fox* (*Le Renard Pâle*, Paris: Institut d'Ethnologie, 1965). Special thanks to griot Tyger Ambimbola-Sodipe, who was a student in CTVA 420, "Screenplay Adaptation," Department of Cinema and Television Arts, California State University, Northridge, 2001, for her additional contributions to the above quotes.
20 Lita Cerqueira, "Bahianas," accessed September 23, 1998, 3, http://brazilonline.com/lita/bonfilm.html.
21 Carlos Diegues, Emanuel Carniero, Carlos Diegues, Paulo Lins, Hamilton Vas Pereira, and Hermano Vianna, *Orfeu*, directed by Carlos Diegues (Rio de Janiero, Brazil: Rio Vermelho Filmes Production and Globo Filmes, 1999); based on the play *Orfeu de Conceição* by Vinicius de Moraes.
22 Fiona Maddocks, "Orpheus in the Underworld; La Traviata; 50 Years of Minimalism; Chamber Music Society of Lincoln Centre – review," *The Observer*, December 3, 2011, accessed August 16, 2013, www.theguardian.com/music/2011/dec/04/orpheus-underworld-traviata-minimalism-review.
23 Maddocks, "Orpheus in the Underworld."
24 Alison McMahan, *Alice Guy-Blaché: Lost Visionary of the Cinema* (New York: Continuum International Publishing Group, 2002), 102.
25 McMahan, *Alice Guy-Blaché*, 105.
26 Millicent Marcus, *Filmmaking by the Book: Italian Cinema and Literary Adaptation* (Baltimore, MD: Johns Hopkins University Press, 1993), 110.
27 Marcus, *Filmmaking by the Book*, 110.
28 Pier Paolo Pasolini, letter to Lucio S. Caruso, Pro Civitate Christiana, quoted in Marcus, *Filmmaking by the Book*, 111.
29 Millicent Marcus, *Filmmaking by the Book*, 114.
30 Claudia Eller, "God Isn't Dead – He's Just in Development at Fox," *Los Angeles Times*, Calendar Section, June 12, 1993, 24.
31 Jim Skotchdopole, quoted in Claudia Eller, "God Isn't Dead," 26.
32 Roger Ebert, "Review: *Monty Python's Life of Brian*," June 18, 2004, accessed April 9, 2017, www.rogerebert.com/reviews/monty-pythongs-life-of-brian-2004.
33 John Leo, "A Holy Furor: Boycotts and Belligerence Greet a Startling New Film about Jesus," *Time*, 132(7) (August 15, 1988), 34.
34 Barbara Kantrowitz and Anne Underwood, "The Bible's Lost Stories," *Newsweek*, December 8, 2003, 49, 54.
35 Special thanks to Anne Allen for her research on French-Canadian cinema for RTVF 415F, "International Cinema," Department of Cinema and Television Arts, California State University, Northridge, May 1999.
36 Denys Arcand, quoted in Ron Burnett, "Denys Arcand – *Jesus of Montreal*: A Discussion," *Melbourne Sunday Herald,* Melbourne, Australia, June 29, 1990, 2.
37 California Newsreel Catalog, *La Gènese*, accessed April 9, 2017, http://newsreel.org/video/LA-GENESE.
38 Cheick Oumar Sissoko, quoted in California Newsreel Catalog, *La Gènese*,
39 Mark Kermode, *The Shawshank Redemption* (London: British Film Institute, 2003), 32–33.
40 Frank Darabont, "The Shawshank Redemption" (screenplay), 107.
41 Alexandra Karova, "*The Social Network* as a Biblical Adaptation," Teaching Assistant lecture, CTVA 420, "Screenplay Adaptation," Department of Cinema and Television Arts, California State University, Northridge, September 19, 2014, 6–7.
42 Karova, "*The Social Network* as a Biblical Adaptation," 3.

43 Karova, "*The Social Network* as a Biblical Adaptation," 5.
44 Karova, "*The Social Network* as a Biblical Adaptation," 5.

SEVENTEEN

Keeping It Literary in China

Most of the films of internationally acclaimed director Zhang Yimou are adaptations of literary work, which he feels is the origin of his creativity:[1]

> Without good literary works, it could be difficult to produce good films. Films are not constitutive of actions only. Motion without thoughts can only be dead actions. In my films, those images that have touched people deeply are mostly originated from literature. And such literary experience has inspired me.[2]

In the case of *Red Sorghum* (China, 1987), internationally acclaimed director Zhang Yimou reasoned that he would give the author of the novel, Nobel laureate Mo Yan, and screenwriter Chen Jianyu first crack at the "literary script" of *Red Sorghum*, a woman's story that ricochets between past and present in a kaleidoscope of seasons spent farming and harvesting sorghum while experiencing the crises of love against backdrops of war.[3] After the "literary script" would come the "film script"[4]: "Film, you know, must always remain filmic."[5] In return, Mo Yan gave Zhang Yimou carte blanche to film the novel any way Zhang Yimou chose, which the director greatly appreciated:

> Some writers are no good; they'll hold up their books and question how you could have neglected to film this sentence – this sentence is so profound, so important! I really applauded Mo Yan when I read his letter. He really understands that film is film ... I feel that film has to find its own means of expression; it can't duplicate literature. ... In adapting *Red Sorghum* to the screen, we had to select the events that went on without any interruption, were simple and succinct, and went by in one breath in the hopes of creating one overall kind of feeling – it's very different from literature.[6]

Screenwriter Lu Wei recalls how Yu Hua, the novelist of *To Live* (China/Hong Kong,1994), sought to write the adaptation himself:

> Zhang Yimou gave him a chance, but he had trouble leaving out his favorite aspect of the story. It is very difficult to ask him to kill his own baby.[7]

Yu Hua's inability to kill off the interior monologues – which similarly plagued Vladimir Nabokov, whose screenplay of *Lolita* would be stripped of so much of its verbal language by Stanley Kubrick – led to Zhang Yimou giving Lu Wei the chance to write a second draft of the epic story of a once-rich gambler struggling to survive as a soldier through the Chinese Civil War and to regain the love of his family as a peasant during the Cultural Revolution. As much as he admires Yu Hua's work, Lu Wei said, "To believe everything in the book is no better than not having reading it."[8] Furthermore, even the craft of screenwriting has its limitations, according to Lu Wei:

> The rules of dramatic screenwriting are not really so important in the actual process of writing. What is important is to stick to the character of Fugui, to understand his personality, and to express his suffering and misfortune. The rules of drama are just rules. They aren't even tangible when you're creating: they're just a method, so you just can't stick strictly to dramatic structure. Actually, from the perspective of dramatic structure, *To Live* doesn't have main plot events. In this movie, every rule serves the sole purpose of supporting the main subject.[9]

Although Zhang Yimou and his screenwriter reduced the novel's time period from the 1940s to the 1970s, instead of unfolding the story to the present day, following "the evolution of the characters,"[10] he and Lu Wei remained faithful to the absurd humor of the novel

> as a reaction to the films of the Cultural Revolution which lacked humor; this style in *To Live*, I like a lot. But again, it depends on the script and the novel I adapt for the screen. In this case, the humor matched the subject well, but this is not always the case and it really depends on the encounter with the text.[11]

Zhang Yimou points out another benefit of the relationship between cinema and literature:

> We, the Chinese directors, have very close relations with the new writers. They are even my friends ... I think that cinema also influenced their literary creation. Additionally, the adaptation of their novels to the screen made them known to a larger public, not only in China, but in Taiwan, Hong Kong, Japan, and in the West. This is stimulating for an artist ... [T]he novelists are as enthusiastic to see their novels adapted to the screen as the directors are to acquire the rights of a new good novel.[12]

Li Yu's recent approach to adapting a story from a literary novel has been wildly successful at the Chinese box office. In writing *Ever Since We Love* (China, 2015), Li Yu and co-screenwriters John Wei and Shaofei Xu kept the literary style of Feng Tang's 2001 young adult novel, *Everything Grows*,[13] "but cast the most popular actors, such as Fan Binbing and Hang Geng ..." to ensure a receptive audience.[14]

Notes

1 Kwok-Kan Tam, "Cinema and Zhang Yimou," 1996. In Frances Gateward (ed.), *Zhang Yimou: Interviews* (Jackson, MS: University of Mississippi Press, 2001), 116.
2 Zhang Yimou, quoted in Tam, "Cinema and Zhang Yimou," 117.
3 Zhang Yimou, quoted in Jiao Xiongping, "Discussing *Red Sorghum*," in Gateward, *Zhang Yimou: Interviews*, 3, reprinted from *Turbulent Meeting: Dialogues with Contemporary Chinese Film*, trans. by Stephanie Deboer (Taipei, Taiwan: Yuanliu Publishing, 1999).
4 Zhang in Jiao, "Dicussing *Red Sorghum*," 3.
5 Zhang in Jiao, "Dicussing *Red Sorghum*," 4.
6 Zhang in Jiao, "Dicussing *Red Sorghum*," 4–5.
7 Lu Wei, quoted in Lu Wei and Wang Tianbing, *The Secret of Screenwriting* (Shanghai: Shanghai Jiao Tong Uuniversity Press, 2013), 82, trans. by May Wu for *Great Adaptations*.
8 Lu in Lu and Wang, *The Secret of Screenwriting*, 84.
9 Lu in Lu and Wang, *The Secret of Screenwriting*, 84–85.
10 Zhang Yimou, quoted in Hubert Niogret, "Interview with Zhang Yimou," in Gateward, *Zhang Yimou: Interviews*, 58; reprinted from *Positif* #410-02 (July–August, 1994), trans. by Lenute Giukin.
11 Zhang in Niogret, "Interview with Zhang Yimou," 59.
12 Zhang Yimou, quoted in Michel Ciment, "Asking the Questions: Interview with Zhang Yimou," in Gateward, *Zhang Yimou: Interviews*, 22–23.
13 Feng Tang, *Everything Grows* (Tianjin, China: Tianjin People's Publishing House, 2001).
14 Siyu Yin, "New Generation Women Directors in Asia," student paper for CTVA 413, "Women As Filmmakers," California State University, Northridge, April 26, 2016, 3.

Part VIII

Embracing and Rethinking Structure

EIGHTEEN
Timing the Times

Timing "Real" Times

When it comes to adapting real life stories, one's approach often depends on the zeitgeist and circumstances of the time in which the adaptation will be viewed. For example, Lin-Manuel Miranda's adaptation of a 731-page biography of Alexander Hamilton, one of America's Founding Fathers, into the smash hit hip-hop musical *Hamilton* (USA, 2015), took into account both modern style and contemporary political concerns in the retelling.[1] It also took liberties with an historical timeline, using deadlines as an excuse. As Lin-Manuel Miranda puts it:

> Hamilton didn't really meet Lafayette, Lawrence, and Mulligan all at once in the same bar, but we're gonna meet them at once because we've got to go. We've got a lot of story to tell and we wanna get you out before Les Mis gets out next door.[2]

In contrast, Kieran Fitzgerald, co-screenwriter with Oliver Stone of *Snowden* (USA, 2016), based on the books *The Time of the Octopus* by Anatoly Kucherena and *The Snowden Files* by Luke Harding, was aware of their protagonist's on-going predicament: Edward Snowden is hoping to return to the country he loves, where he may be judged as either a traitor or a hero. In a Q&A at the Writers Guild Theater, Fitzgerald stated:

> My goal was to basically ensure that the research be accurately portrayed in the movie ... The stories were on-going at the time ... It was very gratifying to be on the cutting edge of history ... We felt responsibility to the history books because his case is going to depend on the perception of him in the US.[3]

In the case of *Hidden Figures*,[4] Margot Lee Shetterly's inspirational story of the black female mathematicians who made it possible for America's astronauts to go to space, many changes were made in order to produce a dramatic story that would fit into one feature. Instead of following dozens of characters who broke through the racism and sexism of the 1950s and 1960s, Schroeder and Melfi's Oscar-nominated screenplay for *Hidden Figures* (USA, 2016) focused on the career trajectories of three friends – Katherine Johnson, Dorothy Vaughan, and Mary Jackson – whose intertwined life stories allowed mainstream audiences and women of color alike to relate more intimately to the injustices these women faced as well as to celebrate their accomplishments against all odds.

Other changes were the prerogative of the producer and the director. Screenwriter Allison Schroeder's initial goal to cover a 40-year span in the history of the characters behind *Hidden Figures* was nixed by producer Donna Gigliotti due to budgetary restrictions.[5] Director and co-screenwriter Theodore Melfi "wanted 40 percent space [program], 60 percent home life," and romantic subplots involving beaus and husbands were given more screen time than in Schroeder's first draft.[6]

At times one woman's ordeal in the book would be substituted for another's in order to make the dramatic arc of the overall story more exciting. For example, Mary Jackson's humiliating ordeal working in a building that didn't have Colored restrooms at a time when segregation ruled the South, becomes Katherine Johnson's plot point in the film. In Shetterly's book, it's Mary who lets off steam after white women laugh at her for trying to use the nearby White restroom. "[S]he ranted about the insult she had experienced on the East Side" to a white male engineer who then took her under his wing, asking her to work for him and guiding her towards fulfilling her ambition of becoming one of Langley Research Center's most successful black female engineers.[7] Katherine Johnson "refused to so much as enter the Colored bathrooms," as it seemed unreasonable to her not to use the unmarked ones for white employees that were much closer to her workplace: "No one ever said another word to her about it," according to the book.[8] But although the movie intertwines the stories of three workplace friends, it's Katherine Johnson who is "the most recognized of all the NASA human computers, black or white."[9] As such, the plot point about the segregated bathrooms, which becomes an arc as integration eventually wins the day, belongs to Katherine, whose meltdown speech begins with:

```
                KATHERINE
There's no bathroom here. There are
no COLORED bathrooms in this building
or ANY building outside the West
Campus. Which is half a mile away!
Did you know that? I have to walk to
Timbuktu just to relieve myself![10]
```

Her outspokenness results in Katherine's boss taking action:

There in front of the group: an inflamed Al Harrison, wielding a crowbar, is bashing the "Colored Restroom" sign on the wall.

AL HARRISON

Damn thing!

On the other side of the corridor … the entire West Computing group, including Dorothy and Mary watch in wonder. Katherine makes her way through, landing between them.[11]

However, Mary does get a dramatic monologue of her own a bit later in the story, when she musters up her courage to go before the city judge for the "'special permission' to attend classes in the whites-only school" that are a pre-requisite towards her becoming an engineer.[12] Shatterly sets up the motivation for Mary's passionate speech with:

> She would let nothing – not even the state of Virginia's segregation policy – stand in the way of her pursuit of the career that had rather unexpectedly presented itself to her. She had worked too hard, her parents had worked too hard; a love of education and a belief that their country would eventually heed the better angels of its nature was one of their greatest bequests to their eleven children.[13]

But in the book, there is no speech. The City of Hampton simply grants Mary the dispensation.[14] It's up to Schroeder and Melfi to dramatize the riveting metaphor between her quest for achievement and American astronauts and the dramatic suspense as to whether the judge will be persuaded by her words:

MARY

The point is, Your Honor…

Mary leans in.

MARY (CONT'D)

No Negro woman in the State of Virginia has ever attended an all-white school. It's unheard of.

THE JUDGE

Yes. It's unheard of.

MARY

And before Alan Shepard sat on top of a rocket, no American had ever touched space. He will forever be

```
          remembered as the Navy man from New
          Hampshire who was the first to touch
          the star.

The smallest opening in the Judge's countenance.

                    MARY (CONT'D)
          And I, sir, plan on being an engineer
          at NASA. But I can't do that without
          taking those classes at that all-
          white high school. And I can't change
          the color of my skin. So … I have no
          choice but to be the first, which I
          can't do without you.

Mary looks around the courtroom.

                    MARY (CONT'D)
          Your Honor, of all the cases you'll
          hear today, which one will matter in
          a hundred years? Which one will make
          you the "first"?[15]
```

Allison Schroeder's passion for undertaking the screenplay adaptation of *Hidden Figures* came from having grown up near Cape Canaveral. Her grandmother worked at NASA as a computer programmer, and Schroeder not only interned at NASA, but worked for a missile launch company later on.[16] Her real life experiences not only motivated her to push hard for the opportunity to write the script, but made their way into the story as well. For example, when Schroeder attended an international economics tutorial in Oxford, England,[17] she recalled:

> [T]he professor said, "I don't know how to teach a woman." I said, "It's the same as teaching a man." I just sat down and he had no choice but to start teaching. When I handed in my first paper, I think that shut him up.[18]

Shroeder's experience with a sexist professor made its way into *Hidden Figures*, in a scene in which Mary Jackson, having received permission to take a previously segregated class that's a prerequisite to becoming an engineer, discovers that she's the only woman in the classroom.

```
The Professor scans the petition. It's official. He's
genuinely confused.
```

```
                              PROFESSOR
              Well. The curriculum is not designed
              for teaching … a woman.

She's unstoppable.

                                MARY
              Well, I imagine it's the same as
              teaching a man.
                        (she smiles at him)
              I don't see a colored section. Should
              I take any seat?

He nods. Mary turns to the class. A few seats left. Few on
the back row. Few in the middle. One on the front row.
Mary steps forward, all eyes on her. She considers her
choices. Then … she plops down. First row. Dead center. She
pulls out her notebook. Let's go.
```

Inserting one's personal experience was also at work in Zhang Yimou's *To Live* (China/Hong Kong,1994), when screenwriter Lu Wei incorporated a true story that his director knew about from the hospital where his mother was working:

> For instance, that doctor [in *To Live*] who ate seven steamed buns … During the Great Chinese Famine, so many people starved. Back then, during the harvest season, they would improve the hospital employees' diets. Some of the employees would eat so much, they had to be operated on for gastric perforations. I wrote this right into the script.[19]

Personal experiences also abound as sources of material in television series. Writer/showrunner Kenya Barris describes his sitcom, *black-ish* (USA, 2014 –), for example, as "based on my life, and actual characters."[20]

In adapting Nobel laureate Günter Grass' novel *Die Blechtrommel* (*The Tin Drum,* West Germany/France/Poland/Yugoslavia, 1979), however, director and co-screenwriter Volker Schlöndorff (along with screenwriters Jean-Claude Carrière and Franz Seitz) credits the novel's female characters' perspectives for his inspiration and emotional involvement in the story:

> It would be better to have lived first and then articulate in your work the experience you lived through, but I started without having ever lived, and that's why I was so dependent on literature.[21]

But Schlöndorff also acknowledges the viewpoint of a female actor/director who was at one point central to his creative and personal life: his wife, Margarethe von Trotta.[22]

When co-writers are involved, their different historical perspectives may further enrich the project. Screenwriter Mark L. Smith and director/co-writer Alejandro González Iñárritu used a four-step process in writing *The Revenant* (USA/Hong Kong/Taiwan, 2015):

> We'd go off and write our 90 pages, then we'd swap. Step Three: We'd argue. Step Four: We'd resolve it. It was a great experience.[23]

But it was also tough work, involving fifteen drafts, some of it extending beyond what was in Michael Punke's bestseller, *The Revenant: A Novel of Revenge*.[24] Smith explains:

> Thematically, Alejandro had some specific ideas that he wanted to bring into it: he wanted to explore the racism of the time. He wanted to make it more powerful with regards to Native Americans. It just grew.[25]

Punke's novel itself already played with historical facts of his protagonist's journey, bending or adding biographical material by John M. Myers[26] and others as needed to weave a dramatic storyline. Punke explains:

> The fur trade era contains a murky mixture of history and legend, and some legend no doubt has invaded the history of Hugh Glass. *The Revenant* is a work of fiction. That said, I endeavored to stay true to history in the main events of the story.[27]

However, Punke continues:

> I took literary and historical liberties in a couple of places that I wish to note. There is persuasive evidence that Glass did finally catch up with Fitzgerald at Fort Atkinson, finding his betrayer in the uniform of the U.S. Army. However, accounts of the encounter are cursory. There is no evidence of a formal proceeding such as I portrayed.[28]

Furthermore, the characters of Cattoire and La Vierge Cattoire, Major Constable and Professeur "are wholly fictional," and "Fort Talbot and its inhabitants are invented."[29]

When we stop to examine the details of description in a novel, other problems of film adaptation can arise. For example, take a look at the following description, rife with atmosphere and dramatic action:

> They put Glass on a horse behind one of the young braves and rode away from the Arikara village. The old woman's dog started to follow behind the horses. One of the [Sioux] Indians stopped, dismounted, and coaxed the dog close. With the dull side of a tomahawk, he bashed the dog's skull, grabbed the animal by the hind legs, and rode to catch the others.[30]

In the novel, we are made to understand that this is the dog of an old blind woman whom the Arikara have left behind to die. (Yes, men have got away with depicting old women as expendable in more than one culture, or leaving them out of the picture.) In contrast, their rivals – the Sioux – are going to rescue our protagonist Glass. But in the movie, the fate of the dog not only may prove to be one subplot too many: its murder by tomahawk paints Indians as stereotypically bloodthirsty. Furthermore, animal rights' activists will do their part to ensure the movie never gets made if dog-bashing is part of the script.

Director Gillian Armstrong, best known in Hollywood for *Little Women* (USA/Canada, 1994), her adaptation of Louisa May Alcott's novel, written by Robin Swicord, has also worked as a narrative and documentary filmmaker in Australia. At the Australian International Documentary Conference (AIDC), she asked a series of questions pertaining to bringing real stories to the screen – specifically as documentaries – although many documentary filmmakers work on their films as both writer and director, with written treatments but without formal scripts per se:

> What is the story? What are you saying? What points are you making? Why? Is it worth it? Is it compelling and unique? Does it matter? Is it rich enough, complicated enough, involving enough to be feature-length? Why this story? Why do you care about it? If you don't have a passion for it, will we (the audience)? What makes it different and special? What is the hook? Why the big screen? Is it powerful, visual, original, unexpected, arresting and sexy? Will it be a transformative experience? An event?[31]

Ultimately, Armstrong points out, powerful documentaries rely on the same dramatic structure as narrative features.[32] If you want to explore reality as a filmmaker, you need to determine whether the subject matter works best as a narrative feature or a documentary, find your most compelling characters, and focus on a time frame.

Time and Fantasy Factors

The use of time in the cinema was described by Andrei Tarkovsky in his book, *Sculpting in Time*: "I think that what a person normally goes to the cinema for is time: for time lost or spent or not yet had. He goes there for living experience."[33]

If reality is out of bounds – whether it's because our dreams get to layers of truth that day-to-day life can leave out, or because the rights to tell the story of a real person, alive or dead, are unavailable, or because of censorship or other factors – then it's important to address your use of time aesthetics in the fictional mode. The work that you are adapting may be a nineteenth-century epic taking place over many years, like *Les Miserables* (USA/UK, 2012),[34] several generations, like *Il Gattopardo* (*The Leopard*, Italy, 1958),[35] or in just one day, like *Ulysses* (UK/USA, 1967).[36]

You need to decide whether to be faithful to the original source material's time frame, or to truncate it for the sake of cinematic intensity. In the case of *The Idiot* (Japan, 1951), Kurosawa tried to remain faithful to most of the events of Dostoevsky's literary masterpiece, although he reset the story from nineteenth-century Russia to twentieth-century Japan.[37] But the producers insisted on a shorter version of Kurosawa's 265-minute film, which killed the flow of the story and made no sense.

Being faithful to epic stories can be easily solved today by writing the adaptation as a mini-series or a series of film sequels. The *Harry Potter* series of eight films (UK/USA, 2001–2011), all but one of which was written by Steve Kloves,[38] granted consultation and approval rights to the novels' author. J.K. Rowling culled several ideas of her bestselling stories from the classic tale of King Arthur, from the elderly wizard as mentor (whose parallel can be found in Harry's headmaster Albus Dumbledore) to the groups of soldiers who follow their leaders Harry and King Arthur into battle.[39] Overall, the *Harry Potter* series forms a character arc that supersedes the arcs of the individual films, following the young protagonist's journey from childhood through his teenage years into adulthood. The fourth film of the series, *Harry Potter and the Goblet of Fire* (UK/USA, 2005) signals the end of childhood for the three main characters as they experience "the many firsts of adolescence ... first friendship, first love, first heartbreak, and first death."[40]

Time is also a significant structural factor in *Cloud Atlas* (Germany/USA, 2012), based on the 2004 novel by David Mitchell.[41] The film covers six different eras ranging from the nineteenth century to the future, with interconnected storylines that explore the impact of one's action in the past on the present and the future. Co-screenwriter/co-director Lilly Wachowski points out yet another time factor that can change how we see a film over the years:

> You watch a movie when you're 20 years old, and you see the same movie when you're 35 years old or 40 years old, and something happens. The movie changes, because we change as individuals.[42]

This is certainly the case with the comedy, *I Served the King of England* (Czech Republic/Slovakia, 2007) directed by Jiří Menzel, who had won the 1967 Academy Award for Best Language Film for *Closely Watched Trains* (UK title: *Closely Observed Trains*) (Czechoslovakia/Yugoslavia/Germany/Hungary, 1966). Both films were based on novels by Czech writer Bohumil Hrabal,[43] whos brilliant wit comes to life in voice-overs that are perfectly matched with Menzel's zany visuals. But *I Served the King of England* has less immediacy than *Closely Watched Trains*, which explored a young man's awkward sexual transition into manhood. The more recent film treats its young protagonist's experiences with sex and money during the Nazi and Communist eras as a series of flashbacks from an old retired waiter. The political buffoonery seems funnier and funnier the older I get, as I quickly approach the age of the old protagonist who has just gotten out of prison, condemned to live out the rest of his life in an obscure forest by the Czech border. He remembers the decadent escapades of his youth, including watching fat, lusting industrialists through the distorting lens of a frosty beer mug, and sprinkling the body of a woman with money that has come his way largely through the happenstance and trickery we've just witnessed.

Age also plays an internal role to Tim Burton's version of *Alice in Wonderland* (USA, 2010), which grossed over a billion dollars worldwide. Screenwriter Linda Woolverton had pitched the project to Disney with the question, "What if Alice was older and went back?"[44] Unlike Lewis Carroll, who had a penchant for underage girls, Woolverton created a 19-year-old Alice who escapes from her engagement party on an English manor, running off to Wonderland in a quest for self-discovery and independence that updates Dorothy's escape from Kansas in *The Wizard of Oz* (USA, 1939).

In Wonderland, when told by a dog that it's time to meet with the Jabberwocky, Alice replies:

```
                ALICE
From the moment I fell down that
rabbit hole, I've been told what
I must do and who I must be. I've
been shrunk, stretched, scratched
and stuffed into a teapot. I've been
accused of being Alice and of not
being Alice. But this is my dream.
I'll decide where it goes from here.
```

And it's wonderful to see, as Alice's dream unfolds in 3-D, details such as the chess pieces and the butterfly that so excited chess player and lepidopterist Vladimir Nabokov, who had translated Lewis Carroll's into Russian before embarking on his masterpiece, *Lolita*.

Alice Through the Looking Glass (USA/UK, 2016), takes even further liberties with time in terms of creating a strong female character with whom contemporary women and girls could identify:

> I have absolutely set out over my career to move the female protagonist forward through time ... Growing up, my favorite movie was Lawrence of Arabia, and I wanted to see a woman lead that life of adventure.[45]

But Woolverton's own journey as a writer in approaching this goal was stymied by writer's block, as she struggled to move past a dark period in her life.

> I really couldn't write it. So I went over to London on a holiday and I was walking in Hyde Park, and there was a bust of Lewis Carroll, and I humbly asked his permission. And the writer's block went away.[46]

Time is an important factor in the life of a writer seeking self-expression and other rewards as months and years tick by. The amount of time in which a script is written, revised, and polished can be limited by studio schedules or an actor's availability. Time can be exploited to provide a sentimental inroad to an audience's sympathy with a character, as in milking family feelings during holidays like Christmas. It can also heighten a sense of urgency in an otherwise banal approach to plot through the addition of a ticking clock. Time, as an aesthetic component of a script, determines the overall span of the characters' lives, and whether we experience key events as flashbacks or chronologically. Time can also be opened up to reveal the intensity in which the moments of epiphany unfold. It may pay to honor the timeframe, characters, and events of the original source material. But often the best way to make the material compelling is to give it a new reincarnation whether in its own or another era, sometimes tying in events which you have personally experienced that reinforce the original story's zeitgeist.

As Kareem Abdul-Jabbar has explained:

> It's impossible to present a fictionalized account of a historic event that is completely accurate. That would make for a dull film. All the artist can hope to do is represent the spirit of the events and people, seeking to tell a larger truth rather than merely recount facts.[47]

Notes

1 Mallory Fencil, "Who Lives? Who Dies? Who Tells Your Story? Authoritative Voice in *Hamilton*'s Hip-Hop Musical Biography," Midterm Presentation, CTVA 420, "Screenplay Adaptation," Department of Cinema and Television Arts, California State University, Northridge, March 14, 2016, 2.

2 Lin-Manuel Miranda, quoted in Alex Horwitz, *Hamilton's America*, directed by Alex Horwitz, Great Performances, PBS, October 21, 2016 (Chicago, IL: The John D. & Catherine MacArthur Foundations; and New York: Radical Media, 2016).

3 Kieran Fitzgerald, interviewed by Andrea Berloff, Moderator, *Snowden* screening and Q&A, Writers's Guild Theater, Beverly Hills, California, September 18, 2016.

4 Margot Lee Shetterly, *Hidden Figures* (New York: William Morrow, 2016).

5 Louise Farr, "Space Odyssey: Alison Schroeder's career trajectory goes into orbit with *Hidden Figures,*" *Written By*, 21(2) (February–March, 2017), 41.

6 Theodore Melfi, quoted in Peter Hanson, "Space Race: Theodore Melfi Finds the Light in Darkness to Reveal *Hidden Figures*," *Written By,* 21(2) (February–March, 2017), 45.

7 Margot Lee Shetterly, *Hidden Figures* (New York: William Morrow, 2016), 109

8 Shetterly, *Hidden Figures*, 129.

9 Shetterly, *Hidden Figures*, 250.

10 Allison Schroeder and Theodore Melfi, *Hidden Figures*, screenplay, May 12, 2015, based on Shetterly, *Hidden Figures*, 65.

11 Schroeder and Melfi, *Hidden Figures*, 66.

12 Shetterly, *Hidden Figures*, 144.

13 Shetterly, *Hidden Figures*, 144.

14 Shetterly, *Hidden Figures*, 144.
15 Allison Schroeder and Theodore Melfi, *Hidden Figures*, 75.
16 Louise Farr, "Space Odyssey: Alison Schroeder's career trajectory goes into orbit with *Hidden Figures*," *Written By*, 21(2) (February–March, 2017), 39.
17 Farr, "Space Odyssey: Alison Schroeder's career trajectory goes into orbit with *Hidden Figures*," 41.
18 Allison Schroeder, quoted in Amy Kaufman, "Meet Allison Schroeder, the NASA-loving Writer of 'Hidden Figures' Who Was Just Nominated for an Oscar," *Los Angeles Times*, January 24, 2017, accessed February 18, 2017, 3, www.latimes.com/entertainment/movies/la-et-mn-hidden-figures-writers-alison-schroeder-20170124-story.htl.
19 Lu Wei, quoted in Lu Wei and Wang Tianbing, *The Secret of Screenwriting* (Shanghai: Shanghai Jiao Tong University Press, 2013), 89, trans. by May Wu.
20 Louise Farr, "black-ish like Me: When Kenya Barris take his homelife to the office, civil rights merge into stories." *WGAW Written By*, 20(4) (Summer, 2016), 26.
21 Volker Schlöndorff, quoted in Hans-Bernhard Moeller and George Lellis, "Heroes without Compromise: An Interview with Volker Schlöndorff," *Journal of Film and Video*, 58(3) (Fall, 2006), 52.
22 Schlöndorff, in Moeller and Lellis, "Heroes without Compromise," 52.
23 Mark L. Smith, quoted at the Q&A following *The Revenant* screening, Writers Guild Theater, Beverly Hills, California, December 13, 2015.
24 Michael Punke, *The Revenant: A Novel of Revenge* (New York: Picador, 2002, Movie Tie-in Edition: November, 2015).
25 Smith, Q&A following *The Revenant* screening.
26 John M. Myers, *The Saga of Hugh Glass: Pirate, Pawnee, and Mountain Man* (Lincoln, NE: University Nebraska Press, 1963).
27 Punke, *The Revenant*, 253.
28 Punke, *The Revenant*, 254.
29 Punke, *The Revenant*, 254.
30 Punke, *The Revenant*, 122.
31 Gillian Armstrong, quoted in Sandy George: "Learning Lessons by Unpacking Florence," *Screen Australia*, February 2013, accessed March 20, 2017, 6, www.screenaustralia.gov.au/getmedia/24fb0967-f43f-4460-bca4-f13b4a524de8/Think-big.pdf?ext=.pdf.
32 Armstrong, in George, "Learning Lessons by Unpacking Florence," 6.
33 Andrei Tarkovsky, *Sculpting in Time: Reflections on the Cinema*, trans. by Kitty Hunter-Blair (Austin, TX: University of Texas Press, 1989), 63.
34 Alain Boublil, Herbert Kretzmer, Claude-Michel Schönberg, and William Nicholson, *Les Misérables*, directed by Tom Hooper (Universal City, CA: Universal); based on the musical *Les Misérables* by Claude-Michel Schönberg and Alain Boublil, and the novel *Les Misérables* by Victor Hugo, first published in 1862.
35 Pascuale Festa Campanile, Suso Cecchi D'Amico, Massimo Franciosa, Enrico Medioli, and Luchino Visconti, *The Leopard*, directed by Luchino Visconti (New York: Criterion Collection), DVD; based on Giuseppe Tomasi di Lampedusa's novel, *Il Gattopardo* (Milan: Casa editrice Feltrinelli, 1958).
36 Fred Haines, *Ulysses* (Rome: Titanus), directed by Joseph Strick; based on James Joyce's novel, *Ulysses*, 1922.
37 Akira Kurosawa and Eijiro Hisaita, *The Idiot*, directed by Akira Kurosawa (New York: New Yorker Video), VHS; based on Fyodor Dostoevsky's *The Idiot*, first published in Russia in 1868.
38 The screenplay for *Harry Potter and the Order of the Phoenix* (Burbank, CA: Warner Bros, 2007) was written by Michael Goldenberg. Steve Kloves wrote the screenplays for *Harry Potter and the Sorcerer's Stone* (2001), *Harry Potter*

and the Chamber of Secrets (2002), *Harry Potter and the Prisoner of Azkaban* (2004), *Harry Potter and the Goblet of Fire* (2005), *Harry Potter and the Half-Blood Prince* (2009), and *Harry Potter and the Deathly Hallows, Parts I and II* (2010, 2011).

39 Brenna O'Neill, "Harry Potter," Midterm Presentation Summary, CTVA 420, "Screenplay Adaptation," Department of Cinema and Television Arts, California State University, Northridge, Fall 2014.

40 Tiffany Katz, "Harry Potter," Midterm Presentation Summary, CTVA 420, "Screenplay Adaptation," Department of Cinema and Television Arts, California State University, Northridge, Fall 2013.

41 *Cloud Atlas*, written and directed by Lilly Wachowski, Lana Wachowski, and Tom Tykwer.

42 Lilly Wachowski, interviewed by Tasha Robinson, "The Wachowskis Explain How Cloud Atlas Unplugs People from the Matrix," *AV Club*, October 25, 2012, accessed March 20, 2017, www.avclub.com/article/the-wachowskis-explain-how-icloud-atlasi-unplugs-p-87900.

43 Bohumil Hrabal, *Ost e sledované vlaky* (*Closely Watched Trains,* 1965); and *Obsluhova jsem anglickeho krúle* (*I Served the King of England*), first published in 1971.

44 Linda Woolverton, interviewed by Scott Myers, "*Written* Interview: Linda Woolverton (*Alice in Wonderland*)," Writers Guild of America (wga.org), March 13, 2010, accessed March 20, 2017, https://gointothestory.blcklst.com/written-interview-linda-woolverton-alice-in-wonderland-8514e62ef3ab#.984aucwts.

45 Linda Woolverton, interviewed by Rebecca Keegan, "First Belle, Now Alice: How Screenwriter and Headbanger Linda Woolverton Is Remaking Disney Heroines for a Feminist Age," May 29, 2016, accessed March 20, 2017, www.latimes.com/entertainment/movies/la-et-mn-linda-woolverton-alice-through-the-looking-glass-20160523-snap-story.html

46 Linda Woolverton, *Alice Through the Looking Glass* Screening and Q&A moderated by Valerie Alexander, at the Writers Guild Theater, Beverly Hills, California, June 11, 2016.

47 Kareem Abdul-Jabbar, "Kareen Abdul-Jabbar Reviews 'Birth of a Nation' ... And Nate Parker: 'Important and Flawed (Guest Column),'" *Hollywood Reporter*, September 9, 2016, accessed September 9, 2016, www.hollywoodreporter.com/news/nate-parkers-troubled-past-importance-926112.

NINETEEN

Alternative Focus Topics for the Story of Malcolm X

In bringing the story of Malcolm X to the screen in 1992, Spike Lee affirmed that it was all right for a filmmaker to make changes in an historical figure's biographical story "as long as you get the essence ... What did Malcolm stand for, where did he come from, where did he arrive?"[1]

According to Cornel West, in his book, *Race Matters*, this is what Malcolm X stood for:

> Malcolm X was the first real black spokesperson who looked ferocious white racism in the eye, didn't blink, and lived long enough to tell America the truth about this glaring hypocrisy in a bold and defiant manner.[2]

Figure 10.1 Malcolm X. Image courtesy of NBC News[3]

Spike Lee based his film, *Malcolm X* (USA, 1992) on *The Autobiography of Malcolm X*,[4] which producer Marvin Worth had optioned in 1969.[5] However, Manning Marable, who spent decades meticulously researching the details of Malcolm X's life, discovered many discrepancies between the *Autobiography* and Malcolm's real life. For example:

> About two-fifths of the book focused exclusively on Malcolm's childhood and juvenile years, describing the criminal exploits of the teenage Malcolm, "Detroit Red." It was only years later that I would learn that much of Detroit Red was fictive, that Malcolm's actual involvement in burglaries and hard-core crime was short-lived.[6]

In contrast, the *Autobiography* minimized the political work of Malcolm X in creating Muslim Mosque, Incorporate, and the Organization of Afro-American Unity in traveling through the Middle East and Africa in 1964.[7]

Tragically, Manning Marable died three days before the publication of his 608-page book, *Malcolm X: A Life of Reinvention*,[8] which won the Pulitzer Prize for History the following year. When rereading Robert McKee's screenwriting book, *Story*, I can't help but wonder how McKee's concept of taking a story "to the end of the line"[9] could be applied to a new biographical film on the life of Malcolm X incorporating Marable's findings. Because as monumentally worthy as Spike Lee's film is, surely for such an important an historical figure as Malcolm X, there's room for plenty of films.

What would a film that makes more of the conflict between Malcolm and the Nation of Islam, and which goes deeper into Malcolm's global vision, chronicling his travels across Africa and finally achieving "a vision of a world without racism"[10] mean for filmmakers and global audiences today? For Spike Lee, taking Malcolm's story "to the end of the line" led him to being the first American filmmaker to shoot part of a Hollywood feature in Mecca. But Malcolm's global vision that Alex Haley largely ignored in the writing of *The Autobiography of Malcolm X* was much more political than the book or the film.

For example, according to Marable, Malcolm X used Islam as "the spiritual platform from which he constructed a politics of Third World revolution, with striking parallels to the Argentinian guerrilla and co-leader of the 1959 Cuban revolution, Che Guevara."[11] Hollywood has also given us a toned-down version of the life of Che Guevara in *The Motorcycle Diaries* (Argentina/US/Chile, 2004), by focusing on the road movie aspect rather than Guevara's later achievements as a revolutionary. Pan-American society might be different today if a more political biopic had been given similar production and distribution opportunities.

As for Malcolm X, Marable points out that Alex Haley, Malcolm X's autobiographer, whose biggest quest in regards to the project may have been fame and financial security, may have reveled in the potentially higher book sales that Malcolm X's orthodoxy might attract, given the "intense interest in the Moslem countries where he is viewed as the most famous Orthodox Brother in America."[12] But, as Spike Lee points out, when James Baldwin wrote the first script to the film adaptation of Malcolm X's life, "the Honorable Elijah Muhammad, the head of the Nation of Islam, was still alive,"[13] and it took many years before people felt free to talk openly "about Malcolm's split with Elijah and the assassination and that whole period of time."[14] There were carefully trained gunmen in the Nation of Islam, and James Baldwin, who was drinking heavily, had a hard time finishing the third act.

> No shit Jimmy was scared. Fornication and adultery were two of the biggest offenses in the Nation, and Malcolm found out about all these young, beautiful intelligent sisters who had Elijah's babies.[15]

After Columbia rejected Baldwin's script for its excessive length regardless of the problems with its third act, several other screenwriters came on board, including Arnold Perl, who had helped Baldwin finish his draft;[16] Calder Willingham, whose version made Malcolm's widow Betty Shabazz throw her food at him;[17] David Mamet, whose version the producer described as "the great American liberals' civil rights dissertation";[18] and novelist David Bradley, who put Alex Haley into the script as a character,[19] much like Steve Biko's reporter friend in *Cry Freedom*. In one scene, Bradley shows Alex Haley drinking with Baker, who was introduced at the beginning of the script as a "crusty-looking newspaper man,"[20] and an editor who says, "Alex, I agree, you're the only writer who can get a book out of Malcolm X. But I'm not sure I want to make a hero out of him,"[21] to which Haley replies, "I don't either. I want to expose him. Look, he could be the most dangerous man in America."[22] Charles Fuller also wrote a script on Malcolm X, but his was too short in comparison to *JFK* (France/USA, 1991), which Oliver Stone was in the process of directing when Fuller completed his draft.[23] Ultimately, screenplay credit went to Arnold Perl and Spike Lee.

There are many great components and memorable details in the writing of Arnold Perl and Spike Lee's *Malcolm X*. The character arc, for example, lets the audience intimately identify with Malcolm through the changes in his hairstyle and what he thinks about his appearance. In the opening of Act I, newly arrived in the big city, Malcolm Little braves fiery lye to "look white" with his first hair-straightening in a barbershop. Later, the composite character Bembry withholds the water necessary to finish the conk long enough for Malcolm to register the necessary pain of ending his addiction to white culture and coming to terms with his real identity; finally, in the prison barbershop, Malcolm X is too busy reading a letter from Elijah Mohammed to pay much attention to his hair. The meaning behind the words as Bembry teaches Malcolm about the Tribe of Shabazz in the prison yard evokes the initiation rites of his West African ancestors. And the scenes shot in Mecca will remain an unforgettable part of film history.

But there are additional approaches that could be taken with Malcolm X in future adaptations as revealed in Manning Marable's extensive research. Some of these include focusing on the protagonist as a revolutionary, instead of the "pragmatic liberal" depicted by Alex Haley;[24] structuring the story around alternative action beats; interpreting the assassination as a passion play; digging further into the mystery of Malcolm's multiple antagonists; exploring the female subplots; and placing Malcolm's story in the contexts of the American folk tradition and black aesthetics. Let's examine these approaches one by one.

According to Marable, *The Autobiography of Malcolm X* provides a mistaken view of its protagonist as a political pragmatist "in the tradition of Benjamin Franklin's autobiography,"[25] instead of as a revolutionary calling for insurrection. In today's political climate of police brutality and racism that is reinforced at the highest levels of government, a more radical approach is likely to find an audience. Additionally, the first part of both the *Autobiography* and the film overemphasizes and exaggerates the role of crime in Malcolm's early life, providing a stereotypical view of Afro-American as gangster. Instead, exploring the mental illness of Malcolm X's mother and the supportive role of his siblings as he moved forward in life, might be a more compassionate way of handling character development.

Marable provides many exciting examples of events that happened to Malcolm X in real life that would resonate well with contemporary audiences and could be easily adapted into visually compelling action scenes and sequences. For example, here is a scene that looks like it could have been jotted down yesterday, although it describes the events of 1965 after Malcolm had risked his life to meet with the young women in Los Angeles who were suing the Nation of Islam leader Elijah Muhammed for child support after he had impregnated them:

> On the day he was to leave town, two carloads of Fruit [Nation of Islam paramilitary fighters] tailed Malcolm's automobile on the highway to the airport. Without any weapon to defend himself, Malcolm found a can in the car, poked it out a side window, and aimed it like a rifle. It was convincing enough; the would-be attackers quickly pulled back. At the airport, though, there were several more Muslim waiting. The LAPD responded by taking Malcolm through an underground tunnel to reach his plane. Prior to embarking, the captain of the flight ordered all the passengers off and had the plane thoroughly searched for bombs.[26]

The demise of some of those who witnessed Malcolm X's assassination also makes for compelling action scenes: Leon 4X Ameer survived a savage beating only to be found dead of a sleeping pill overdose in a hotel room the day after "claiming he had evidence that the U.S. government was involved in Malcolm's death."[27] Another victim was Robert 35X Smith, one of Malcolm's rostrum guards at the assassination. "Karate Bob," as he was called, died when he either jumped or was pushed in front of a speeding subway car.[28]

Marable describes the assassination of Malcolm X as "a passion play representing his beliefs," comparing Malcolm's desire for a symbolic death to that of Husayn ibn Ali (626–680), a Shi'ite martyr for justice.[29] The absence of police,[30] the death of witnesses, the passionate subplot of Malcolm's wife Betty, who watched him being murdered ... How would Paul Thomas Anderson depict this, I wonder?

Settling on an antagonist or combination of antagonists is a particular challenge in updating the story of Malcolm X. First of all, it's a security risk: Some of the individuals or entities allegedly implicit in the assassination are still alive. Louis Farrakhan, who not only replaced Malcolm as minister of the NOI's Mosque No. 7 in Harlem, but moved into Malcolm's house, had described Malcolm as a man "worthy of death."[31] Marable also investigates the roles of the CIA, the FBI, the police, and Willie Bradley in the assassination.

The character of Willie Bradley deserves a narrative feature of his own, beginning with his life as a bank robber. He may have been an FBI informant before or after Malcolm X's assassination, which might "explain why Bradley took a different exit from the murder scene than the two other shooters, shielding him from the crowd's retaliation."[32] Bradley's character arc is full of surprising twists, from his romantic relationship with boxer Rubin "Hurricane" Carter's defending lawyer who owned a boxing gymnasium, which led to Bradley being inducted into the Newark Athletic Hall of Fame in 2009, and finally, to an investigation into Bradley's role in the killing of Malcolm X called for by Leith Mullings, Distinguished Professor of Anthroplogy at the Graduate Center, CUNY, and Manning Marable's widow.

Yet another variable for a new adaptation of Malcolm X's life involves the female subplots. Ella, Malcolm's older sister, introduced him to a better way of life: the black bourgeoisie (although she financed her lifestyle through crime, providing a multi-dimensional character). She made sure, when he had to go to prison, that it would be a relatively safe one, where he eventually earned the equivalent of a PhD in self-learning. Ella saved her money for a hajj to Mecca, only to give it to her brother so that he could have this life-changing experience. She also purchased a new home for Malcolm X and his family under her name at a time when he was such a controversial figure "that it would have been impossible for him to purchase a home in an integrated neighborhood" – a neighborhood which was "predominantly Jewish," though Spike Lee chose to leave that detail as well as Ella's character out of his film.[33] I had thought that the exclusion of Ella was because of Lee's misogyny, but actually it was because of Betty Shabazz's influence. According to Marable, when Ella found out that "Betty was retained as a paid consultant," she was outraged enough to complain to a reporter that Betty "doesn't know enough about Malcolm to consult on anything pertaining to his life." Betty took revenge "by eliminating any references to Ella in Lee's movie."[34]

Ultimately, Marable places Malcolm's story in the American folk tradition of men of resistance such as Nat Turner, Stagger Lee, and Tupac Shakur,[35] and reminds us that Malcolm's legacy extends beyond America's shores, encouraging blacks "to celebrate their culture and the tales of black resistance to European colonialism and white domination."[36] According to the poet Amiri Baraka, Malcolm X's "great contribution was to preach Black Consciousness to the Black Man."[37]

Malcolm's travels through Africa undoubtedly contributed to the further development of such thinking, more recently expressed by African writers such as Ngũgĩ Wa Thiong'o, the Kenyan novelist and playwright who described writers as "surgeons of the heart and souls of a community."[38] Ngũgĩ has called on African writers to cultivate "a truly African sensibility"[39] in lieu of the Afro-European novels and essays written in English and French, that could have been written "in Ibo ... Dhuluo or Maasai"[40] and translated into other African languages "to create a progressive movement in the African novel and literature."[41]

Today, we can extend such thinking to the Pan-Africanization of the cinematic arts as well. As Anjali Prabhu, author of *Contemporary Cinema of Africa and the Diaspora* has written, Haitian/Congolese writer/director Raoul Peck's French and English-language documentary *Lumumba: Death of a Prophet* (France/Switzerland/Germany, 1992), about Patrice Lumumba, the Congolese prime minister who was assassinated in 1961,

> adopts the form of Henri Lopès' [Congolese writer/diplomat] poem, in which the poet laments the death of the prophet in terms of the story his mother told him. This is mirrored by the voice-over of the narrator/filmmaker, who reflects upon his arrival from Haiti in Africa by referring to the stories his mother has told him.[42]

Peck directed a narrative feature on the same subject, *Lumumba* (France/Belgium/Germany/Haiti, 2000), that begins with the democratically elected leader's death, "after CIA and other classified information were released on this assassination,"[43] and an extensively researched book by Belgian author Ludo de Witte, *The Assassination of Lumumba*, had also been published.[44] Prabhu suggests that we view the 2000 film – which is in Lingala as well as French and English[45] – together with the documentary as "an interconnected whole" which, she states, is "the most Africanizing gesture of the current moment ... in the contemporary world of African and diaspora cinema."[46]

Studying African-American culture and co-directing the documentary *Beale Street* (USA, 1978, 1981), inspired me on a personal level to turn to my Jewish roots, shooting a film in Eastern Europe (*Exile*, USA/Austria/Czechoslovakia, 1984) which explored how my ancestors had escaped pogroms and avoided the Holocaust, and examined the process which had alienated me and my immediate family from being in touch with our souls. Later I supported a center for Yiddish culture in Massachusetts which has preserved thousands of Yiddish books from extinction – wondering which one was written by an ancestor whose name and language I don't know, though I'd heard there was a poet in the family, back in Vilna. It was important to my assimilationist mother and grandmother to forget our ancestors in order to focus on trying to pass in mainstream American culture, and I can't pick up the broken pieces of my history.

Notes

1 Spike Lee, quoted in Terry Pristin, "By All Necessary Means: It Took Producer Marvin Worth 25 Years to Turn Malcolm X's Story into a Movie. Why Didn't He Give Up and What Made It Happen (Besides Spike, Of Course)," *Los Angeles Times*, November 15, 1992, accessed March 22, 2017, 3, http://articles.latimes.com/1992-11-15/entertainment/ca-648_1_marvin-worth/3.
2 Cornel West, *Race Matters* (New York: Vintage Books, 1994), 151.
3 Still from "Remembering Malcolm X 50 Years later," *The Big Picture RT*, February 24, 2015, illustrating "Malcolm X Remembered on Assassination Anniversary," *NBC News*, February 21, 2015, accessed November 15, 2016, www.nbcnews.com/news/us-news/malcolm-x-remembered-assassination-anniversary-n310096; also accessed June 6, 2017, "Remembering Malcolm X 50 Years later," *The Big Picture RT,* February 24, 2015, YouTube, www.bing.com/videos/search?q=Remembering+Malcolm+X+50+Years+Later&view=detail&mid=9D2CE20D088159EB537E9D2CE20D088159EB537E&FORM=VIRE.
4 Malcolm X, as told to Alex Haley, *The Autobiography of Malcolm X* (New York: Grove Press, 1965).
5 Spike Lee, with Ralph Wiley, *By Any Means Necessary: The Trials and Tribulations of the Making of* Malcolm X (New York: Hyperion, 1992), 24.
6 Manning Marable, *Malcolm X: A Life of Reinvention* (New York: Viking, 2011), 489.
7 Marable, *Malcolm X*, 489.
8 Larry Richter, "On Eve of Redefining Malcolm X, Biographer Dies," *New York Times*, April 1, 2011, accessed March 22, 2017, www.nytimes.com/2011/04/02/books/malcolm-x-biographer-dies-on-eve-of-publication-of-redefining-work.html.
9 Robert McKee, *Story: Style, Structure, Substance, and the Principles of Screenwriting* (New York: HarperCollins, 1997), 140.
10 Marable, *Malcolm X*, 493.
11 Marable, *Malcolm X*, 12.
12 Alex Haley correspondence, quoted in Manning Marable, op.cit., 402.
13 Lee, *By Any Means Necessary*, 24.
14 Lee, *By Any Means Necessary*, 24.
15 Lee, *By Any Means Necessary*, 25.
16 Lee, *By Any Means Necessary*, 24.
17 Lee, *By Any Means Necessary*, 25.
18 Lee, *By Any Means Necessary*, 26.
19 Lee, *By Any Means Necessary*, 26.
20 David Bradley, "The Autobiography of Malcolm X," screenplay, edited first revision, July 17, 1987, Warner Brothers, p.1. Margaret Herrick Library, Academy of Motion Picture Arts & Sciences.
21 Bradley, "The Autobiography of Malcolm X," 39.
22 Bradley, "The Autobiography of Malcolm X," 40.
23 Lee, *By Any Means Necessary*, 27, 30.
24 Marable, *Malcolm X*, 466.
25 Marable, *Malcolm X*, 466.

26 Marable, *Malcolm X*, 409.
27 Marable, *Malcolm X*, 459.
28 Marable, *Malcolm X*, 459.
29 Marable, *Malcolm X*, 433
30 Marable, *Malcolm X*, 433.
31 Louis Farrakhan, quoted in Marable, *Malcolm X*, 477.
32 Marable, *Malcolm X*, 475.
33 Marable, *Malcolm X*, 422.
34 Marable, *Malcolm X*, 472.
35 Marable, *Malcolm X*, 480.
36 Marable, *Malcolm X*, 481.
37 Amiri Baraka, 1965, quoted in Marable, *Malcolm X*, 481.
38 Ngũgĩ Wa Thiong'o, *Decolonising the Mind: The Politics of Language in African Literature* (Rochester, NY: James Currey, 1986), p. ix.
39 Ngũgĩ, *Decolonising the Mind*, 84.
40 Ngũgĩ, *Decolonising the Mind*, 84.
41 Ngũgĩ, *Decolonising the Mind*, 85.
42 Anjali Prabhu, *Contemporary Cinema of Africa and the Diaspora* (Malden, MA: Wiley Blackwell, 2014), 175.
43 Anjali Prabhu, quoted in an email from Joanne Webb, Marketing Representative, Global Education, Wiley, September 30, 2014.
44 Ludo de Witte, *The Assassination of Lumumba* (London, New York: Verso, 2001).
45 "*Lumumba* (2000)," imdb.com, accessed March 24, 2017, www.imdb.com/title/tt0246765/?ref_=nv_sr_1.
46 Prabhu, *Contemporary Cinema of Africa and the Diaspora*, 186.

Part IX
Censorship

TWENTY

Retelling, Limited

Censorship has played a role in what can be seen on screen in many parts of the world. In the US back in the early 1930s, the Hays Office had attempted to ban Mae West's play "Diamond Lil" from being made into a film. Mae West's clever use of double-entendres and gestures of innuendo instead of overt sexual dialogue not only allowed *She Done Him Wrong* (USA,1933) to pass the censors, but made it such a huge success at the box office that she was credited from saving Paramount Studios from bankruptcy, although the Hays Office later succeeded in locking the film in a Paramount vault.[1] Currently, the US operates with a ratings system, the MPPA (Motion Picture Association of America), established in 1968.[2] In Russia, censors called for a ban of *Beauty and the Beast* (USA, 2017) because it featured Disney's first gay character, LeFou.[3] In India, where kissing is not allowed in public, the Central Board of Film Certification (CBFC) not only blocked a watered-down *Fifty Shades of Grey* from being released, but also required that two kissing scenes in the James Bond movie *Spectre* (US/UK, 2015) based on characters by Ian Fleming be shortened.[4] Censorship of sexual issues is also practiced in the Middle East and countries like China, Kenya, and Malaysia.

Two or Three Lolitas

One of the most problematic adaptations involving censorship of sexual subject matter is Stanley Kubrick's *Lolita* (USA, 1962). When the director and his producer James Harris were considering buying Vladimir Nabokov's bestselling novel in 1957, MGM wrote a memo detailing Kubrick and Harris' reaction to the suggestion "that the subject-matter, 'an elderly man having an affair with a twelve-year old girl' would probably fall into the area of sex perversion, prohibited by the Code."[5]

> They maintained vehemently that the treatment of the story would not deal offensively with their sex relationship, but that the humor

arose from the problems of a mature man married to a gum-chewing teenager ... Any further judgment of course would have to be reserved until we see what treatment they submit.[6]

Irrespective of MGM's final judgment, a December 7, 1961 letter from MGM to Kubrick sums up the Examiners' reaction to the project:

> "The first thing that disturbs us is your intention to play this essentially as comedy. We can see the possibilities of an acceptable film on this book if it had the mood of Greek tragedy, if it showed the tragedy of a man who through an obsession brought ruin and disaster to himself and to those around him, but it seems to us fantastic to play it for cheap laughs." The Examiners saw the book as a masterpiece.[7]

History bears out the insignia of "masterpiece," although the novel itself was "banned for two years by the French government" when first published there in 1955.[8] The French critic, booklover, and world-famous director François Truffaut included *Lolita* on a pile of burned books in his film *Fahrenheit 451* (UK, 1961), an adaptation of Ray Bradbury's sci-fi story about a fireman whose job it was to burn books until he realizes that it's possible – though illegal – for people to actually read the books, and to think. The book *Lolita* continues to garner the wrath of critics and readers "because they feel Nabokov turned the rape of a twelve-year-old into an aesthetic experience,"[9] although in Iran, where the book is still banned and where it has been illegal for women to attend the university, a clandestine class of young women studying *Lolita* along with their teacher Azar Nafisi identified with what Vera Nabokov (Vladimir Nabokov's wife) described as Lolita's "heartrending courage..."[10] Nafisi cautions us:

> Those who tell us Lolita is a little vixen who deserved what she got should remember her nightly sobs in the arms of her rapist and jailer, because you see, as Humbert reminds us with a mixture of relish and pathos, "she had absolutely nowhere else to go."[11]

I try to imagine Nafisi sharing this line, "She had absolutely nowhere else to go," with young Iranian college-age women, all in long black chadors the minute they leave their professor's house, who can't leave Tehran, and can be stoned not only for expressing their sexuality by kissing in public, but for allowing a lock of hair or a painted fingernail to be seen outside of their chadors.

Whether one feels bamboozled or inspired by his language and content, the style that Nabokov used in *Lolita* is singularly cinematic and poetic, from the rhythm and alliteration of "Lolita, light of my life, fire of my loins. My sin, my soul..."[12] which opens the novel, to the end of the novel, where Humbert Humbert is "thinking of aurochs and angels, the secret of durable pigments, prophetic sonnets, the refuge of art. And this is the only immortality you and I may share, my Lolita."[13] Nabokov's love of interpretation, puzzles, associative thinking, and dream-like plot construction are also recognized by T. Jefferson Kline as characteristics of poetry.[14]

Alfred Appel, Jr. sleuths through Nabokov's word-play in order to determine the source of his underage heroine's name:

> Lo-lee-ta: the middle syllable alludes to "Annabel Lee" (1849), by Edgar Allan Poe (1809–1849). H.H. will lead one to believe that "Annabel Leigh" is the cause of his misery: "Annabel Haze, alias Dolores Lee, alias Loleeta," he says on p.167.[15]

Appel further substantiates the tie-in by providing the poem, "Annabel Lee," which includes the following lines:

> *She* was a child and *I* was a child,
> In this kingdom by the sea,
> But we loved with a love that was more than love –
> I and my Annabel Lee –[16]

However, Nabokov may have been thinking of additional characters – both fictional and real – in choosing "Lolita" as the name of his female character. In Nobel laureate Rabindranath Tagore's 1924 novel, *Gora*, Lolita is a rebellious young woman who risks scandal to take an unchaperoned trip with Binoy, who says to himself,

> "Lolita and I now stand alone, side by side, against the rest of Society," and he could not put out of his mind the fact that in her trouble Lolita had left every one else to come and join him. ... All her own people were far away while he was near, and this sense of nearness thrilled in his heart like a tremor of an impeding flash in clouds laden with lightning.
>
> When Lolita had retired to her cabin for the night, Binoy felt unable to sleep.[17]

Later in the novel by Tagore, we see that Lolita has "retired to her room, to weep, as she had made herself weep so many times before."[18]

Before the novel *Lolita* was originally published in 1955 in France, a Puerto Rican revolutionary by the name of Lolita Lebron had led an attack, opening fire on the U.S. Congress on March 1, 1953, "when we demanded freedom for Puerto Rico and we told the world that we are an invaded nation, occupied and abused by the United States of America."[19] Lolita was jailed for 27 years for her participation in this attack,[20] but in the meantime, is it possible that Nabokov, ardently criticizing American bourgeois values in *Lolita*, was also writing metaphorically about imperialism when Humbert took over the body of his unruly little stepdaughter?

With or without this Puerto Rican metaphor which Alfred Appel overlooked in his copious annotations of *Lolita*, metaphors from a myriad of other sources abound – a record number of them, if you don't include Flaubert's *Bouvard et Pécuchet* – including chess, lepidoptery, literature, and poetry. When Nabokov was given the chance to write the screenplay adaptation of his novel, he said, "The screenplay became poetry, which was my original purpose."[21] But it clocked in at over 400 pages. "You couldn't make it," said the producer. "You couldn't *lift* it."[22]

Although Nabokov received screenplay credit, Kubrick's *Lolita* was mostly written by the director and the producer. In order to obtain the right to publish his own screenplay, Nabokov had to agree not to say "anything derogatory about Kubrick's film either in writing or verbally."[23] In other words, he was not at liberty to bemoan the loss of a backstory to Humbert's fixation on underage girls, the omission of Lolita's misery in favor of jollifying and expanding the rivalry between the two men who lusted after her, or to condemn the fact that what should be an American road movie for its second half was mostly filmed in England. Still, some of Kubrick's *mise-en-scène* aspires to Nabokov's greatness as a prose stylist.

Had Nabokov lived until 1997, would he have approved of Adriane Lyne's adaptation of *Lolita* (USA/France, 1997), given its relative fidelity to the novel's plot points, or would he have shuddered at the casting of 17-year-old Dominique Swain to play a pre-teenage nymphet? What would he have thought of Marielle Heller's *The Diary of a Teenage Girl* (USA, 2015), based on Phoebe Gloeckner's graphic novel with the same title?[24] Both the graphic novel and the film examine a relationship between a grown man and an underage girl, but what motivated Heller to tackle the adaptation was the point of view of its narrator/protagonist, Minnie Goetze:

> This was the most honest depiction of a girl ... that I ever came across. I'd never seen female characters as brazen about exploring their sexuality as their male counterparts who were exploring up the wazoo. It felt like she was just an empowering exciting character to get to know, so honest, so smart, so interested in the world, so vulnerable and willing to be flawed.[25]

Minnie, age 15, can't match Humbert's eloquence, but she sure can draw comic strips that express not only her inner feelings about her trysts with her mother's boyfriend, but her aspirations to record her 1970s San Francisco-era sexual experiences through art.

Heller's first adaptation of the graphic novel was an off-Broadway play, but when she brought the project to the screen, Gloeckner's comic strips were brought to life by combining animation with live-action storytelling of characters that Heller further developed in the course of attending the Sundance Labs and writing twenty drafts.[26] As Gloeckner points out, in addition to this hybrid visual approach, "instead of writing, Minnie records the diary out loud. This just worked much better for film."[27]

Of the finished product, Manohla Dargis of *The New York Times* comments:

> It would be easy to call Minnie a victim, and Monroe the villain, even if that's not at all how it plays out in the movie. Monroe may not be exactly the light of Minnie's life, but for much of the story, he is the fire of her loins, to borrow and bend some opening words from Nabokov's Lolita.[28]

Stieg Larsson's 2005 international best-seller *The Girl with the Dragon Tattoo*, the first novel of his posthumously published *Millenium* trilogy, features a 23-year-old female computer hacker who is tortured and raped by a sadistic legal guardian. Lisbeth Salander achieves her revenge against the legal guardian by literally branding him a rapist and regaining control of her life and finances. Her computer skills bring her to the attention of Mikael Blomkvist, who seeks her help in investigating the disappearance of Harriet Vanger, a member of a wealthy, ultra-right wing family, as well as discovering all he can about a billionaire industrialist who had had Blomkvist imprisoned for his first investigation of him. Ultimately, they discover vast networks of corruption by the Swedish-based corporation owned by the Vanger family, as well as the tortures and murders of women by CEO Martin Vanger. The film and television mini-series adaptations of this thriller and the subsequent volumes of the *Millenium* series have amassed a fortune: $114,947,100 worldwide for the Swedish film adaptation[29] and $232,617,430 worldwide for the American adaptation alone.[30]

Eva Gabrielsson, the author's life partner, explains how the characters of the *Millenium* trilogy may have been influenced by Astrid Lindgren's much-beloved Swedish children's book series, *Pippi Longstocking*[31] (itself adapted into films and television shows in Canada, the Soviet Union, the U.S. and Sweden).[32] The protagonist of these children's books – both strong and cute – not only "doesn't depend on anyone, [she] can use a revolver." Reminiscent of Mary Shelley sitting around the fire with Lord Byron and her husband back in 1816, concocting ghost stories as a prelude to *Frankenstein*,[33] Gabrielsson recalls:

> One evening toward the end of the 1990s, Stieg and some journalists at TT had fun imagining what all the favorite storybook idols of Swedish children might really have grown up to be. Pippi Longstocking? Lisbeth Salander, perhaps. And what about Kalle Blomkvist (or Bill Bergson, as he's known in English), the young hero of Astrid Lindgren's trilogy about an ordinary boy who loves to solve mysteries and even real crimes that baffle the police and other adults? Maybe Mikael Blomkvist.[34]

In an interview before his death, Larsson ruminated on the idea of a grown-up Pippi:

> What would she be called? A sociopath? Somebody suffering from attention-deficit/hyperactivity disorder? I made her like Lisbeth Salander, 25 years old, with a ginormous exclusion complex. She knows nobody and has no social skills whatsoever.[35]

Sometimes the censorship of an author can take the form of death, or even murder. Eva Gabrielsson, Larsson's companion for 32 years, wrote, "In the 1990s, more than a dozen people were murdered in Sweden for political reasons by individuals involved with neo-Nazi groups,"[36] and Larsson received numerous death threats. However, when he died in 2004, it was due to a heart attack. After his death, his estate hired David Lagercrantz to write a sequel to Larsson's *Millenium* triology, entitled *The Girl in the Spider's Web*,[37] currently being cast with an eye towards a 2018 movie release.

In some ways, film and television adaptations can be thought to extend the life of an author's work. But Eva Gabrielsson, who has fought – so far unsuccessfully – to be the person in charge of his literary estate, deplores the "Stieg Larsson industry" which has sprung up since his death, commercializing and minimizing the significance of the political content in his work. Marie-Françoise Colombani describes Gabrielsson's viewpoint of this industry as:

> the complete antithesis of everything he stood for: TV series, films, books by false friends, all kinds of rumors. ... The real Stieg Larsson – the militant, the feminist, the journalist, the autodidact of a vast and eclectic culture – gradually disappeared, leaving the blockbuster author alone in the spotlight.[38]

The Swedish adaptation of *The Girl with the Dragon Tattoo* (Sweden/Denmark/Germany/Norway, 2009), co-written by Nikolaj Arcel and Rasmus Heisterberg and directed by Niels Arden Oplev, remains fairly faithful to Larsson's novel and was well-received. But while the American version (USA/Sweden/Norway, 2011), written by Steven Zaillian and directed by David Fincher, was praised for its strong action-picture-type heroine at a time when women were rarely depicted as multi-dimensional characters,[39] many women bridled at what Melissa Silverstein described as Lisbeth Salander's "pornification" in the international 2011 advertising campaign.[40]

Working on major films supported by governments or corporations can be constraining to filmmakers with unique aesthetic visions or political outlooks that vary from official policy, whether in the former Soviet Union, China, or the US. Sergei Paradjanov suffered four years of hard labor after creating two masterpieces of adaptation: *Shadows of Forgotten Ancestors* (Soviet Union, 1964), based on a Ukranian folk tale, and *The Color of Pomegranates* (Soviet Union, 1968), a uniquely poetic treatment of the life of Sayat Nova, an Armenian monk – which was shelved when Paradjanov refused to comply with the censors' cuts, and completed only after his release from prison.[41] In China, Zhang Yimou's films *Ju Dou, Raise the Red Lantern,* and *Qiu Ju* were considered "poisonous fumes" – fit only for foreigners to view, until July 1992, after the publication of an interview by Mayfair Mei-Hui Yang about the censorship of Chinese cinema in China.[42] In the US, censorship sometimes takes the form of barriers to funding (and to the agents and managers who serve as gatekeepers).

Ellen Stewart, who founded La MaMa Experimental Theatre Club in 1961, told me back in the early 1980s that if one was making important work with social consciousness which one couldn't get produced properly through mainstream studios or networks, one could still stand on a street corner and sell the VHS. Of course, today, that would mean raising funds for low-budget production on funding sites such as IndieGoGo, and streaming the work-in-progress and the completed films or webisodes through the internet – in many cases, an effective way to bypass censorship. If your story is compelling, it is possible that you may be able to forego the bigger budgets of blockbuster films that may be fascistic or simply innocuous. It really depends on your and your producer's passion for your message and your dedication to the means of expression, and whether those factors can overrule your lust for gambling for the big box office. With independent film festivals, cable, and the internet, there are more and more venues for getting polemical work out – as well as more and more competition. On a more hopeful note, some of the films and programs whose subject matter may have been self-censored to the point of non-existence in the past are now getting major accolades and distribution.

Notes

1 Jill Watts, *Mae West: An Icon in Black and White* (Oxford: Oxford University Press, 2001), 154, 156, 158, 169, 265.
2 Motion Picture Association of America. "Film Ratings," accessed March 12, 2017, www.mpaa.org/film-ratings/.
3 Ivan Nechepurenko, "Russian Official Seeks to Ban 'Beauty and the Beast' Over Gay Character," *New York Times*, March 6, 2017, accessed March 12, 2017, https://nyti.ms/2n6DVzX.
4 "India board censors James Bond's kissing scenes in Spectre," *Telegraph Film*, November 19, 2015, accessed March 12, 2017, www.telegraph.co.uk/film/james-bond-spectre/India-board-censors-Bond-kissing-in-SPECTRE/.
5 "Memo for the files, RE: LOLITA, signed G.M.S," MGM files, September 11, 1957, Margaret Herrick Library, Academy of Motion Picture Arts & Sciences, 1.
6 "Memo for the files, RE: LOLITA, signed G.M.S," 1.
7 Letter to Stanley Kubrick from MGM, signed [BLANK] "Secretary," December 7, 1961, Margaret Herrick Library, Academy of Motion Picture Arts & Sciences, 1.
8 Richard Corliss, *Lolita* (London: British Film Institute Film Classics, 1994), 6.
9 Azar Nafisi, *Reading Lolita in Tehran: A Memoir in Books* (New York: Random House, 2004), 40.
10 Vera Nabokov, quoted from her diary, in Nafisi, *Reading Lolita in Tehran*, 40.
11 Azar Nafisi, *Reading Lolita in Tehran*, 36, quoting Vladimir Nabokov, *The Annotated Lolita*, ed. with preface, introduction, and notes by Alfred Appel, Jr. (New York: Vintage Books, 1991), 142.
12 Vladimir Nabokov, *The Annotated Lolita*, ed. with preface, introduction, and notes by Alfred Appel, Jr. (New York: Vintage Books, 1991), 9.

13 Nabokov, *The Annotated Lolita*, 309.
14 T. Jefferson Kline, "Cinema and/as Poetry," *Unraveling French Cinema: from L'Atalante to Caché* (Chichester: Wiley-Blackwell, 2010), 18.
15 Nabokov, *The Annotated Lolita*, 328.
16 Nabokov, *The Annotated Lolita*, 329.
17 Rabindranath Tagore, *Gora* (London: Macmillan and Co., 1924), 153.
18 Tagore, *Gora*, 161.
19 Lolita Lebron, quoted in Berta Ceci-Joubert, "Report from Vieques: Tribunal condemns U.S. Crimes in Puerto Rico," *Workers World,* December 7, 2000, accessed March 13, 2017, www.workers.org/ww/2000/vieques1207.php.
20 Aurora Levins Morales, "From Self-Sacrifice to Self-Preservation," review of Lolita Lebron's granddaughter Irene Vilar's *A Message from God in the Atomic Age*, in *The Women's Review of Books*, 14(8) (May, 1997), 10.
21 Vladimir Nabokov, quoted in Richard Corliss, *Lolita* (London: British Film Institute, 1994), 19.
22 James B. Harris, quoted in Richard Corliss, *Lolita,* 19.
23 Corliss, *Lolita*, 65.
24 Phoebe Gloeckner, *The Diary of a Teenage Girl* (Berkeley, CA: North Atlantic Books, 2002, 2015).
25 Marielle Heller interviewed in Anne Thompson, "Marielle Heller on the Road to 'The Diary of a Teenage Girl,'" *IndieWire*, August 3, 2015, accessed June 17, 2016, www.indiewire.com/2015/08/marielle-heller-on-the-road-to-the-diary-of-a-teenage-girl-185693/.
26 Heller, in Thompson, "Marielle Heller on the Road."
27 Phoebe Gloeckner, "Phoebe Gloeckner's *Diary of a Teenage Girl*: From Graphic Novel to Feature Film," interview by Stamps School of Art & Design at the University of Michigan, 2014, accessed March 14, 2017, http://stamps.umich.edu/creative-work/stories/phoebe.
28 Manohla Dargis, "Review: In *The Diary of a Teenage Girl,* a Hormone Bomb Waiting to Explode," *New York Times*, August 6, 2015, accessed March 14, 2016, www.nytimes.com/2015/08/07/movies/review-in-the-diary-of-a-teenage-girl-a-hormone-bomb-waiting-to-explode.html?_r=0.
29 "*The Girl with the Dragon Tattoo* (2009): Total Life-Time Grosses," Box Office Mojo, accessed March 17, 2017, www.boxofficemojo.com/movies/?id=girldragontattoo11.htm&adjust_yr=2017&p=.htm.
30 "*The Girl with the Dragon Tattoo* (2011): Total Life-Time Grosses," Box Office Mojo, accessed March 17, 2017, www.boxofficemojo.com/movies/?id=girldragontattoo11.htm.
31 Astrid Lindgren, *Pippi Longstocking* (New York: Puffin, 2005). First published in Sweden, 1945.
32 "Pippi Longstocking," Wikipedia.org, accessed March 17, 2017, https://en.wikipedia.org/wiki/Pippi_Longstocking.
33 Mary Shelley, *Frankenstein* (New York: Dover, 1994), pp. vi–viii.
34 Eva Gabrielsson, *"There Are Things I Want You to Know" About Stieg Larsson and Me*, with Marie-Françoise Colombani, trans. by Linda Coverdale (New York: Seven Stories Press, 2011), 96.
35 Stieg Larson, quoted in Nathaniel Rich, "The Mystery of the Dragon Tattoo: Stieg Larsson, the World's Bestselling – and Most Enigmatic – Author" *Rolling Stone*, December 23, 2010, accessed March 17, 2017, www.rollingstone.com/culture/news/the-mystery-of-the-dragon-tattoo-stieg-larsson-the-worlds-bestselling-and-most-enigmatic-author-20110105.
36 Gabrielsson, *"There Are Things I Want You to Know,"* 55.
37 Steven Erlanger, "In Stieg Larsson's Head, but His Own Man," *New York Times*, August 28, 2015, accessed August 29, 2015, http://yti.ms/1JB9wwX.
38 Marie-Françoise Colombani, "Preface," in Gabrielsson, *"There Are Things I Want You to Know,"* p. x.

39 Roger Ebert, "The Girl with the Dragon Tattoo," December 19, 2011, accessed March 17, 2017, www.rogerebert.com/reviews/the-girl-with-the-dragon-tattoo-2011.
40 Melissa Silverstein, "The Pornification of Lisbeth Salander," *IndieWire,* June 8, 2011, accessed March 17, 2017, www.indiewire.com/2011/06/the-pornification-of-lisbeth-salander-212281/.
41 Gerald Mast and Bruce F. Kawin, *A Short History of the Movies*, 6th edn. (Boston, MA: Allyn and Bacon, 1996), 536.
42 Mayfair Mi-Hui Yang, "Of Gender, State, Censorship, and Overseas Capital: An Interview with Chinese Director Zhang Yimou." In Frances Gateward (ed.), *Zhang Yimou: Interviews* (Jackson, MS: University of Mississippi Press, 2001), 43, reprinted by permission of Duke University Press from *Public Culture,* 5(2) (Summer, 1993), 297–313.

Part X
Future Adaptations

TWENTY-ONE

Future Adaptations

In describing the visual effects of "an old Pathé Film from France"[1] in which books, dishes, clothing, carpets, and furniture transport themselves magically on Moving Day, the poet and critic Vachel Lindsay wrote in 1915, "The ability to do this kind of a thing is fundamental in the destinies of the art."[2] Lindsay criticized *Moving Day* (France, 1908)[3] as crassly lacking "the touch of the creative imagination,"[4] like other films that are "mere voodooism."[5] Over a hundred years later, we can see his critique of *Moving Day* reverberate in many of the visual effects-driven blockbusters of today, and wish that earlier producers had taken heed:

> A picture that is all action is a plague, one that is all elephantine and pachydermatous pageant is a bore, and, most emphatically, a film that is all mechanical legerdemain is a nuisance.[6]

Yet Vachel Lindsay predicted the emergence of cinematic "prophet-wizards"[7] in whose hands, he proclaimed, "this lantern of wizard-drama is going to give us in time the visible things in the fullness of their primeval force, and some that have been for a long time invisible."[8] He wanted us to wake up and realize that there was more to the future of the photoplay than scientific inventors and the kinds of producer who "imagines the people want nothing but a silly lark."[9]

Every generation has new technology to play with. By now, we've made the shift from Kurosawa's film *Dreams*, which includes a story based on the painting "Wheat Field with Crows" by Vincent van Gogh, to a virtual reality film of van Gogh's "Starry Night." Although at the time of writing, an extensive body of adaptation work in virtual reality doesn't exist, in the meantime experiments such as being able to watch "Circle of Life" in 360° from the musical adaptation of *The Lion King* indicate technological progress in new directions.[10]

In his book, *Jane Austen, Game Theorist*, Michael Suk-Young Chwe re-examines Austen's focus on "insisting upon the right to choose according to one's own preferences (over whom to marry, for example)," as a model for game theory.[11] For example, in *Pride and Prejudice*, "Elizabeth [Bennet] is set up with strategic skills right from the start,"[12] and Mr. Darcy "learns the hard way that a proposal is a strategic situation: the proposer must consider whether the proposee will actually accept or not."[13] Similarly, in *Sense and Sensibility*, "Elinor is good at making decisions, while Marianne overspecializes in thinking about other people's motives. The two sisters thus exemplify two skills both necessary for strategic thinking," and for winning at the game of love.[14] It's entirely possible that Jane Austen's best future adaptations will be videogames.

Perhaps this is why, in this already late age of filmmaking and early age of videogames, *The Jane Austen Book Club* novel and film seem so trivial. Both are well-crafted and intelligent, yet seem small-minded, as if written with a pair of tweezers rather than a computer or a pen. At least the videogame would give us the semblance of individual choice as it's played.

Will the universe as we've come to know it by watching and writing movies break down if we stop relying on Hollywood formulas like John Truby's "Universal Structure" with its "twenty-two building blocks of every great story?"[15] What hidden realms might we discover if we use string theory, pushing past six dimensions to ten, eleven, or even twenty-six dimensions, for example? String theory's extra dimensions may prove especially valuable as we orchestrate the relationships between structure and content when writing virtual reality scripts.

Prior to string theory, the Standard Model of particle physics explained three of the forces of the universe, but not the gravitational force. String theory unified all four forces. According to *The Fabric of the Cosmos: What Is Space?*, the vibrations of the strings at the center of quarks that make the protons and electrons that in turn make atoms, make our universe a cosmic symphony.[16]

As screenwriters, thinking metaphorically, how do the minutiae of looks, gestures, and words that a character uses change the lives of other characters in the story, as well as the lives of members of the audience? What is our relationship to each detail of a writer's imagination that makes it to our screens and monitors? Can this become a way of structuring a story from the inside out, while harkening to the cosmic forces beyond the day-to-day scope of the "Person with the Problem?"

The answers may lie as much in spiritual practice as in scientific inquiries. For example, in discussing the Tiwa language of northern New Mexico, Native American elder Joseph Rael says:

> I came to the realization that sounds, especially vowel sounds, are the vibrations of principal ideas, encoded in the human gene pool, and words made from these sounds will carry within them the principal ideas that are the same, no matter what language a person is speaking.[17]

Rael, who has addressed the United Nations as well as the U.S. Pentagon on the role of the warrior in the modern world,[18] identifies the vowels as having the following meanings: "A = purification; E = placement; I = awareness; O = childlike innocence; and U = carrying."[19] The French poet, Arthur Rimbaud, proclaimed the power of vowels and silences in *A Season in Hell*, saying "I invented the colors of the vowels! ... I made rules for the form and movement of each consonant ... At first this was an academic study. I wrote of silences and of nights, I expressed the inexpressible."[20] Tibetan Buddhists describe an alchemy of written syllables:

> My mind, in the aspect of the undifferentiable suchness of myself and the deity, becomes a moon mandala, upon which the very aspect of the tone of the mantra resounding in space is set down, having the form of written syllables. The sounds and the written letters [of the mantra] are mixing, like very pure mercury adhering to grains of gold...
>
> The (syllables) transform into a thousand-petaled lotus, as brilliant as refined gold, marked at the center by the mantra, OM MANI PADME HUM. From the tips of the multicolored light rays emitted from the moon, lotus and mantra, innumerable holy bodies of the Arya (Avalokiteshvara) spread out, pervading all the realms of space.[21]

All of these examples address the relationship between the microcosms of vowels and syllables and the macrocosms they convey – a heavy responsibility for writers whose craft involves working with letters and words to express what it means to be human (or even superhuman!) in terms of our emotions, experiences, and fantasies.

Arthur Rimbaud prophesized a future in which the poet "would give more than the formula of his thought," and described the poems made to last as "[a]lways full of *Number* and *Harmony*."[22] Perhaps it was this French poet who inspired Jean Cocteau to give the protagonist of *Orphée* (France, 1950) such an obsession with reciting mathematical poetry – much to the disdain of the avant-garde literati of Orphée's milieu. Still ahead of his time in the twentieth century, Cocteau may have recognized the interconnection between the arts and sciences, although he was more involved with the arts as a form of magic than as a form of healing.

In traditional Chinese medicine, the human energy system "shares the same basic elements and energies that constitute the entire universe," and contains multiple subsystems and supersystems.[23] As screenwriters in tune with our bodies and our universe, we can reexamine our role as we zoom in from the cosmos to our planet; from our country to a particular city; from a cineplex to a particular audience; from the movie the audience watches to its acts, sequences, scenes, beats, and dialogue; from its lines of dialogue to words, images, and gestures; down to the very syllables and white space in the script that we have written.

To give ourselves permission to think outside the box – that big black hole of "been there, done that" – it can help to carry relatively new concepts that have worked in other forms of art to our own, so that we can at least catch up. In jazz, Ornette Coleman, who won the Pulitzer Prize for his album "Sound Grammar" in 2007, developed "new structures of composition"[24] between harmony, movement, and melody called "harmolodics." Coleman says:

> To me, human existence exists on a multiple level, not just on a two-dimensional level, not just having to be identified with what you do and what you say ... That's how I have always wanted musicians to play with me: on a multiple level. I don't want them to follow me. I want them to follow themself, but to be with me.[25]

Can this concept affirm the necessity of making an adaptation more alive by being in sync with but not enslaved to the original author's words? The freedom to improvise while being in loose harmony with some of the great cinematic, literary, and musical ideas of one's contemporaries and predecessors, can be the key to one's own greatness. As Klara Szlezák and D.E. Wynter state in *Referentiality and the Films of Woody Allen*:

> For four decades as a filmmaker, Allen has been "jamming" with his literary and cinematic "idols" (Houpt) – or companions – using the referential, intertextual, and intermedial aspects of cinema to improvise, harmonize, and bring transcendence to the works of the masters and in the process creating his very own masterpieces.[26]

Stephon Alexander, a jazz musician and a physics professor, digs into the details of the relationship between jazz and spoken language:

> Jazz vocabulary is analogous to phrases in spoken language. We use letters to make up words, and then string together words into phrases or sentences. Notes are like letters, scales and chords are like words, and jazz "licks" or patterns are like spoken phrases.[27]

Furthermore, states Alexander, "From the symmetric patterns of quarks that organize to form nuclear matter, to the helical structure in DNA, to patterns of galaxies in super-clusters, the universe is teeming with structure."[28] Putting two and two together (with occasional references to Eisenstein to provide a complex mathematical justification), Alexander makes the case that the universe "has a musical character."[29]

John Coltrane, the jazz saxophonist, "realized that he had to go beyond the Western and classic jazz idiom to make his music cosmic and express the cosmic through music."[30] The mandala that he used to structure his improvisations incorporates a pentatonic scale used in ancient Greek, Chinese, African, and Indian music along with other scales, "the same way space-time transformation relates length contraction to time dilation, electric fields to magnetic fields."[31] Not only is this thinking cyclical rather than linear, but it applies the principle of asymmetry to what screenwriting teachers have traditionally taught as the steps that every hero must take.

What rich promises the study of time, cosmology, and neuroscience of the twenty-first century hold for the re-examination of story structure in a constantly evolving universe! We can now be free to think in more than one dimension, as well as applying the terms of relativity to relationships between characters.

Critic Manohla Dargis observes:

> We live in interesting narrative times, cinematically. In *Cloud Atlas* characters jump across centuries, space and six separate stories into a larger tale about human interconnectedness ... while in *Life of Pi* a boy and a tiger share a small boat in a very big sea amid long silences, hallucinatory visuals and no obvious story arc. In movies like these ... filmmakers are pushing hard against, and sometimes dispensing with, storytelling conventions, and audiences seem willing to follow them ... [It] can be thrilling to see something that feels new, risky or unusual, and even to venture into the realm of the confounding.[32]

Applying theories of cosmology and medicine can help us to apply the systems, supersystems, and subsystems of the human condition in our plot structures and character arcs so that our audience as well as our characters can heal. In Part I we applied current thinking about posttraumatic stress disorder to character arc as an example of how to use the healing arts to enrich our work as screenwriters. But there are many more templates available to transform the structure as well as the content of adaptations in the future.

For example, as Mikio Sankey points out in suggesting that acupuncture be brought "into alignment with the needs and thinking of society today, especially here in the West,"[33] it is possible to go beyond traditional theories

Figure 21.1 Life of Pi, directed by Ang Lee, written by David Magee (USA, 2012), based on the novel by Yann Martel. Image courtesy of 20th Century Fox. Produced by Ingenious Media, Haishang Films, and Netter Productions

in applying four basic principles of acupuncture to the field of screenwriting. The first principle, "to unlock the gateways to the finer frequency levels of consciousness that are stored in the planes above the dense mental planes of consciousness,"[34] reminds me of *High and Low* (*Tengoku to Jigoku*, literally "Heaven and Hell," Japan, 1963), the transcendent masterpiece of cinematic art that Akira Kurosawa created in adapting Ed McBain's pulp fiction book, *The King's Ransom*. The second principle, "to balance and strengthen the opposing energy fields of the heart and love versus the kidneys and fear,"[35] lets us rethink the old genres of love story and thriller, among other applications. The third principle, "assisting the client to find or discover his or her puzzle piece in life"[36] by enabling him or her to access the great teachings and to reach a higher consciousness sounds like a template for a character arc that involves an inner journey; and the fourth principle, "to expand both the vocabulary and the field of acupuncture to bring this grand traditional system more into alignment with the needs of the people in the Western countries in the twenty-first century,"[37] is akin to the purpose of this book in the field of screenwriting.

It will be interesting to see how Jill Soloway's adaptation of Chris Kraus's novel, *I Love Dick* (USA, 2016) on Amazon evolves. The first season is much more coherent than experimental, apart from title cards that seem to have floated out of the films of the early French New Wave by Agnès Varda and Jean-Luc Godard, and a few experimental films used as cutaways. It's possible that this relatively conservative approach will help Soloway's *I Love Dick* series survive.

In contrast, Joan Hawkins describes Kraus's work as "theoretical fiction ... in which theory becomes an intrinsic part of the 'plot'."[38] However, theory isn't everything. As the great Chinese director Zhang Yimou states, "I don't think a film should carry too much theory. After all, it is not philosophy or a concept to be taught in a classroom ... I tend to believe that films are about emotions. An artist's ideas should be understood naturally through emotions."[39] What enables us to feel so deeply about films like Zhang Yimou's *To Live* (China, 1994), or Oliver Stone's *Born on the Fourth of July* (USA, 1989), is experiencing the trauma of war the way the author and the filmmakers experienced it in their personal lives and then dramatized it to reach us. Jack Davis points out that "Stone encourages viewers to experience history not on an intellectual level but on an emotional one, as he and Kovic experienced the Vietnam era."[40] Jill Soloway is similarly committed to the feeling that emanates from Chris Kraus's work. Soloway explains:

> For us, *I Love Dick* is not just about adapting the book, but about trying to record the feeling of what happens when you read the book. Chris is so comfortable with her desire and her creativity that it shocks everyone who reads it into their own artistic awakening.[41]

As you embark on the practice of screenwriting and adaptation, trust your own emotions regarding the work that lies ahead of you.

Mikio Sankey reminds us that:

> If you find any teacher or school of thought that tells you their style is the only way, I would suggest that you go to your heart and re-evaluate that teacher and style of teaching. [T]here is no One Way or One Pathway. There are infinite choices.[42]

Notes

1 Vachel Lindsay, *The Art of the Moving Picture* (New York: Liveright Publishing, 1970), 61, originally published by Macmillan, 1915.
2 Lindsay, *The Art of the Moving Image*, 62.
3 Segundo de Chomón, *Moving Day* (Paris: Pathé Brothers, 1908).
4 Lindsay, *The Art of the Moving Image*, 63.
5 Lindsay, *The Art of the Moving Image*, 295.
6 Lindsay, *The Art of the Moving Image*, 142.
7 Lindsay, *The Art of the Moving Image*, 291.
8 Lindsay, *The Art of the Moving Image*, 290.
9 Lindsay, *The Art of the Moving Image*, 290.
10 "Circle of Life," *The Lion King*, Musical (Disney Broadway, 2015), accessed October 20, 2016, www.youtube.com/watch?v=7T57kzGQGto.
11 Michael Suk-Young Chwe, *Jane Austen: Game Theorist* (Princeton, NJ: Princeton University Press, 2013), 9.
12 Chwe, *Jane Austen*, 50.
13 Chwe, *Jane Austen*, 52.
14 Chwe, *Jane Austen*, 54.
15 John Truby, "Why Story Structure Is the Key to Success," *Writer's Store*, accessed August 25, 2016, www.writersstore.com/why-story-structure-is-the-key-to-success/ 1982-2016.
16 Graham Judd and Sabin Street, producers/directors, *The Fabric of the Cosmos: What Is Space?* PBS-TV/NOVA. WGBH Educational Foundation. Based on the book by Brian Greene, *The Fabric of the Cosmos* (New York: Vintage Series, Random House, 2005). Broadcast in Los Angeles on November 2, 2011, www.pbs.org/wgbh/nova/physics/fabric-of-cosmos.html#fabric-space.
17 Joseph Rael, *Ceremonies of the Living Spirit* (Tulsa, OK: Council Oak Books, 1997), 5.
18 Joseph Rael (Beautiful Painted Arrow), Manatake American Indian Council, accessed August 25, 2016, www.manataka.org/page1627.html.
19 Rael, *Ceremonies of the Living Spirit*, 5.
20 Arthur Rimbaud, "Une Saison en Enfer: Ravings II – Alchemy of the Word." In Oliver Bernard (ed., trans.), *Rimbaud* (Baltimore, MD: Penguin Books, 1962), 327.
21 His Holiness the Dalai Lama, "The Yoga Method of Avalokiteshvara, the Buddha of Compassion," teaching given in New York City, September 24, 2005, including: "3. The Deity of Syllables" and "4. The Deity of Form" in "The Actual Practice," *The Self-generation Sadhana of Avalokiteshvara,* ed. by Nichola Ribush, accessed August 25, 2016, www.lamayeshe.com/article/yoga-method-avalokiteshvara-buddha-compassion.
22 Arthur Rimbaud, letter to Paul Demeny (Douai) from Charleville, France, in Bernard, *Rimbaud*, p. xxxii.
23 Daniel Reid, *The Shambhala Guide to Traditional Chinese Medicine* (Boston, MA: Shambhala Publications, 1996), 22.
24 AAJ Staff, "A Fireside Chat with Marc Ribot," *All About Jazz*, February 21, 2004, accessed November 28, 2015, www.allaboutjazz.com/a-fireside-chat-

with-marc-ribo-marc-ribot-by-aaj-staff.php, quoted in Stephon Alexander, *The Jazz of Physics: The Secret Link Between Music and the Structure of the Universe* (New York: Basic Books, 2016), 97.

25 Michael Jarrett, "Ornette Coleman Interview," *Cadence Magazine*, 1995 (recorded November 8, 1987 in Atlanta, GA), www2.york.psu.edu/~jmj3/p_ornett.htm.

26 Klara Stephanie Szlezák and D.E. Wynter, eds., *Referentiality and the Films of Woody Allen* (New York: Palgrave Macmillan, 2015), 8.

27 Stephon Alexander, *The Jazz of Physics: The Secret Link Between Music and the Structure of the Universe* (New York: Basic Books, 2016), 172–173.

28 Alexander, *The Jazz of Physics*, 215.

29 Alexander, *The Jazz of Physics*, 215.

30 Alexander, *The Jazz of Physics*, 217.

31 Alexander, *The Jazz of Physics*, 227.

32 Manohla Dargis, in A.O. Scott and Manohla Dargis, "When Do We 'Get It'?: Films Dispense with Storytelling Conventions, accessed November 23, 2012, 1–2, www.nytimes.com/2012/11/25/movies/films-dispense-with-storytelling-conventions.html.

33 Mikio Sankey, *Antahkarana, Celestial Fullness: Esoteric Acupuncture AI. VI.* (Inglewood, CA: Mountain Castle, 2014), 2.

34 Sankey, *Antahkarana, Celestial Fullness*, 3.

35 Sankey, *Antahkarana, Celestial Fullness*, 3.

36 Sankey, *Antahkarana, Celestial Fullness*, 3.

37 Sankey, *Antahkarana, Celestial Fullness*, 3–4.

38 Joan Hawkins, "Afterword," in Chris Kraus, *I Love Dick* (Los Angeles, CA: Semiotext(e), 1998, 2006), 263.

39 Zhang Yimou, quoted in Tan Ye, "From the Fifth to the Sixth Generation: An Interview with Zhang Yimou," 1999. In Frances Gateward (ed.), *Zhang Yimou Interviews* (Jackson, MS: University of Mississippi Press, 2001), 154. First published in *Film Quarterly*, 53(2) (Winter, 1999–2000).

40 Jack E. Davis, "New Left, Revisionist, In-Your-Face History: Oliver Stone's *Born on the Fourth of July* Experience." In Robert Brent Toplin (ed.), *Oliver Stone's USA* (Lawrence, KS: University Press of Kansas, 2000), 141.

41 Jill Soloway, quoted in Amanda Hess, "Chris Kraus and Jill Soloway Talk About the Show 'I Love Dick,'" *The New York Times*, May 5, 2017, accessed May 7, 2017, 3, https://nyti.ms/2pdr2Vo.

42 Sankey, *Antahkarana, Celestial Fullness,* 661.

Select Bibliography

Achebe, Chinua (2009) *The Education of a British-Protected Child: Essays*. New York: Anchor Books.

Agha-Jaffar, Tamara (2002) *Demeter and Persephone: Lessons from a Myth*. Jefferson, NC: McFarland & Company.

Alexander, LaVeria and Alexis Krasilovsky (1999) "*Cinderella* and *Ever After*: Retrieving the Heroine's Journey." *Creative Screenwriting* 6(3) (May–June), 55–57.

Anzaldúa, Gloria E. (2015) *Light in the Dark – Luz en lo Oscuro: Rewriting Identity, Spirituality, Reality*. Edited by Analouise Keating. Durham NC: Duke University Press.

Aronson, Linda (2010) "'Cinderella' Structured According to the Basic Nine-Point Plan." In *The 21st Century Screenplay: A Comprehensive Guide to Writing Tomorrow's Films*. Los Angeles, CA: Silman-James Press.

Bauer, Eric (2015) "Re-Revealing Shakespeare: An Interview with Baz Luhrmann." *Creative Screenwriting*, January 7, accessed June 1, 2017, https://creativescreenwriting.com/re-revealing-shakespeare-baz-lurhmann-on-romeo-juliet/.

Bignell, Jonathan (2000) "A Taste of the Gothic: Film and Television Versions of *Dracula*." In Robert Giddins and Erica Sheen (eds), *The Classic Novel: From Page to Screen*. Manchester: Manchester University Press.

Buchanan, Judith (2005) *Shakespeare on Film*. Harlow: Pearson Longman.

Cahir, Linda Costanzo (2006) *Literature into Film: Theory and Practical Approaches*. Jefferson, NC: McFarland & Company.

Carter, Angela (1995) "*Ashputtle* or *The Mother's Ghost*: Three Versions of One Story." In *Burning Your Boats: The Collected Short Stories*. New York: Henry Holt.

Chahine, Youssef (2003) Interview in "Caméra Arabe: The Young Arab Cinema." Special features DVD. *Asfar al-sath Halfaouine: Child of the Terraces*. Directed by Ferid Boughedir. New York: Kino on Video.

Chattopadhyay, Saratchandra (2002) *Devdas: A Novel*. Translated by Sreeiata Guha. New York: Penguin.

Choueiti, Mare and Stacy L. Smith (2014) *Gender Disparity On Screen and Behind the Camera in Family Films: An Executive Summary*. Los Angeles, CA: Geena Davis Institute on Gender in Media and Annenberg School for Communication

& Journalism at University of Southern California (September 22, 2014), 14–17.

Chwe, Michael Suk-Young (2013) *Jane Austen: Game Theorist*. Princeton, NJ: Princeton University Press.

Cocteau, Jean (1972) *Beauty and the Beast: Diary of a Film*. Translated by Ronald Duncan. New York: Dover.

Conway, Jill Ker (1998) *When Memory Speaks: Reflections on Autobiography*. New York: Alfred A. Knopf.

Crowl, Samuel (1994) "The Bow is Bent and Drawn: Kurosawa's *Ran* and the Shakespearean Arrow of Desire." *Literature/Film Quarterly* 22(2) (April), 109–115.

Curti, Lidia (1998) *Female Stories, Female Bodies: Narrative, Identity and Representation*. New York: New York University Press.

Dalton, Mary M. (2014) "Conquer or Connect: Power, Patterns, and the Gendered Narrative." *Journal of Film & Video* 65(1–2) (Spring–Summer), 23–29.

del Toro, Guillermo and Chuck Hogan (2009) "Why Vampires Never Die." The Opinion Pages, *New York Times*, July 3, accessed April 19, 2017, www.nytimes.com/2009/07/31/opinion/31deltoro.html?_r=0.

Desmond, John M. and Peter Hawkins (2006) *Adaptation: Studying Film & Literature*. Boston, MA: McGraw Hill.

Donaldson, Michael C. and Lisa A. Callif (2014) *Clearance & Copyright: Everything You Need to Know for Film and Television*. 4th edn. Los Angeles, CA: Silman-James Press.

Downing, Christine (1994) *The Long Journey Home: Re-visioning the Myth of Demeter and Persephone for Our Time*. Boston, MA: Shambhala.

Edson, Eric (2012) *The Story Solution: 23 Steps All Great Heroes Must Take*. Los Angeles, CA: Michael Wiese.

Estés, Clarissa Pinkola (1992/1996) *Women Who Run with the Wolves: Myths and Stories of the Wild Woman Archetype*. New York: Ballantine Books.

Evenson, J. M. (2013) *Shakespeare for Screenwriters*. Studio City, CA: Michael Wiese.

Faivre, Antoine (1993) *The Golden Fleece and Alchemy*. Albany, NY: State University of New York Press.

Farr, Louise (2016) "Black-ish Like Me: Kenya Barris Writes What His Family Knows." *WGAW Written By* 20(4) (Summer), 24–32.

Farr, Louise (2015) "Partners in Crime: Jim Kouf & David Greenwalt Brew Police Procedural with Fantasy-Horror to Concoct 'Grimm.'" *WGAW Written By* 19(4) (Summer), 26–32.

Frankel, Valerie Estelle (2010) *From Girl to Goddess: The Heroine's Journey through Myth and Legend*. Jefferson, NC: McFarland & Company.

Gabrielsson, Eva (2011) *"There Are Things I Want You to Know" About Stieg Larsson, Eva and Me*. Translated by Linda Coverdale. New York: Seven Stories Press.

Gateward, Frances, (ed.) (2001) *Zhang Yimou: Interviews*. Jackson, MS: University of Mississippi Press.

Gates, Henry Louis, Jr (2008) "General Editor Essay" and "Afterword," in Solomon Northup, *Twelve Years a Slave*. New York: Penguin.

Ghali, Noureddine (1987) "An Interview with Sembène Ousmane." In John D.H. Downing (ed.), *Film & Politics in the Third World*. New York: Autonomedia.

Gilligan, Carol (1982) *In a Different Voice: Psychological Theory and Women's Development*. Cambridge, MA: Harvard University Press.

Goldsmith, Jeff (2009) "Still *Slumming...*" *Creative Screenwriting* (March–April), 41–43.

Hanel, Rachel (2017) "Video Games Redefine the Classics." *Poets & Writers* (July–August), accessed July 24, 2017, www.pw.org/content/video_games_redefine_the_classics.

Harrison, Stephanie (2005) *Adaptations: From Short Story to Big Screen – 35 Great Stories that Have Inspired Great Films*. New York: Three Rivers Press.

Harrison, Stephanie (2006) "You Ought to Be in Pictures: A Story Writer's Guide to Film Adaptation." *Poets & Writers* (September–October), 69–73.

Hirsch, Marianne (1989) *The Mother/Daughter Plot: Narrative, Psychoanalysis, Feminism*. Bloomington, IN: Indiana University Press.

Hudson, Kim (2009/2010) *The Virgin's Promise: Writing Stories of Feminine Creative, Spiritual, and Sexual Awakening*. Studio City, CA: Michael Wiese.

Humphries-Brooks, Stephenson (2006) *Cinematic Christ: Hollywood's Making of the American Christ*. Westport, CT: Praeger.

Hunt, Darnell and Ana-Christine Ramón (2015) *2015 Hollywood Diversity Report: Flipping the Script*. Hollywood, CA: Ralph J. Bunche Center for African American Studies at UCLA, accessed April 19, 2017, www.bunchecenter.ucla.edu/wp-content/uploads/2015/02/2015-Hollywood-Diversity-Report-2-25-15.pdf.

Krasilovsky, Alexis (1998) "All About *All About Eve*." *Creative Screenwriting* 5(1) (January–February), 57–59.

Krasilovsky, Alexis (1994) "Issues in Adaptation: A Screenwriter's Journey into Myths and Fairy Tales." *Creative Screenwriting* 1(1) (Spring), 111–122.

Krasilovsky, Alexis (1994) "Of Spinners & Screenplays." *Creative Screenwriting* 1(3) (Fall), 67–84.

Lauzen, Martha (2017) *The Celluloid Ceiling: Behind-the-Scenes Employment of Women on the Top 100, 250, and 500 Films of 2016*. Center for the Study of Women in Television and Film. San Diego, CA: San Diego State University, accessed June 6, 2017, http://womenintvfilm.sdsu.edu/wp-content/uploads/2017/01/2016_Celluloid_Ceiling_Report.pdf

Lee, Spike and Ralph Wiley (1992) *By Any Means Necessary: The Trails and Tribulations of the Making of Malcolm X*. New York: Hyperion.

Leed, Eric J. (1991) *The Mind of the Traveler: From Gilgamesh to Global Tourism*. New York: Basic Books.

Le Fanu, Mark (2005) *Mizoguchi and Japan*. London: British Film Institute.

Lindsay, Vachel (1970) *The Art of Moving Pictures*. Introduction by Stanley Kauffmann. New York: Liveright. Originally published by Macmillan, 1915.

Lispector, Clarice (1977) *The Hour of the Star*. Translated by Giovanni Pontiero. Manchester: Carcanet Press.

Llosa, Mario Vargas (1991) *A Writer's Reality*. New York: Syracuse University Press.

Lu Wei and Wang Tianbing (2013) *The Secret of Screenwriting* (in Chinese). Shanghai: Shanghai Jiao Tong University Press.

Mahfouz, Maguib (2011) *Midaq Alley: A New Translation*. Translated by Humphrey Davies. New York: American University in Cairo Press.

Marable, Manning (2011) *Malcolm X: A Life of Reinvention*. New York: Viking Press.

Marcus, Millicent (1993) *Filmmaking by the Book: Italian Cinema and Literary Adaptation*. Baltimore, MD: Johns Hopkins University Press.

Margolis, Harriet (ed.) (1999) *Jane Campion's The Piano*. Cambridge: Cambridge University Press.

McDonald, Keiko (ed.) (1993) *Ugetsu: Kenji Mizoguchi, Director*. New Brunswick, NJ: Rutgers University Press.

McKee, Robert (1997) *Story: Substance, Structure, Style, and the Principles of Screenwriting*. New York: HarperCollins.

McMahan, Alison (2002) *Alice Guy-Blaché: Lost Visionary of the Cinema*. New York: Continuum International.

Meador, Betty De Shong (1992) *Uncursing the Dark: Treasures from the Underworld*. Asheville, NC: Chiron Publications.

Meletinsky, Eleazar Moiseevich (1998) *The Poetics of Myth: Mythification in Twentieth Century Literature*. Translated by Guy Lanoue and Alexandre Sadetsky. New York: Garland.

Mirandé, Alfredo (2013) "Hombres y Machos." In Shira Tarrant (ed.), *Men Speak Out: Views on Gender, Sex, and Power.* 2nd edn. New York: Routledge.

Murdock, Maureen (1990) *The Heroine's Journey*. Boston, MA: Shambhala.

Nabokov, Vladimir (1951) *Speak, Memory: An Autobiography Revisited*. New York: Knopf Doubleday.

Nabokov, Vladimir (1962) *Lolita: A Screenplay*. New York: McGraw-Hill.

Nabokov, Vladimir (1991) *The Annotated Lolita: Revised and Updated*. New York: Vintage Books.

Nafisi, Azar (2004) *Reading Lolita in Tehran: A Memoir in Books*. New York: Random House.

Nelmes, Jill and Jule Selbo (eds.) (2015) *Women Screenwriters: An International Guide*. New York: Palgrave Macmillan.

Orlean, Susan (1998) "Q&A with Susan Orlean." In *The Orchid Thief*. New York: Ballantine Books.

Ovid (1994) *The Metamorphoses of Ovid*. Translated by David R. Slavitt. Baltimore, MD: Johns Hopkins University Press.

Perera, Sylvia Brinton (1981) *Descent to the Goddess: A Way of Initiation for Women*. Toronto, OH: Inner City Books.

Perrault, Charles (2002) "Cinderella, or the Little Glass Slipper." In Maria Tatar, *The Annotated Classic Fairy Tales*. New York: W. W. Norton.

Potter, Sally (1992) *Orlando: A Biography – Film Screenplay*. London: Faber & Faber.

Purkiss, Diane (1992) "Women's Rewriting of Myth." In Carolyne Larrington (ed.), *The Feminist Companion to Mythology*. London: Pandora, 441–455.

Rahn, Suzanne (2003) "Introduction: Analyzing Oz: The First Hundred Years." In *L. Frank Baum's World of Oz: A Class Series at 100*. Lanham, MD: Scarecrow Press.

Rankin, Walter (2007) *Grimm Pictures: Fairy Tale Archetypes in Eight Horror and Suspense Film*. Jefferson, NC: McFarland & Company.

Reis, Patricia (1991/1995) *Through the Goddess: A Woman's Way of Healing*. New York: Continuum.

Rhys, Jean (1998) *Wide Sargasso Sea*. Edited by Judith L. Raiskin. New York: W. W. Norton.

Richie, Donald (1996) *The Films of Akira Kurosawa*. 3rd edn. Berkeley, CA: University of California Press.

Sabal, Joana (1998) "Great Adaptations." *Independent* (August–March), 32–35.

Sanders, Julie (2007) *Adaptation and Appropriation*. London: Routledge.

Sierra, Judy (1992) *Cinderella*. Phoenix, AZ: Oryx Press.

Sokoloff, Alexandra (2009) "How to Become a Novelist in Your Spare Time." *WGAW Written By* 13(1) (August–September), 17.

Stayton, Richard (2012) "Taming the Tiger: They Said 'Life of Pi' Couldn't Be Made into a Movie. David Magee Proved Them Wrong." *WGAW Written By* 16(6) (November–December), 22–29.

Szlezák, Klara Stephanie and D.E. Wynter (eds.) (2015) *Referentiality and the Films of Woody Allen*. New York: Palgrave Macmillan.

Tarkovsky, Andrei (1987) *Sculpting in Time: Reflections on the Cinema*. Translated by Kitty Hunter-Blair. Austin, TX: University of Texas Press.

Thompson, Emma (1996) *The Sense and Sensibility Screenplay and Diaries*. New York: Newmarket Press.

Toplin, Robert Brent (ed.) (2000) *Oliver Stone's USA: Film, History, and Controversy*. Lawrence, KS: University Press of Kansas.

Truffaut, François (1978) "What Do Critics Dream About?" In *The Films in My Life*. New York: Simon & Schuster.

Vogler, Christopher (2007) *The Writer's Journey: Mythic Structure for Writers*. 3rd edn. Los Angeles, CA: Michael Wiese.

Walker, Alice (1996) *The Same River Twice: Honoring the Difficult – A Meditation on Life, Spirit, Art, and the Making of the Film 'The Color Purple' Ten Years Later*. New York: Scribner.

Warner, Marina (1994) *From the Beast to the Blonde*. London: Farrar, Straus and Giroux.

Index

Note: Italic page numbers indicate pages with figures